Graphic Classics:
O. HENRY

Graphic Classics Volume Eleven
2005

Edited by Tom Pomplun

EUREKA PRODUCTIONS
8778 Oak Grove Road, Mount Horeb, Wisconsin 53572
www.graphicclassics.com

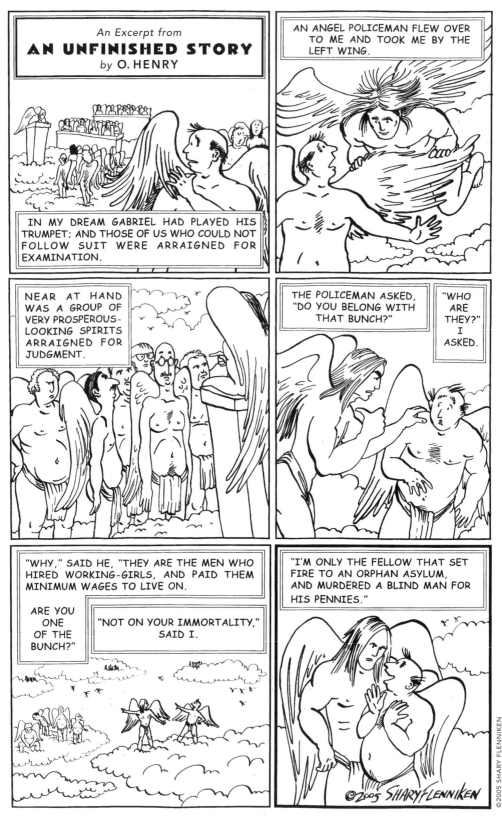

An Excerpt from
AN UNFINISHED STORY
by O. HENRY

IN MY DREAM GABRIEL HAD PLAYED HIS TRUMPET; AND THOSE OF US WHO COULD NOT FOLLOW SUIT WERE ARRAIGNED FOR EXAMINATION.

AN ANGEL POLICEMAN FLEW OVER TO ME AND TOOK ME BY THE LEFT WING.

NEAR AT HAND WAS A GROUP OF VERY PROSPEROUS-LOOKING SPIRITS ARRAIGNED FOR JUDGMENT.

THE POLICEMAN ASKED, "DO YOU BELONG WITH THAT BUNCH?"

"WHO ARE THEY?" I ASKED.

"WHY," SAID HE, "THEY ARE THE MEN WHO HIRED WORKING-GIRLS, AND PAID THEM MINIMUM WAGES TO LIVE ON.

ARE YOU ONE OF THE BUNCH?"

"NOT ON YOUR IMMORTALITY," SAID I.

"I'M ONLY THE FELLOW THAT SET FIRE TO AN ORPHAN ASYLUM, AND MURDERED A BLIND MAN FOR HIS PENNIES."

©2005 SHARY FLENNIKEN

Graphic Classics:
O. HENRY

Cover illustration by Esao Andrews / Back cover illustration by Lisa K. Weber

Graphic Classics: O. Henry is published by Eureka Productions. ISBN 978-0-9746648-2-0. Price US $11.95. Available from Eureka Productions, 8778 Oak Grove Road, Mount Horeb, WI 53572. Tom Pomplun, designer and publisher, tom@graphicclassics.com. Eileen Fitzgerald, editorial assistant. This compilation and all original works ©2005 Eureka Productions. All rights revert to creators after publication. Graphic Classics is a trademark of Eureka Productions. The Graphic Classics website is at http://www.graphicclassics.com. Printed in Canada.

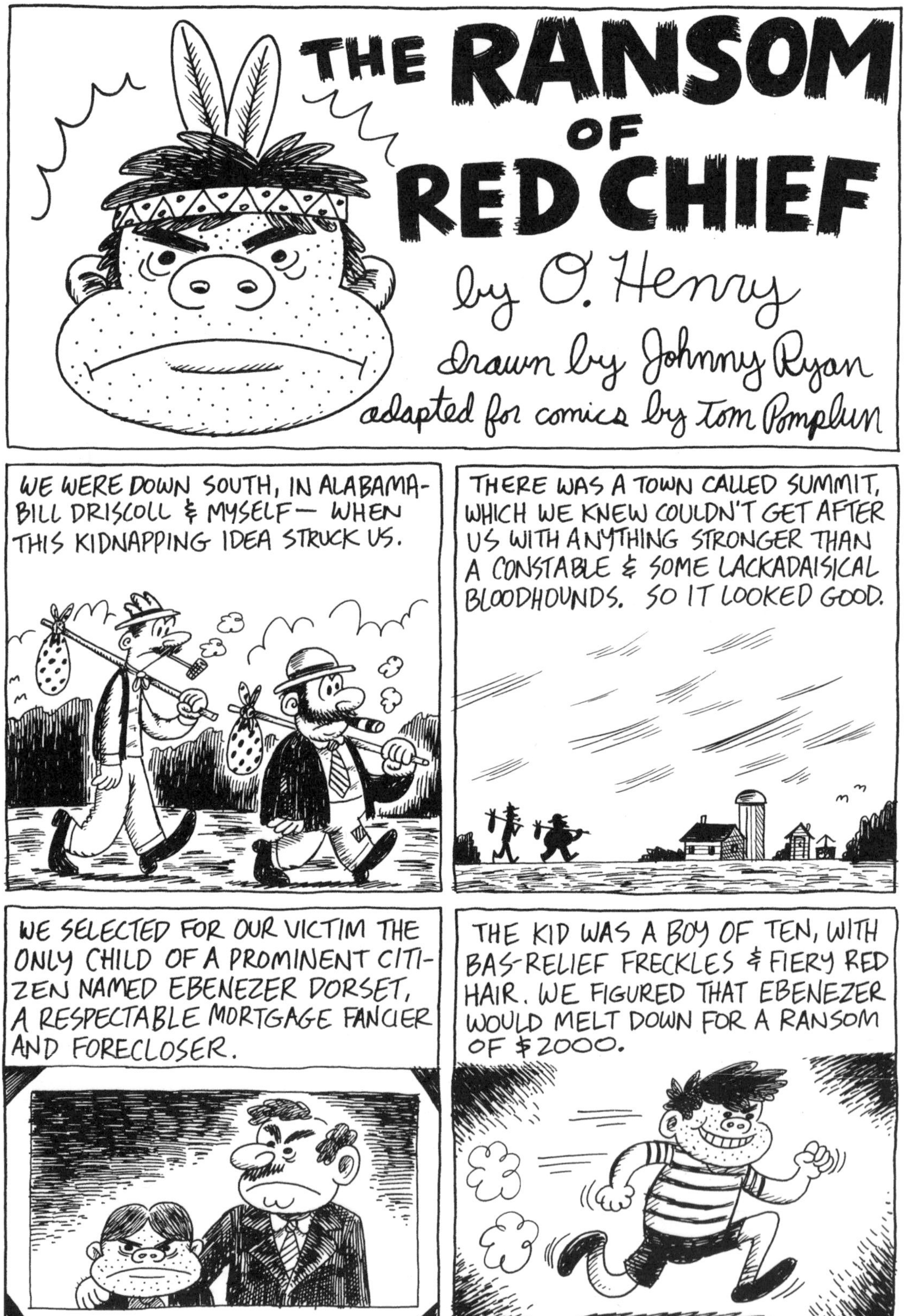
THE RANSOM OF RED CHIEF
by O. Henry
drawn by Johnny Ryan
adapted for comics by Tom Pomplun
WE WERE DOWN SOUTH, IN ALABAMA- BILL DRISCOLL & MYSELF— WHEN THIS KIDNAPPING IDEA STRUCK US.
THERE WAS A TOWN CALLED SUMMIT, WHICH WE KNEW COULDN'T GET AFTER US WITH ANYTHING STRONGER THAN A CONSTABLE & SOME LACKADAISICAL BLOODHOUNDS. SO IT LOOKED GOOD.
WE SELECTED FOR OUR VICTIM THE ONLY CHILD OF A PROMINENT CITIZEN NAMED EBENEZER DORSET, A RESPECTABLE MORTGAGE FANCIER AND FORECLOSER.
THE KID WAS A BOY OF TEN, WITH BAS-RELIEF FRECKLES & FIERY RED HAIR. WE FIGURED THAT EBENEZER WOULD MELT DOWN FOR A RANSOM OF $2000.

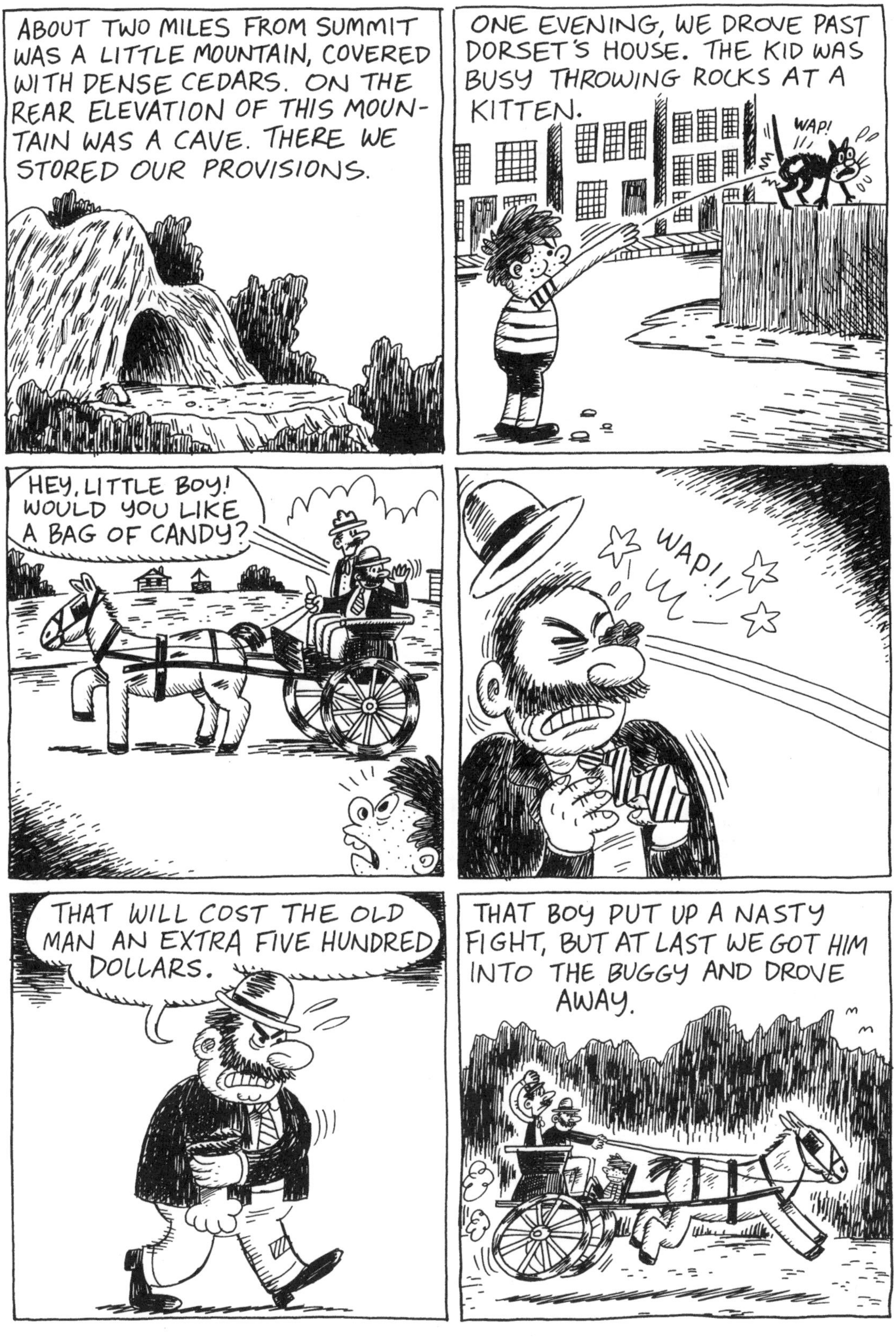
ABOUT TWO MILES FROM SUMMIT WAS A LITTLE MOUNTAIN, COVERED WITH DENSE CEDARS. ON THE REAR ELEVATION OF THIS MOUNTAIN WAS A CAVE. THERE WE STORED OUR PROVISIONS.
ONE EVENING, WE DROVE PAST DORSET'S HOUSE. THE KID WAS BUSY THROWING ROCKS AT A KITTEN.
WAP!
HEY, LITTLE BOY! WOULD YOU LIKE A BAG OF CANDY?
WAP!
THAT WILL COST THE OLD MAN AN EXTRA FIVE HUNDRED DOLLARS.
THAT BOY PUT UP A NASTY FIGHT, BUT AT LAST WE GOT HIM INTO THE BUGGY AND DROVE AWAY.

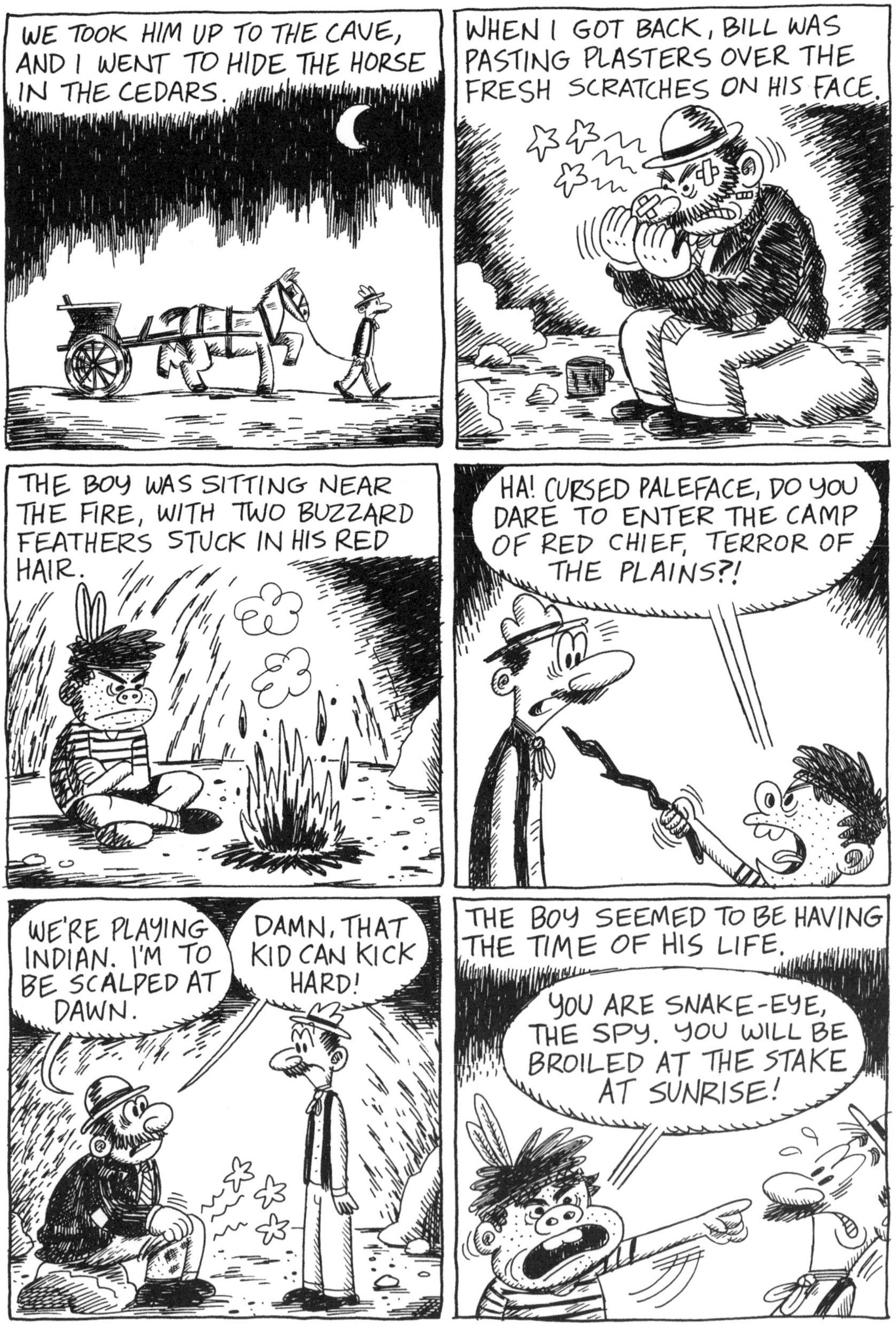
WE TOOK HIM UP TO THE CAVE, AND I WENT TO HIDE THE HORSE IN THE CEDARS.
WHEN I GOT BACK, BILL WAS PASTING PLASTERS OVER THE FRESH SCRATCHES ON HIS FACE.
THE BOY WAS SITTING NEAR THE FIRE, WITH TWO BUZZARD FEATHERS STUCK IN HIS RED HAIR.
HA! CURSED PALEFACE, DO YOU DARE TO ENTER THE CAMP OF RED CHIEF, TERROR OF THE PLAINS?!
WE'RE PLAYING INDIAN. I'M TO BE SCALPED AT DAWN.
DAMN, THAT KID CAN KICK HARD!
THE BOY SEEMED TO BE HAVING THE TIME OF HIS LIFE.
YOU ARE SNAKE-EYE, THE SPY. YOU WILL BE BROILED AT THE STAKE AT SUNRISE!

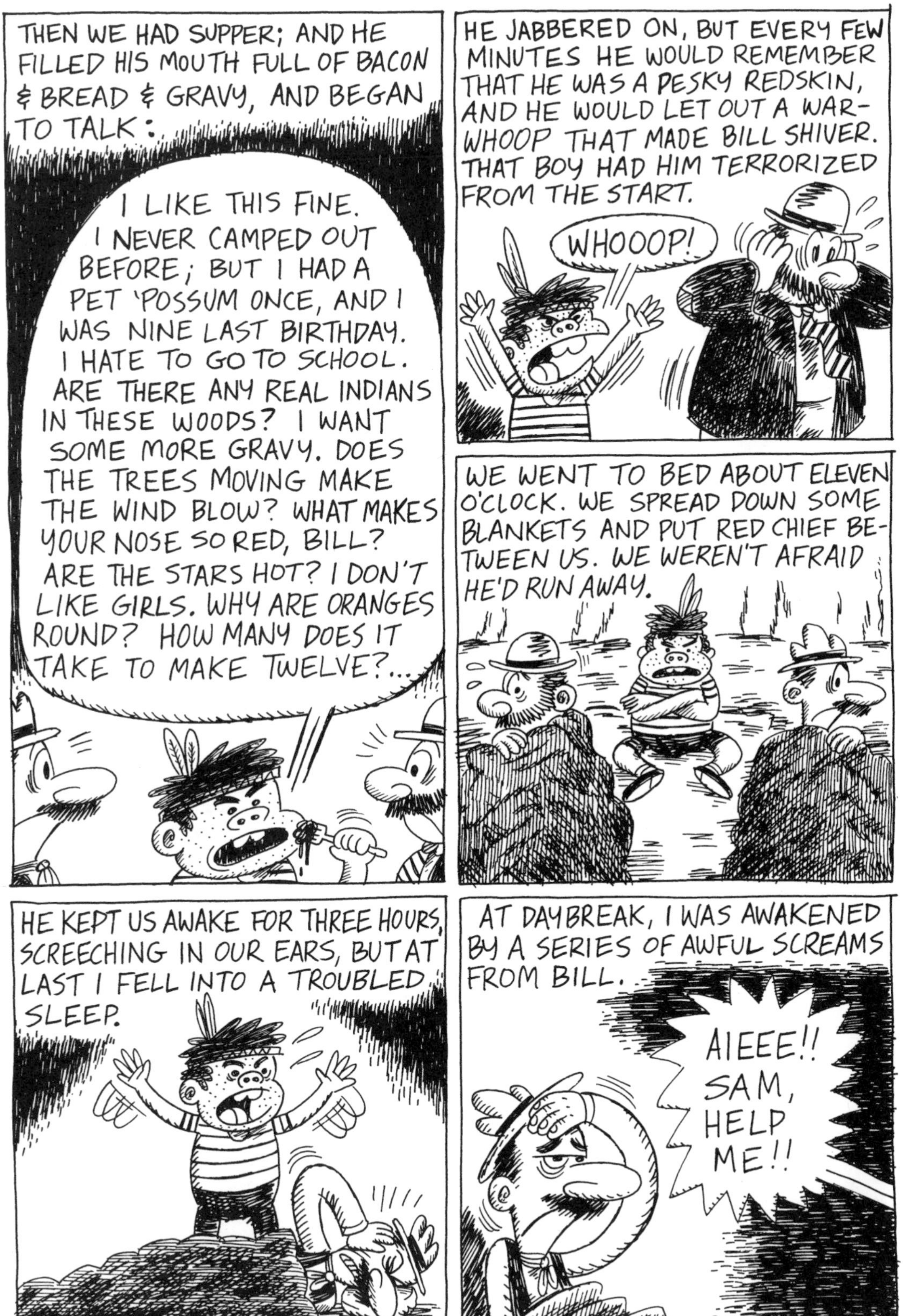
THEN WE HAD SUPPER; AND HE FILLED HIS MOUTH FULL OF BACON & BREAD & GRAVY, AND BEGAN TO TALK:
I LIKE THIS FINE. I NEVER CAMPED OUT BEFORE; BUT I HAD A PET 'POSSUM ONCE, AND I WAS NINE LAST BIRTHDAY. I HATE TO GO TO SCHOOL. ARE THERE ANY REAL INDIANS IN THESE WOODS? I WANT SOME MORE GRAVY. DOES THE TREES MOVING MAKE THE WIND BLOW? WHAT MAKES YOUR NOSE SO RED, BILL? ARE THE STARS HOT? I DON'T LIKE GIRLS. WHY ARE ORANGES ROUND? HOW MANY DOES IT TAKE TO MAKE TWELVE?...
HE JABBERED ON, BUT EVERY FEW MINUTES HE WOULD REMEMBER THAT HE WAS A PESKY REDSKIN, AND HE WOULD LET OUT A WAR-WHOOP THAT MADE BILL SHIVER. THAT BOY HAD HIM TERRORIZED FROM THE START.
WHOOOP!
WE WENT TO BED ABOUT ELEVEN O'CLOCK. WE SPREAD DOWN SOME BLANKETS AND PUT RED CHIEF BE-TWEEN US. WE WEREN'T AFRAID HE'D RUN AWAY.
HE KEPT US AWAKE FOR THREE HOURS, SCREECHING IN OUR EARS, BUT AT LAST I FELL INTO A TROUBLED SLEEP.
AT DAYBREAK, I WAS AWAKENED BY A SERIES OF AWFUL SCREAMS FROM BILL.
AIEEE!! SAM, HELP ME!!

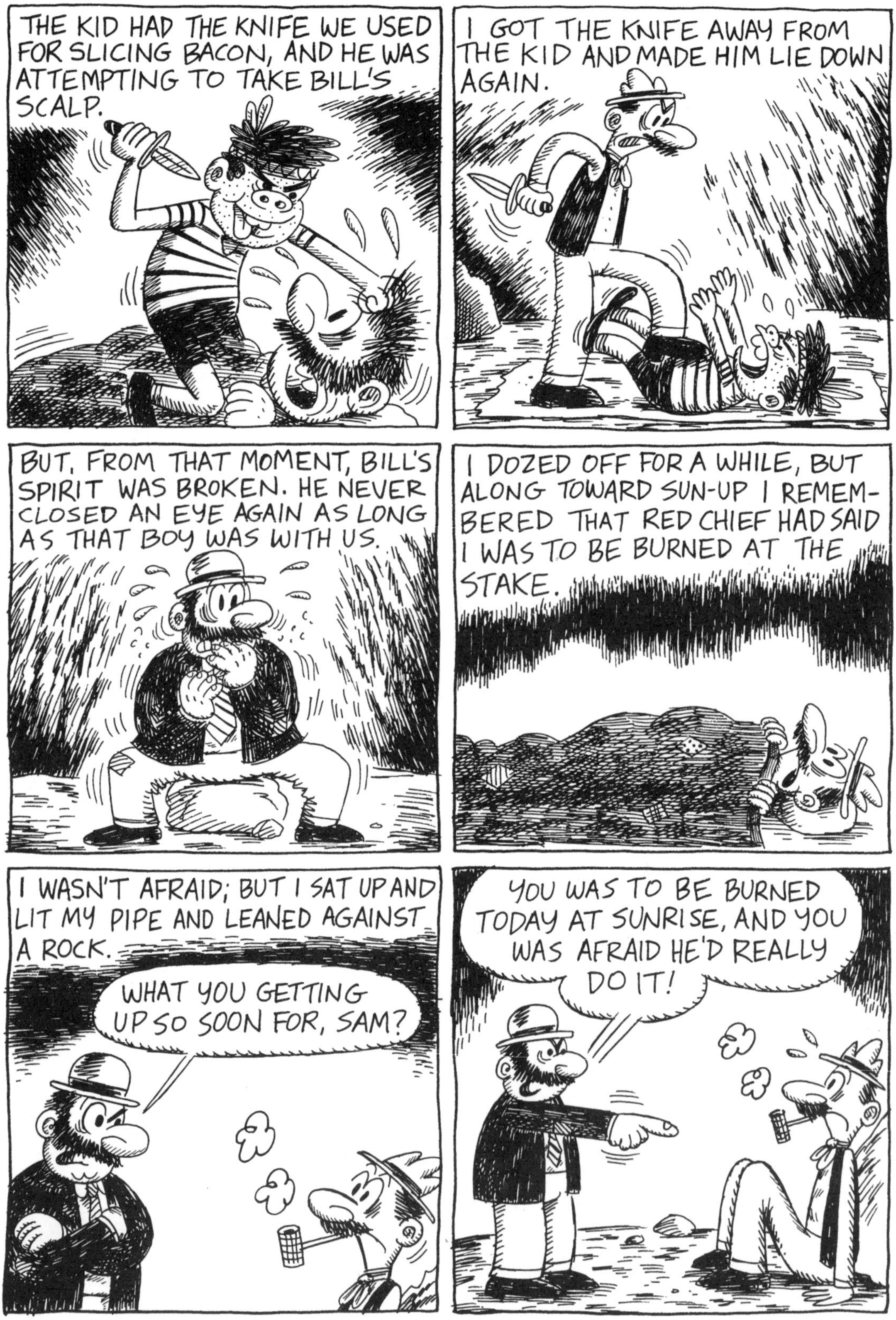
THE KID HAD THE KNIFE WE USED FOR SLICING BACON, AND HE WAS ATTEMPTING TO TAKE BILL'S SCALP.
I GOT THE KNIFE AWAY FROM THE KID AND MADE HIM LIE DOWN AGAIN.
BUT, FROM THAT MOMENT, BILL'S SPIRIT WAS BROKEN. HE NEVER CLOSED AN EYE AGAIN AS LONG AS THAT BOY WAS WITH US.
I DOZED OFF FOR A WHILE, BUT ALONG TOWARD SUN-UP I REMEMBERED THAT RED CHIEF HAD SAID I WAS TO BE BURNED AT THE STAKE.
I WASN'T AFRAID; BUT I SAT UP AND LIT MY PIPE AND LEANED AGAINST A ROCK.
WHAT YOU GETTING UP SO SOON FOR, SAM?
YOU WAS TO BE BURNED TODAY AT SUNRISE, AND YOU WAS AFRAID HE'D REALLY DO IT!

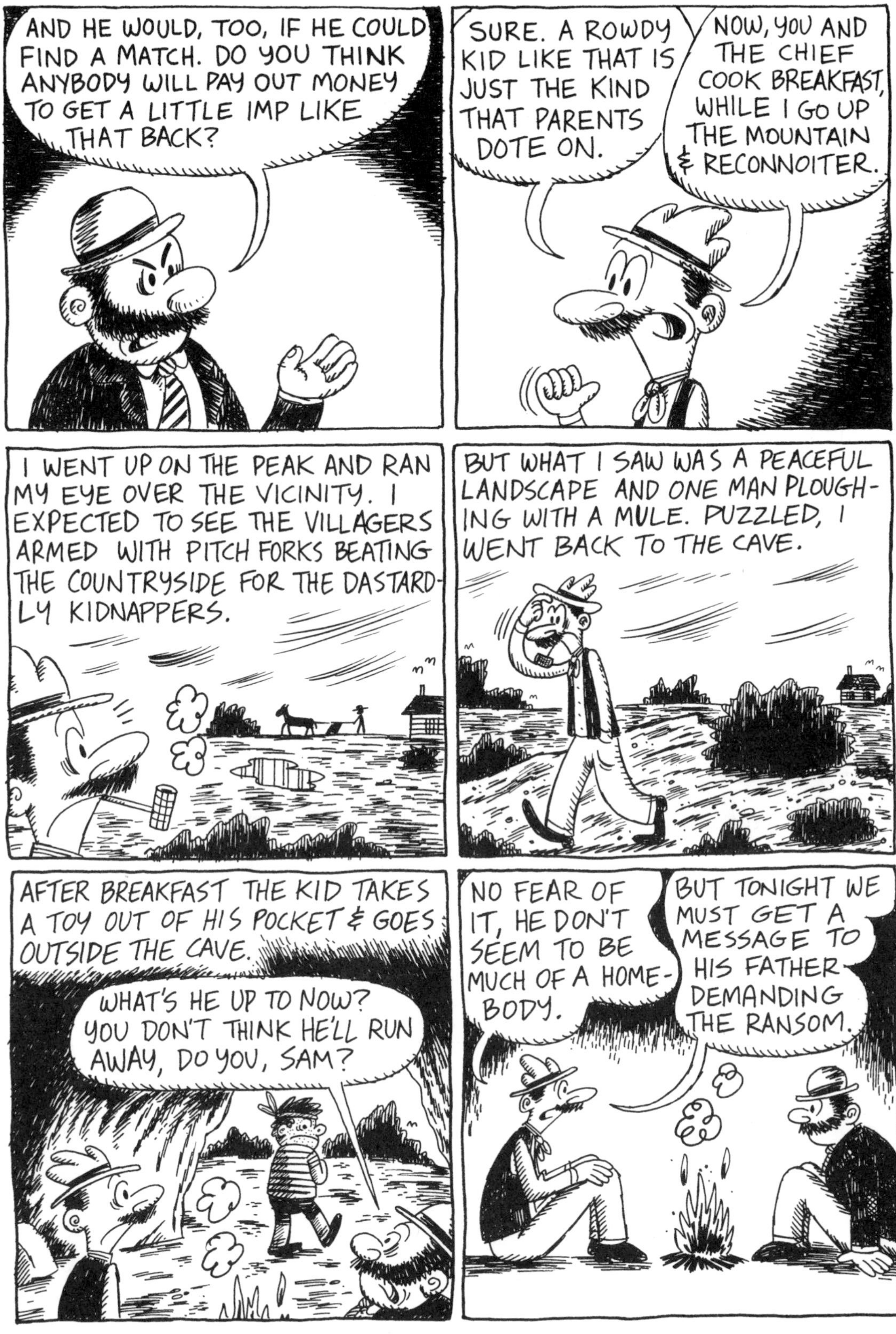
AND HE WOULD, TOO, IF HE COULD FIND A MATCH. DO YOU THINK ANYBODY WILL PAY OUT MONEY TO GET A LITTLE IMP LIKE THAT BACK?
SURE. A ROWDY KID LIKE THAT IS JUST THE KIND THAT PARENTS DOTE ON.
NOW, YOU AND THE CHIEF COOK BREAKFAST, WHILE I GO UP THE MOUNTAIN & RECONNOITER.
I WENT UP ON THE PEAK AND RAN MY EYE OVER THE VICINITY. I EXPECTED TO SEE THE VILLAGERS ARMED WITH PITCH FORKS BEATING THE COUNTRYSIDE FOR THE DASTARDLY KIDNAPPERS.
BUT WHAT I SAW WAS A PEACEFUL LANDSCAPE AND ONE MAN PLOUGHING WITH A MULE. PUZZLED, I WENT BACK TO THE CAVE.
AFTER BREAKFAST THE KID TAKES A TOY OUT OF HIS POCKET & GOES OUTSIDE THE CAVE.
WHAT'S HE UP TO NOW? YOU DON'T THINK HE'LL RUN AWAY, DO YOU, SAM?
NO FEAR OF IT, HE DON'T SEEM TO BE MUCH OF A HOME-BODY.
BUT TONIGHT WE MUST GET A MESSAGE TO HIS FATHER DEMANDING THE RANSOM.

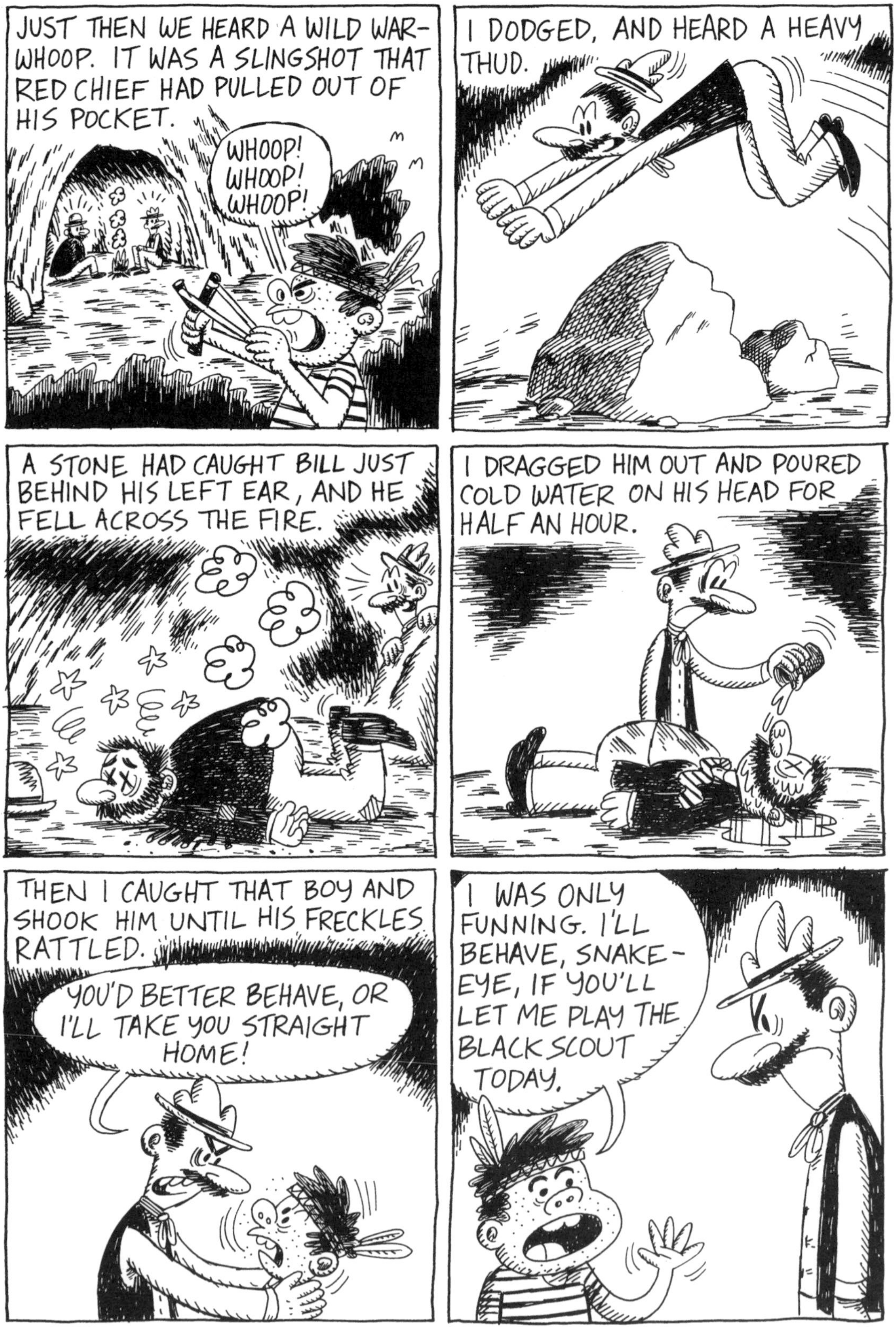
JUST THEN WE HEARD A WILD WAR-WHOOP. IT WAS A SLINGSHOT THAT RED CHIEF HAD PULLED OUT OF HIS POCKET.
WHOOP! WHOOP! WHOOP!
I DODGED, AND HEARD A HEAVY THUD.
A STONE HAD CAUGHT BILL JUST BEHIND HIS LEFT EAR, AND HE FELL ACROSS THE FIRE.
I DRAGGED HIM OUT AND POURED COLD WATER ON HIS HEAD FOR HALF AN HOUR.
THEN I CAUGHT THAT BOY AND SHOOK HIM UNTIL HIS FRECKLES RATTLED.
YOU'D BETTER BEHAVE, OR I'LL TAKE YOU STRAIGHT HOME!
I WAS ONLY FUNNING. I'LL BEHAVE, SNAKE-EYE, IF YOU'LL LET ME PLAY THE BLACK SCOUT TODAY.

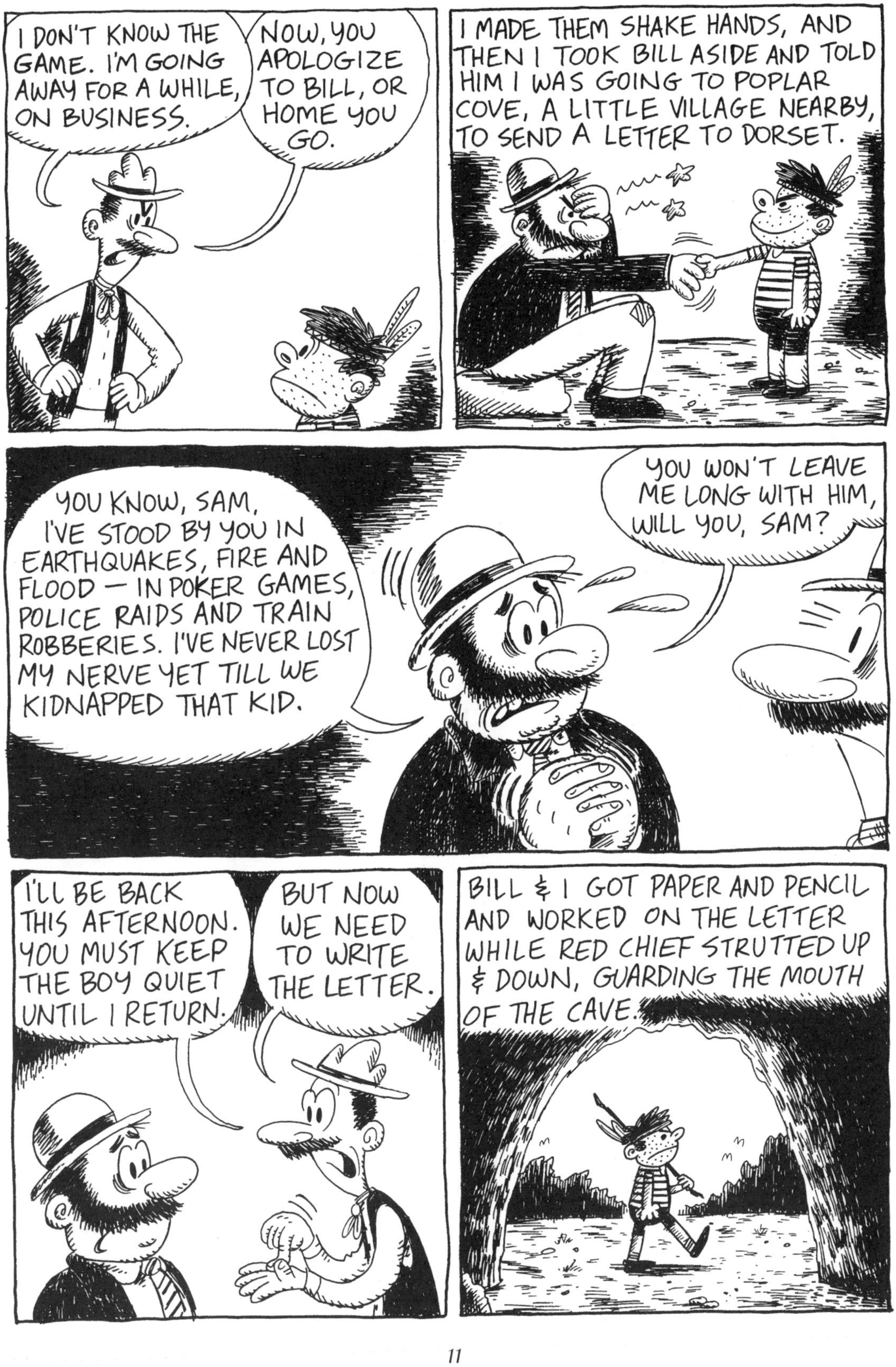
I DON'T KNOW THE GAME. I'M GOING AWAY FOR A WHILE, ON BUSINESS.
NOW, YOU APOLOGIZE TO BILL, OR HOME YOU GO.
I MADE THEM SHAKE HANDS, AND THEN I TOOK BILL ASIDE AND TOLD HIM I WAS GOING TO POPLAR COVE, A LITTLE VILLAGE NEARBY, TO SEND A LETTER TO DORSET.
YOU KNOW, SAM, I'VE STOOD BY YOU IN EARTHQUAKES, FIRE AND FLOOD — IN POKER GAMES, POLICE RAIDS AND TRAIN ROBBERIES. I'VE NEVER LOST MY NERVE YET TILL WE KIDNAPPED THAT KID.
YOU WON'T LEAVE ME LONG WITH HIM, WILL YOU, SAM?
I'LL BE BACK THIS AFTERNOON. YOU MUST KEEP THE BOY QUIET UNTIL I RETURN.
BUT NOW WE NEED TO WRITE THE LETTER.
BILL & I GOT PAPER AND PENCIL AND WORKED ON THE LETTER WHILE RED CHIEF STRUTTED UP & DOWN, GUARDING THE MOUTH OF THE CAVE.

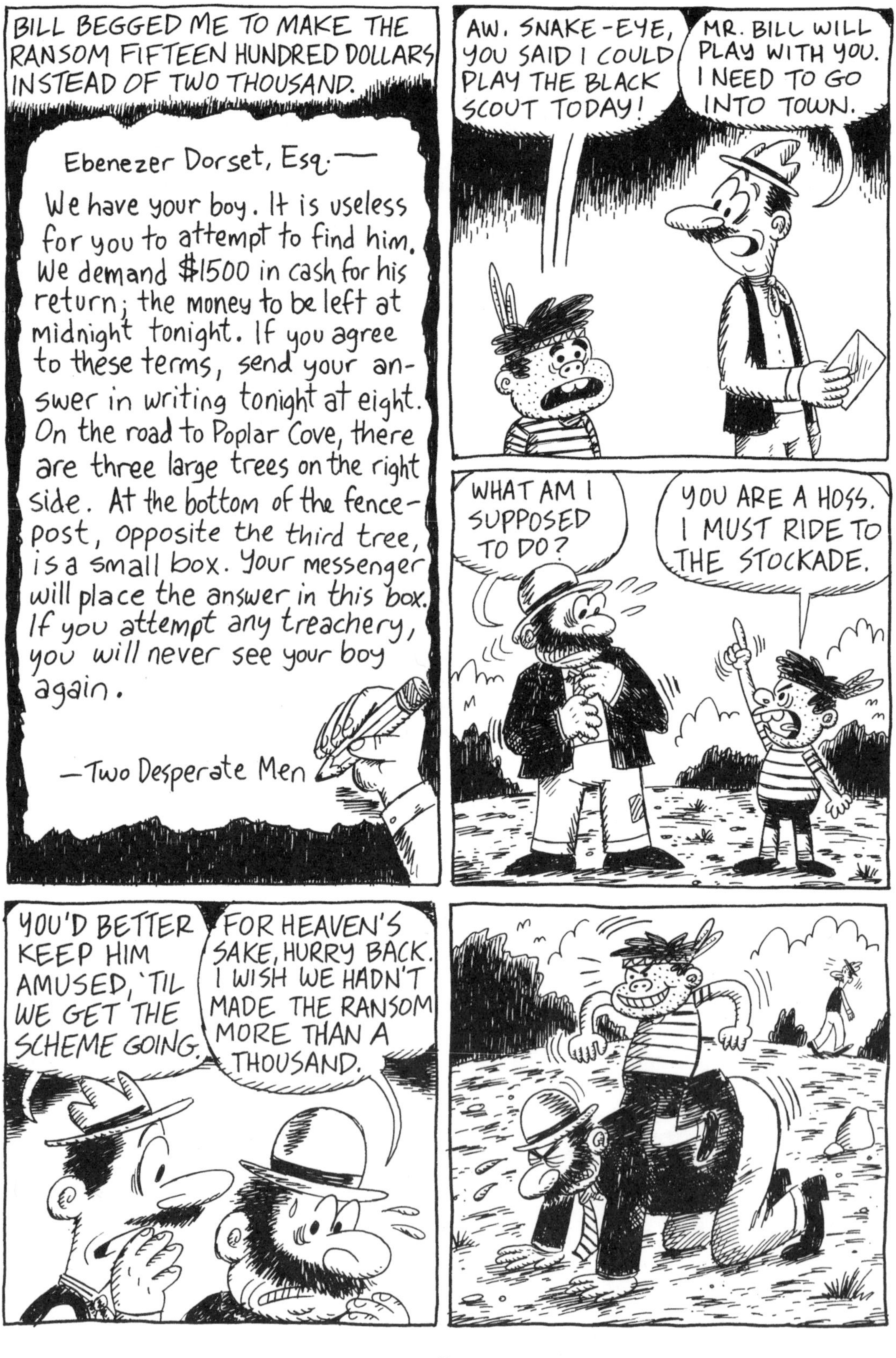
BILL BEGGED ME TO MAKE THE RANSOM FIFTEEN HUNDRED DOLLARS INSTEAD OF TWO THOUSAND.
Ebenezer Dorset, Esq.—
We have your boy. It is useless for you to attempt to find him. We demand $1500 in cash for his return; the money to be left at midnight tonight. If you agree to these terms, send your answer in writing tonight at eight. On the road to Poplar Cove, there are three large trees on the right side. At the bottom of the fence-post, opposite the third tree, is a small box. Your messenger will place the answer in this box. If you attempt any treachery, you will never see your boy again.
—Two Desperate Men
AW, SNAKE-EYE, YOU SAID I COULD PLAY THE BLACK SCOUT TODAY!
MR. BILL WILL PLAY WITH YOU. I NEED TO GO INTO TOWN.
WHAT AM I SUPPOSED TO DO?
YOU ARE A HOSS. I MUST RIDE TO THE STOCKADE.
YOU'D BETTER KEEP HIM AMUSED, 'TIL WE GET THE SCHEME GOING.
FOR HEAVEN'S SAKE, HURRY BACK. I WISH WE HADN'T MADE THE RANSOM MORE THAN A THOUSAND.

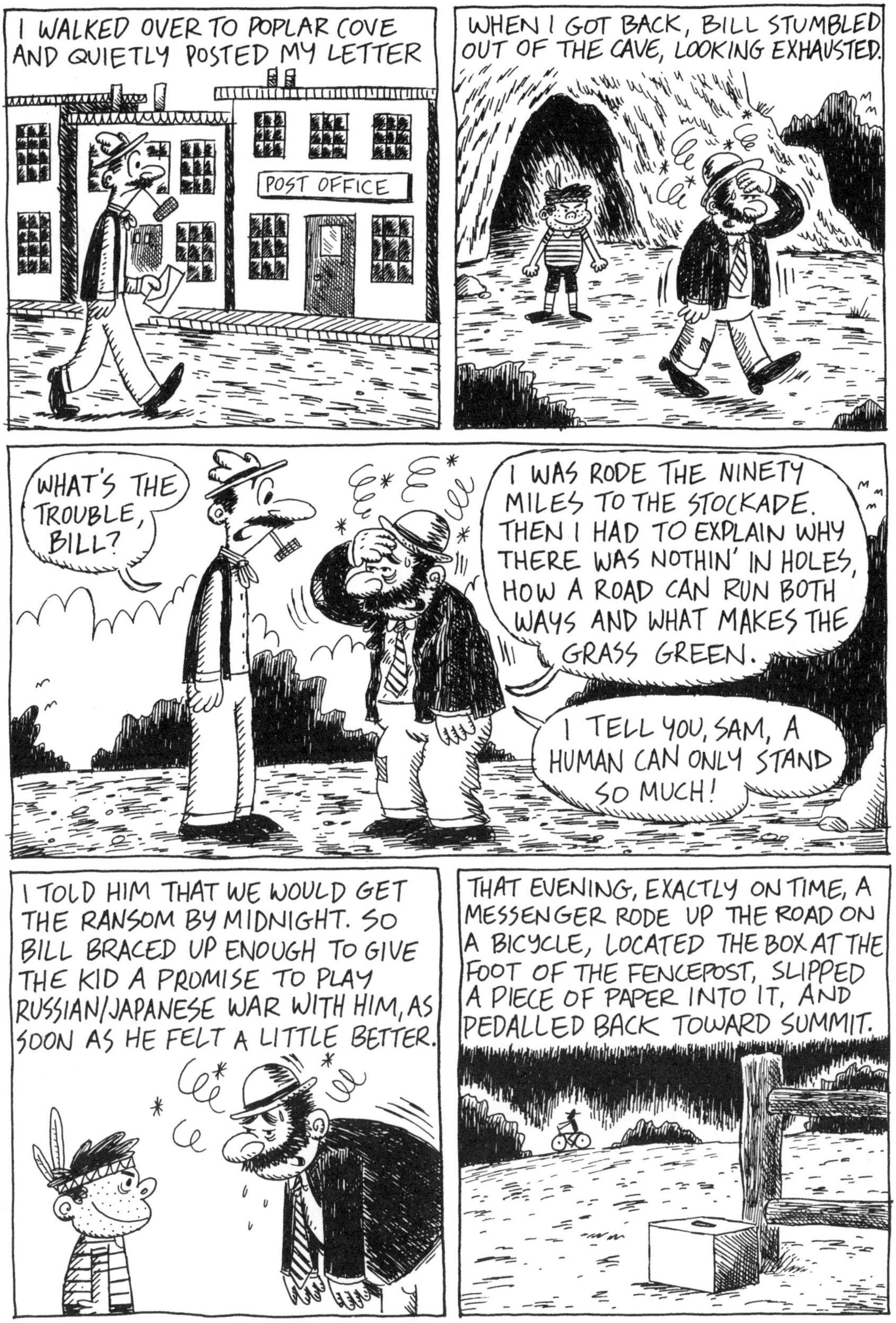
I WALKED OVER TO POPLAR COVE AND QUIETLY POSTED MY LETTER
POST OFFICE
WHEN I GOT BACK, BILL STUMBLED OUT OF THE CAVE, LOOKING EXHAUSTED.
WHAT'S THE TROUBLE, BILL?
I WAS RODE THE NINETY MILES TO THE STOCKADE. THEN I HAD TO EXPLAIN WHY THERE WAS NOTHIN' IN HOLES, HOW A ROAD CAN RUN BOTH WAYS AND WHAT MAKES THE GRASS GREEN.
I TELL YOU, SAM, A HUMAN CAN ONLY STAND SO MUCH!
I TOLD HIM THAT WE WOULD GET THE RANSOM BY MIDNIGHT. SO BILL BRACED UP ENOUGH TO GIVE THE KID A PROMISE TO PLAY RUSSIAN/JAPANESE WAR WITH HIM, AS SOON AS HE FELT A LITTLE BETTER.
THAT EVENING, EXACTLY ON TIME, A MESSENGER RODE UP THE ROAD ON A BICYCLE, LOCATED THE BOX AT THE FOOT OF THE FENCEPOST, SLIPPED A PIECE OF PAPER INTO IT, AND PEDALLED BACK TOWARD SUMMIT.

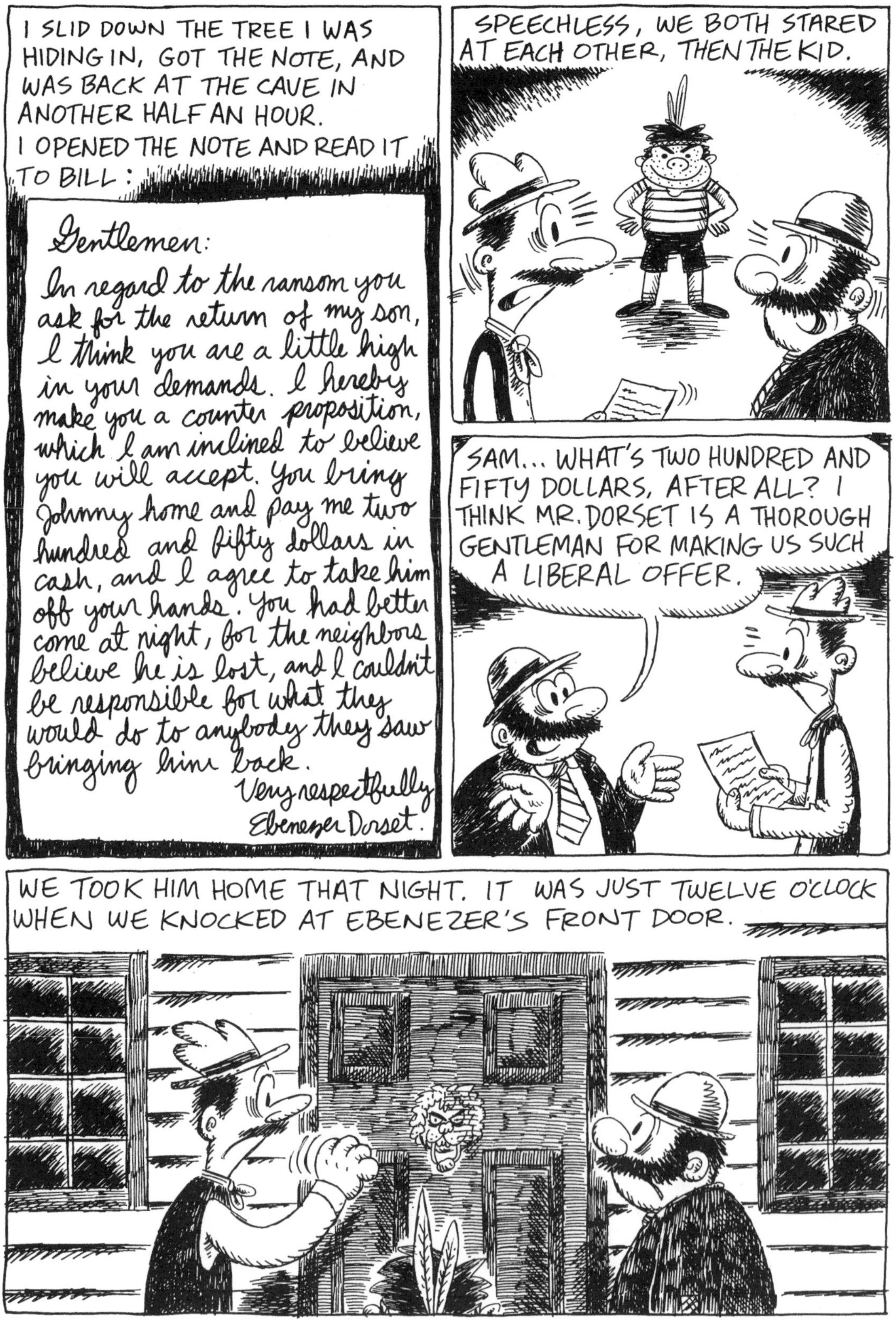
I SLID DOWN THE TREE I WAS HIDING IN, GOT THE NOTE, AND WAS BACK AT THE CAVE IN ANOTHER HALF AN HOUR.
I OPENED THE NOTE AND READ IT TO BILL:
Gentlemen:
In regard to the ransom you ask for the return of my son, I think you are a little high in your demands. I hereby make you a counter proposition, which I am inclined to believe you will accept. You bring Johnny home and pay me two hundred and fifty dollars in cash, and I agree to take him off your hands. You had better come at night, for the neighbors believe he is lost, and I couldn't be responsible for what they would do to anybody they saw bringing him back.
Very respectfully
Ebenezer Dorset.
SPEECHLESS, WE BOTH STARED AT EACH OTHER, THEN THE KID.
SAM... WHAT'S TWO HUNDRED AND FIFTY DOLLARS, AFTER ALL? I THINK MR. DORSET IS A THOROUGH GENTLEMAN FOR MAKING US SUCH A LIBERAL OFFER.
WE TOOK HIM HOME THAT NIGHT. IT WAS JUST TWELVE O'CLOCK WHEN WE KNOCKED AT EBENEZER'S FRONT DOOR.

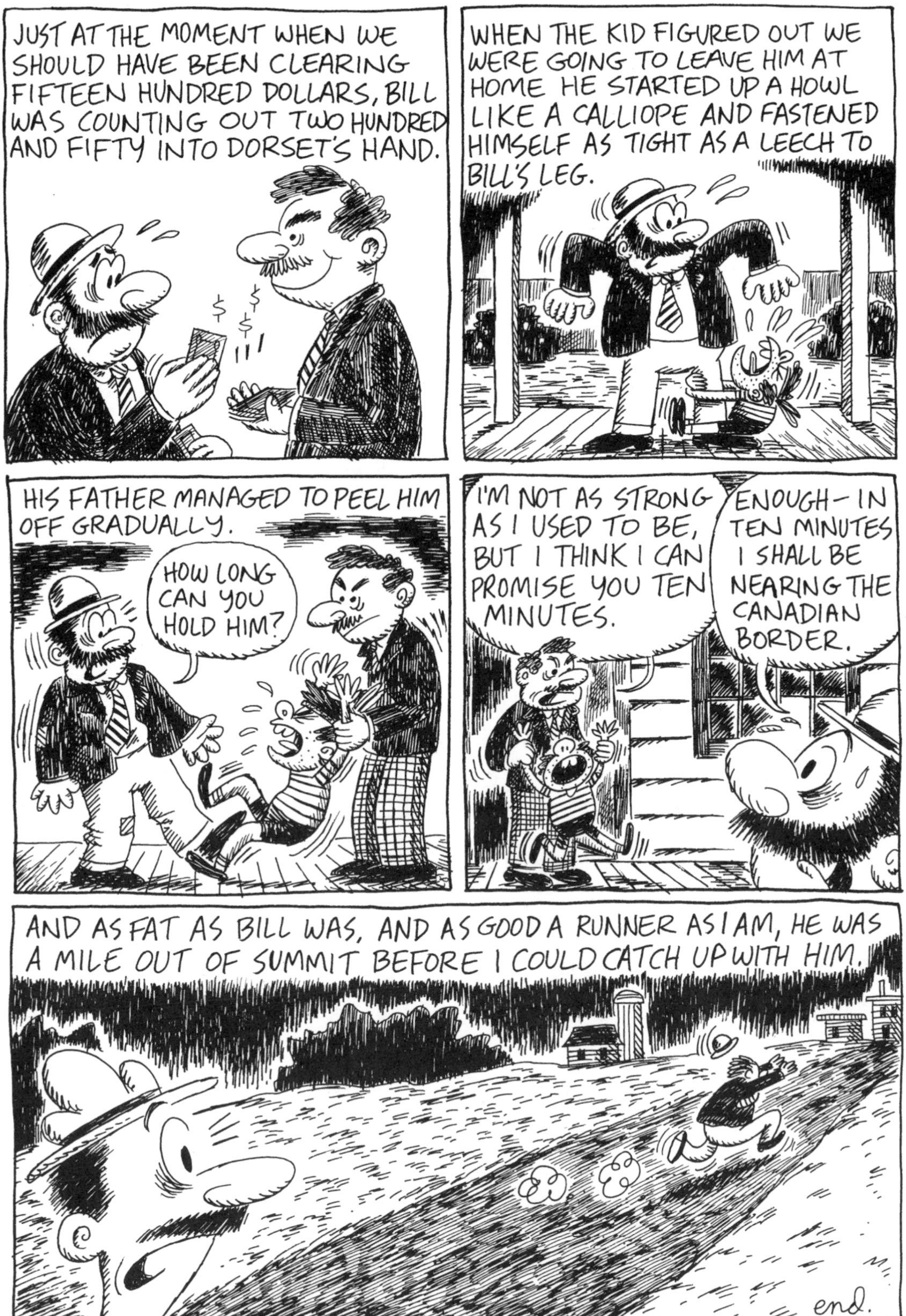
JUST AT THE MOMENT WHEN WE SHOULD HAVE BEEN CLEARING FIFTEEN HUNDRED DOLLARS, BILL WAS COUNTING OUT TWO HUNDRED AND FIFTY INTO DORSET'S HAND.
WHEN THE KID FIGURED OUT WE WERE GOING TO LEAVE HIM AT HOME HE STARTED UP A HOWL LIKE A CALLIOPE AND FASTENED HIMSELF AS TIGHT AS A LEECH TO BILL'S LEG.
HIS FATHER MANAGED TO PEEL HIM OFF GRADUALLY.
HOW LONG CAN YOU HOLD HIM?
I'M NOT AS STRONG AS I USED TO BE, BUT I THINK I CAN PROMISE YOU TEN MINUTES.
ENOUGH— IN TEN MINUTES I SHALL BE NEARING THE CANADIAN BORDER.
AND AS FAT AS BILL WAS, AND AS GOOD A RUNNER AS I AM, HE WAS A MILE OUT OF SUMMIT BEFORE I COULD CATCH UP WITH HIM.
end.

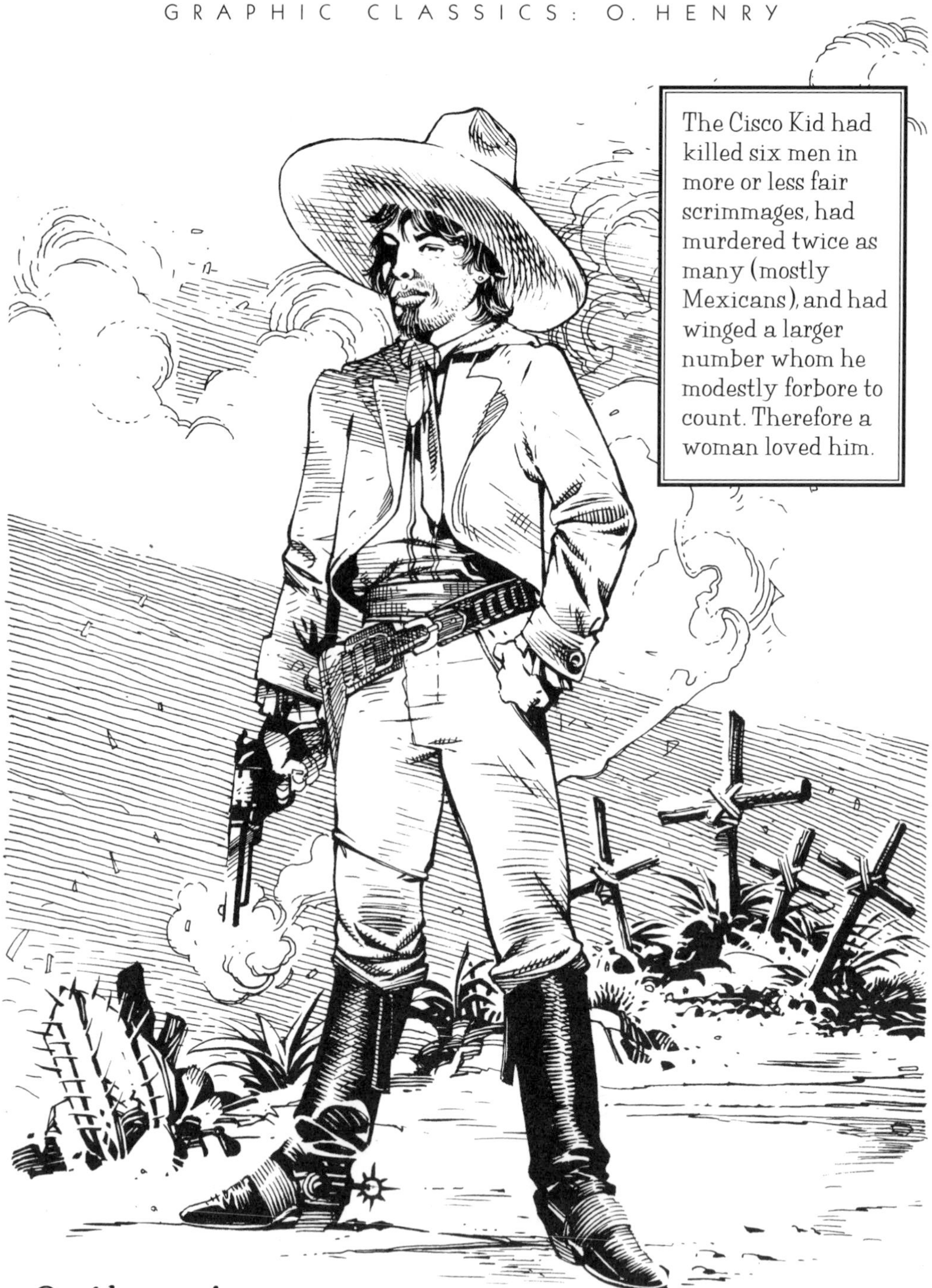
The Cisco Kid had killed six men in more or less fair scrimmages, had murdered twice as many (mostly Mexicans), and had winged a larger number whom he modestly forbore to count. Therefore a woman loved him.

O. Henry's

THE CABALLERO'S WAY

A Tale of The Cisco Kid ~ Illustrated by Mark A. Nelson

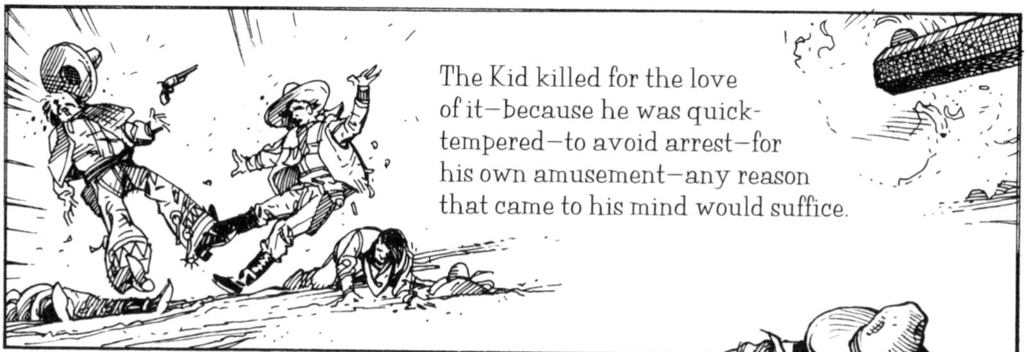
The Kid killed for the love of it—because he was quick-tempered—to avoid arrest—for his own amusement—any reason that came to his mind would suffice.

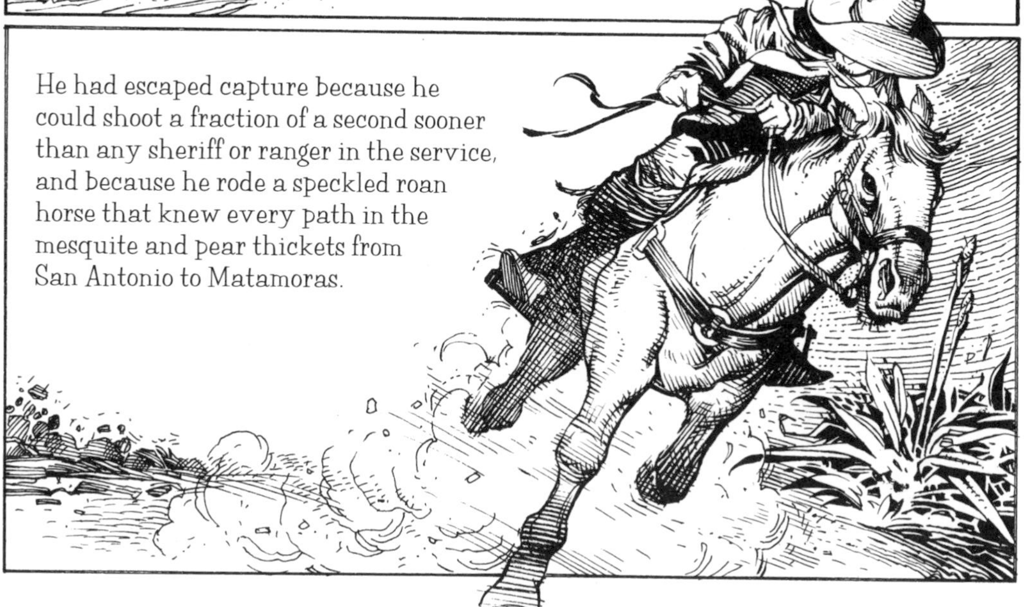
He had escaped capture because he could shoot a fraction of a second sooner than any sheriff or ranger in the service, and because he rode a speckled roan horse that knew every path in the mesquite and pear thickets from San Antonio to Matamoras.

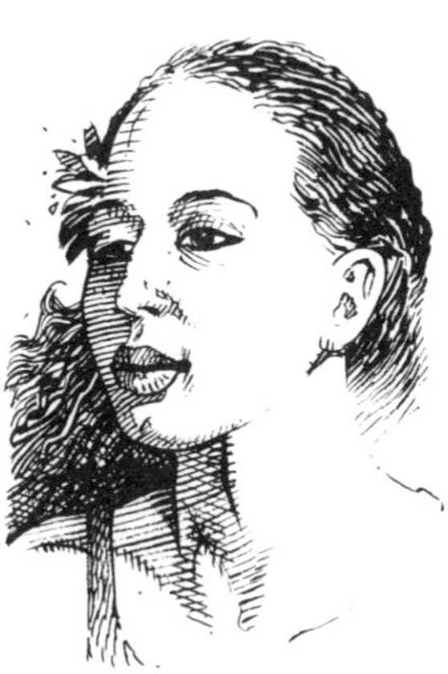

Tonia Perez, the girl who loved the Cisco Kid, lived in a grass-roofed hut near the Lone Wolf Crossing of the Frio. With her lived a grandfather, who herded goats and lived in a continuous drunken dream from drinking mescal.

Back of the hut, a tremendous forest of bristling cactus crowded almost to its door. It was along the bewildering maze of this spinous thicket that the speckled roan would bring the Kid to see his girl.

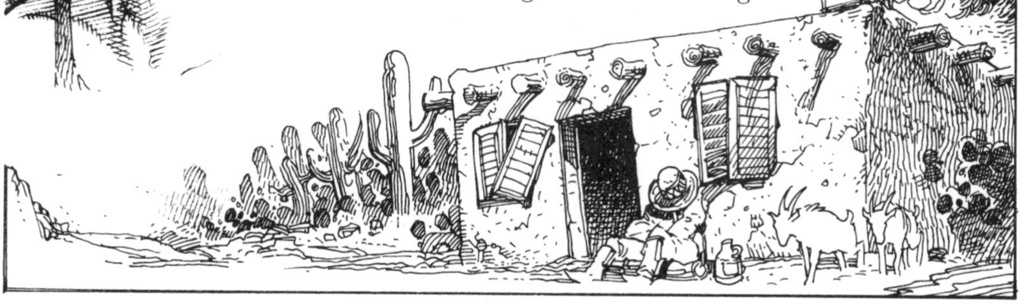

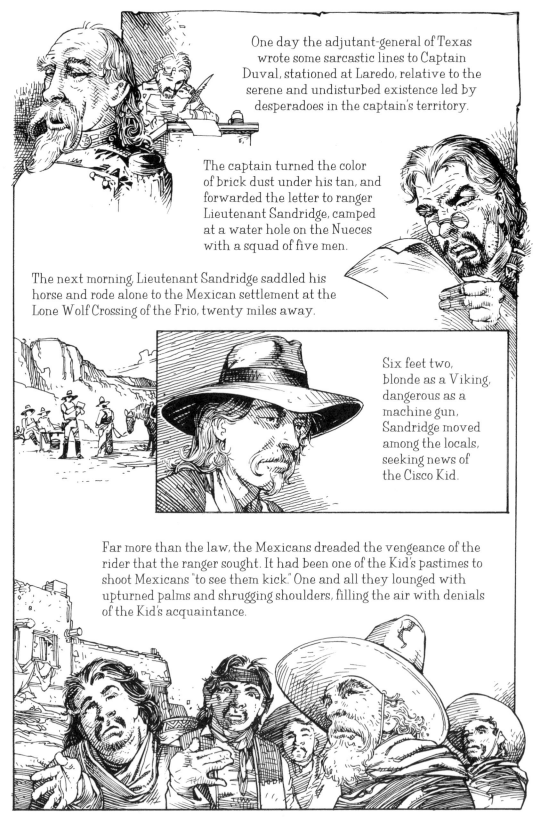

One day the adjutant-general of Texas wrote some sarcastic lines to Captain Duval, stationed at Laredo, relative to the serene and undisturbed existence led by desperadoes in the captain's territory.

The captain turned the color of brick dust under his tan, and forwarded the letter to ranger Lieutenant Sandridge, camped at a water hole on the Nueces with a squad of five men.

The next morning, Lieutenant Sandridge saddled his horse and rode alone to the Mexican settlement at the Lone Wolf Crossing of the Frio, twenty miles away.

Six feet two, blonde as a Viking, dangerous as a machine gun, Sandridge moved among the locals, seeking news of the Cisco Kid.

Far more than the law, the Mexicans dreaded the vengeance of the rider that the ranger sought. It had been one of the Kid's pastimes to shoot Mexicans "to see them kick." One and all they lounged with upturned palms and shrugging shoulders, filling the air with denials of the Kid's acquaintance.

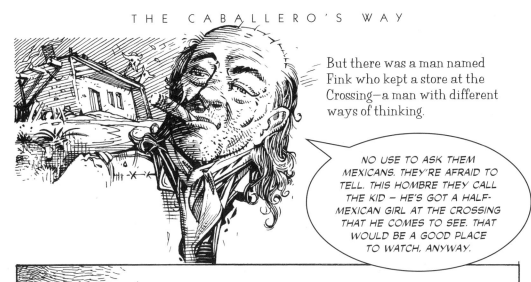

But there was a man named Fink who kept a store at the Crossing—a man with different ways of thinking.

NO USE TO ASK THEM MEXICANS. THEY'RE AFRAID TO TELL. THIS HOMBRE THEY CALL THE KID — HE'S GOT A HALF-MEXICAN GIRL AT THE CROSSING THAT HE COMES TO SEE. THAT WOULD BE A GOOD PLACE TO WATCH, ANYWAY.

Sandridge rode down to the girl's home. The sun was low, and the goats were corralled for the night.

The old Mexican lay upon a blanket, already in a stupor from his mescal, and dreaming.

And in the door of the hut stood Tonia.

Lieutenant Sandridge sat in his saddle staring at her, unable to move.

Her blue-black hair, smoothly divided in the middle and bound close to her head, and her large eyes full of Latin melancholy, gave her the Madonna touch, while her motions and air spoke of a concealed fire.

As for Tonia, never before had she seen such a man as this. The men she had known had been small and dark.

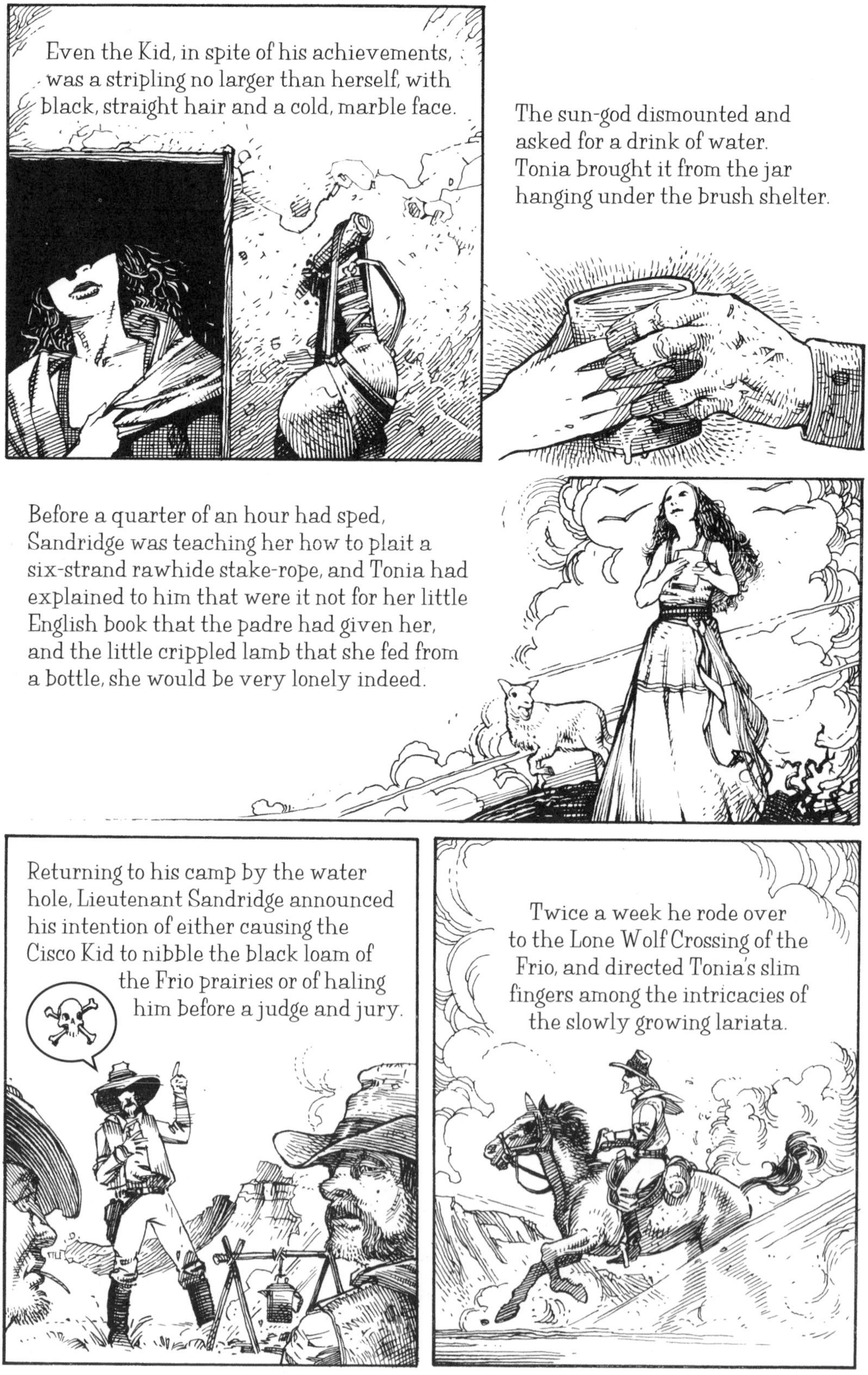
Even the Kid, in spite of his achievements, was a stripling no larger than herself, with black, straight hair and a cold, marble face.
The sun-god dismounted and asked for a drink of water. Tonia brought it from the jar hanging under the brush shelter.
Before a quarter of an hour had sped, Sandridge was teaching her how to plait a six-strand rawhide stake-rope, and Tonia had explained to him that were it not for her little English book that the padre had given her, and the little crippled lamb that she fed from a bottle, she would be very lonely indeed.
Returning to his camp by the water hole, Lieutenant Sandridge announced his intention of either causing the Cisco Kid to nibble the black loam of the Frio prairies or of haling him before a judge and jury.
Twice a week he rode over to the Lone Wolf Crossing of the Frio, and directed Tonia's slim fingers among the intricacies of the slowly growing lariata.

The ranger knew that he might find the Kid there at any visit. He kept his armament ready, and had a frequent eye for the pear thicket at the rear of the hut.

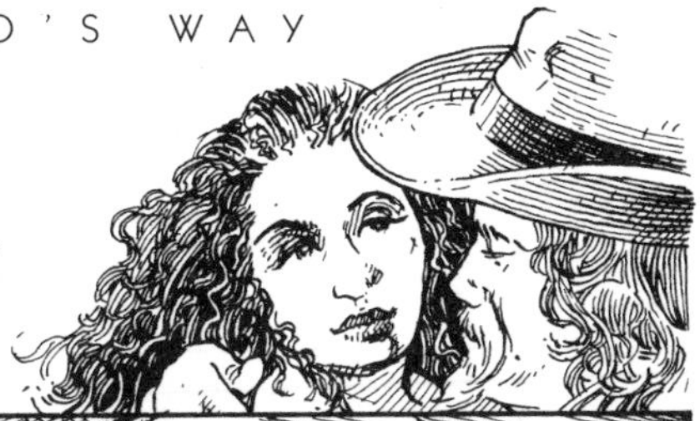

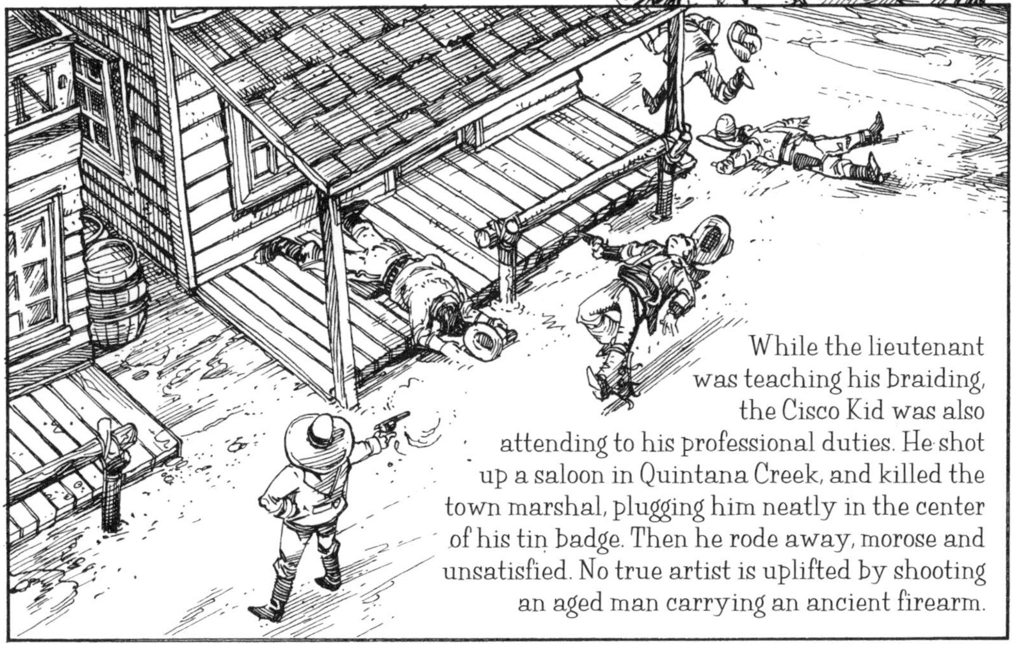
While the lieutenant was teaching his braiding, the Cisco Kid was also attending to his professional duties. He shot up a saloon in Quintana Creek, and killed the town marshal, plugging him neatly in the center of his tin badge. Then he rode away, morose and unsatisfied. No true artist is uplifted by shooting an aged man carrying an ancient firearm.

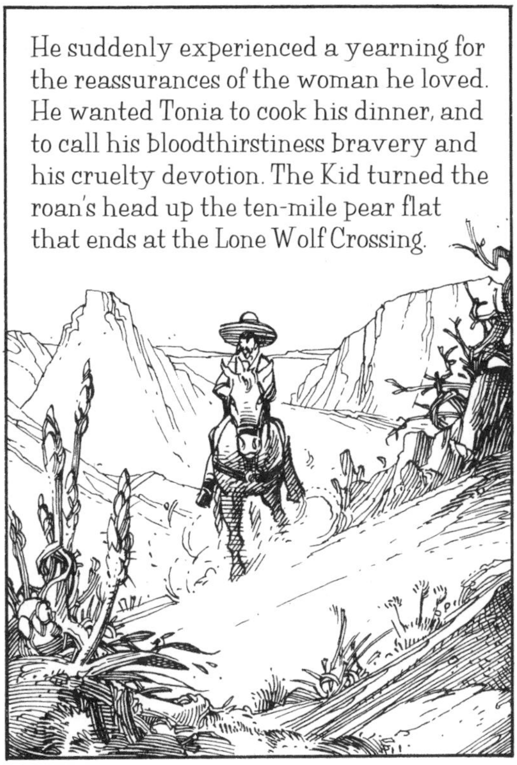
He suddenly experienced a yearning for the reassurances of the woman he loved. He wanted Tonia to cook his dinner, and to call his bloodthirstiness bravery and his cruelty devotion. The Kid turned the roan's head up the ten-mile pear flat that ends at the Lone Wolf Crossing.

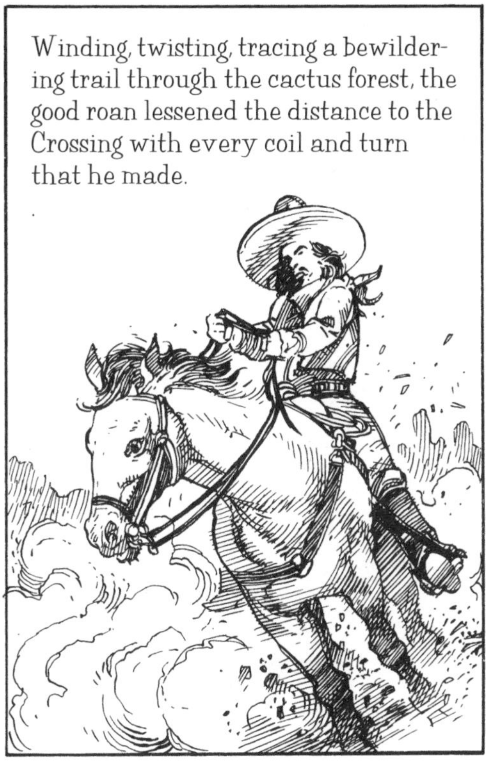
Winding, twisting, tracing a bewildering trail through the cactus forest, the good roan lessened the distance to the Crossing with every coil and turn that he made.

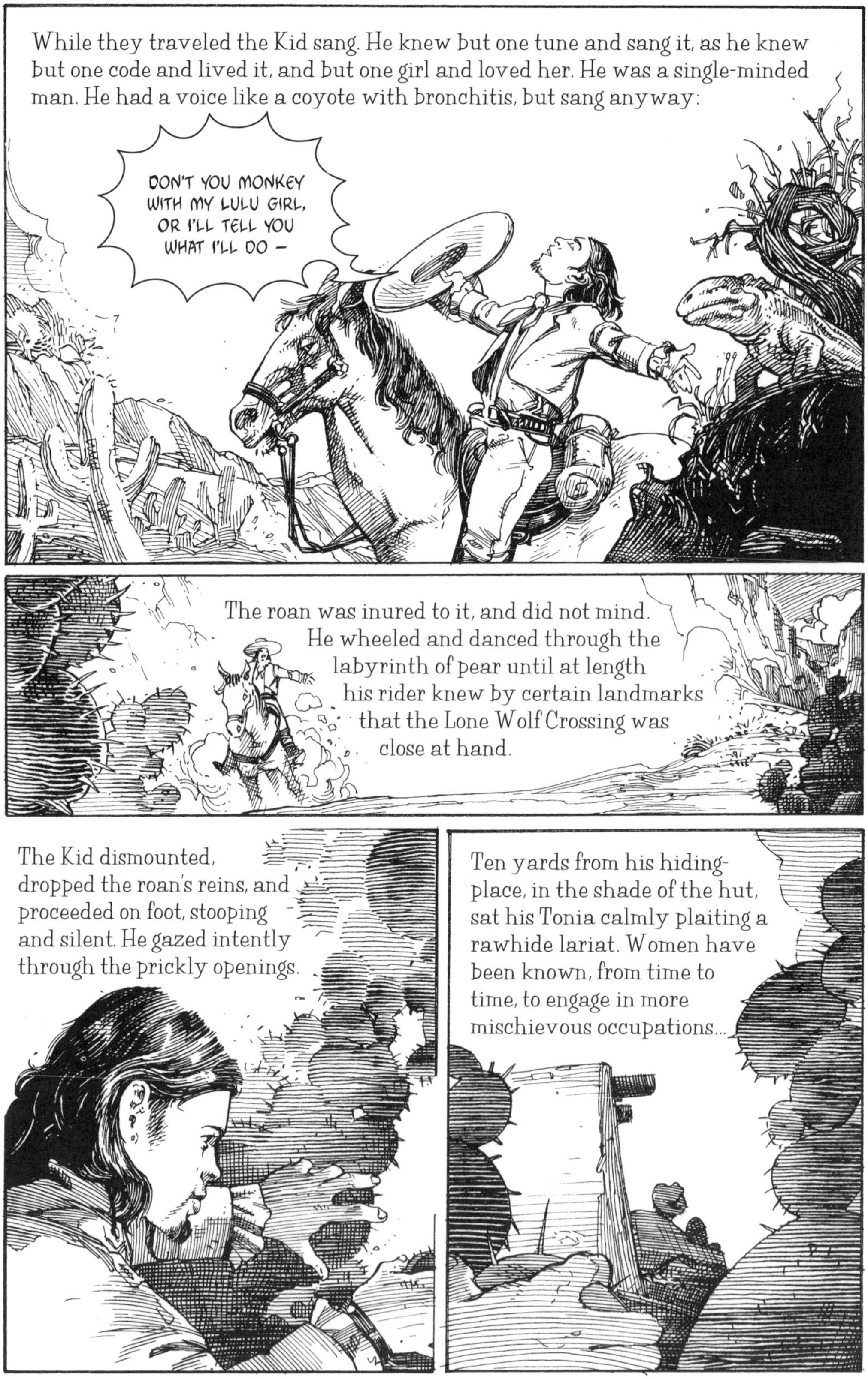
While they traveled the Kid sang. He knew but one tune and sang it, as he knew but one code and lived it, and but one girl and loved her. He was a single-minded man. He had a voice like a coyote with bronchitis, but sang anyway:
DON'T YOU MONKEY WITH MY LULU GIRL, OR I'LL TELL YOU WHAT I'LL DO –
The roan was inured to it, and did not mind. He wheeled and danced through the labyrinth of pear until at length his rider knew by certain landmarks that the Lone Wolf Crossing was close at hand.
The Kid dismounted, dropped the roan's reins, and proceeded on foot, stooping and silent. He gazed intently through the prickly openings.
Ten yards from his hiding-place, in the shade of the hut, sat his Tonia calmly plaiting a rawhide lariat. Women have been known, from time to time, to engage in more mischievous occupations...

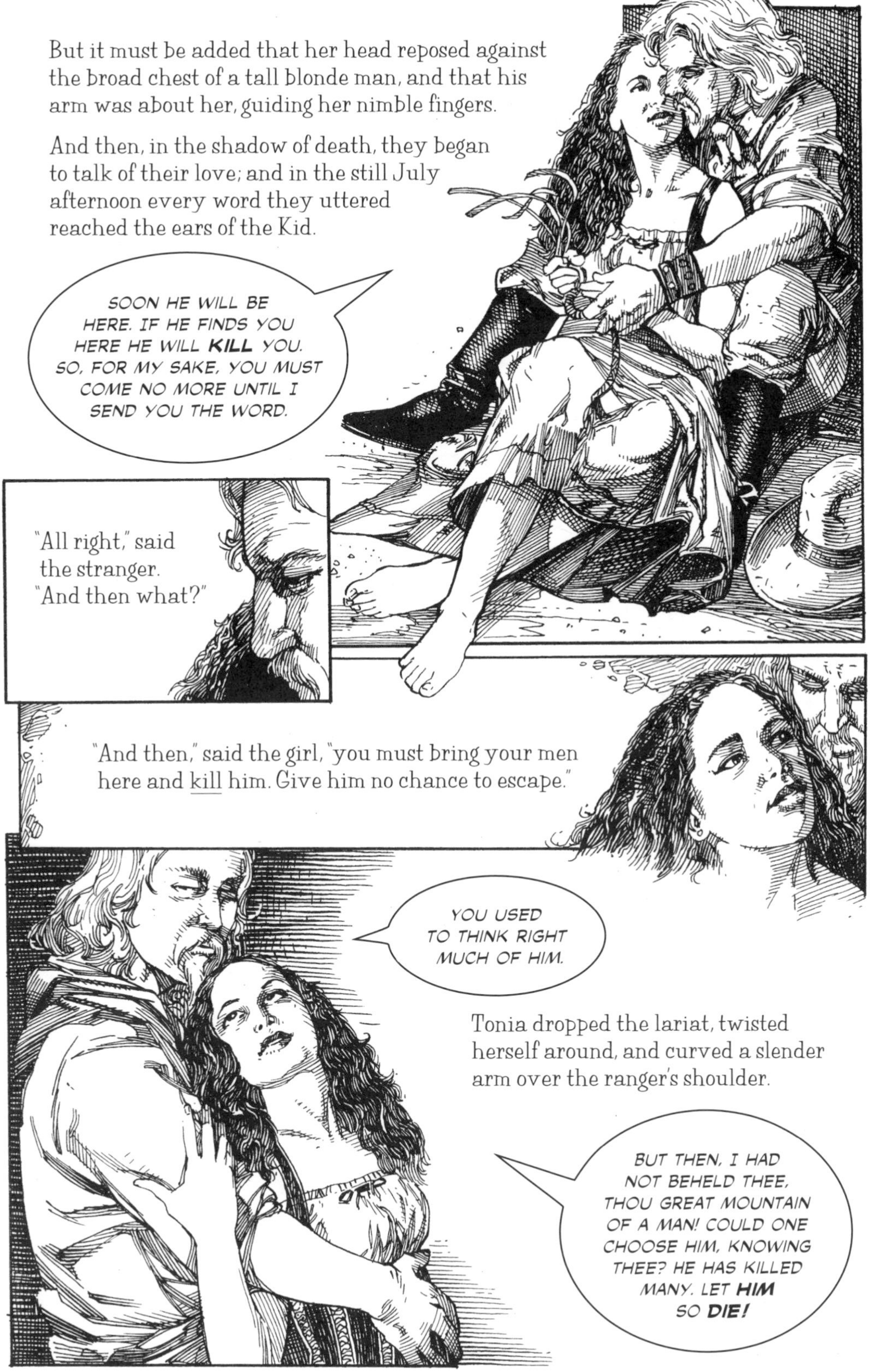
But it must be added that her head reposed against the broad chest of a tall blonde man, and that his arm was about her, guiding her nimble fingers.
And then, in the shadow of death, they began to talk of their love; and in the still July afternoon every word they uttered reached the ears of the Kid.
SOON HE WILL BE HERE. IF HE FINDS YOU HERE HE WILL KILL YOU. SO, FOR MY SAKE, YOU MUST COME NO MORE UNTIL I SEND YOU THE WORD.
"All right," said the stranger. "And then what?"
"And then," said the girl, "you must bring your men here and kill him. Give him no chance to escape."
YOU USED TO THINK RIGHT MUCH OF HIM.
Tonia dropped the lariat, twisted herself around, and curved a slender arm over the ranger's shoulder.
BUT THEN, I HAD NOT BEHELD THEE, THOU GREAT MOUNTAIN OF A MAN! COULD ONE CHOOSE HIM, KNOWING THEE? HE HAS KILLED MANY. LET HIM SO DIE!

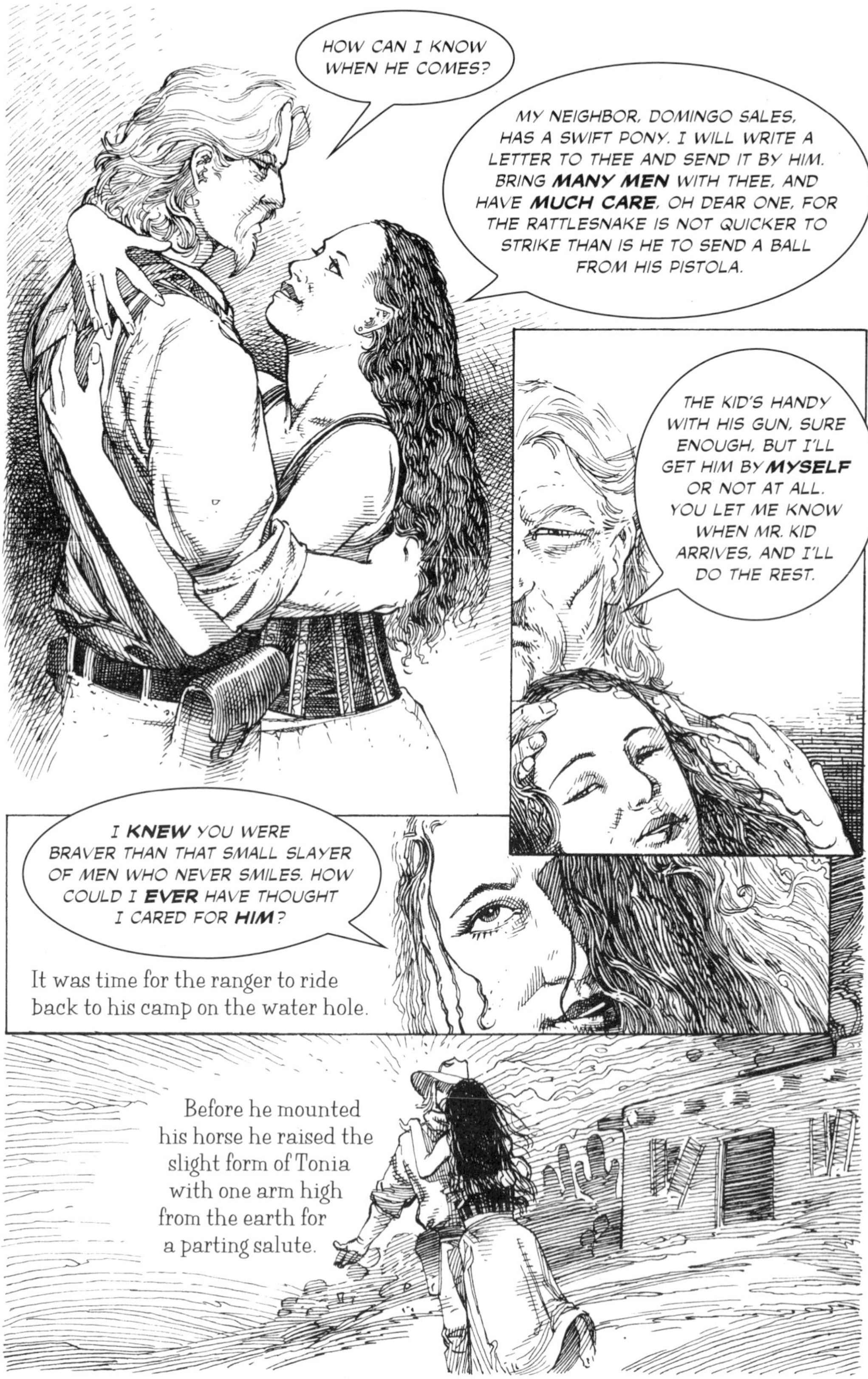
HOW CAN I KNOW WHEN HE COMES?
MY NEIGHBOR, DOMINGO SALES, HAS A SWIFT PONY. I WILL WRITE A LETTER TO THEE AND SEND IT BY HIM. BRING **MANY MEN** WITH THEE, AND HAVE **MUCH CARE**, OH DEAR ONE, FOR THE RATTLESNAKE IS NOT QUICKER TO STRIKE THAN IS HE TO SEND A BALL FROM HIS PISTOLA.
THE KID'S HANDY WITH HIS GUN, SURE ENOUGH, BUT I'LL GET HIM BY **MYSELF** OR NOT AT ALL. YOU LET ME KNOW WHEN MR. KID ARRIVES, AND I'LL DO THE REST.
I **KNEW** YOU WERE BRAVER THAN THAT SMALL SLAYER OF MEN WHO NEVER SMILES. HOW COULD I **EVER** HAVE THOUGHT I CARED FOR **HIM**?
It was time for the ranger to ride back to his camp on the water hole.
Before he mounted his horse he raised the slight form of Tonia with one arm high from the earth for a parting salute.

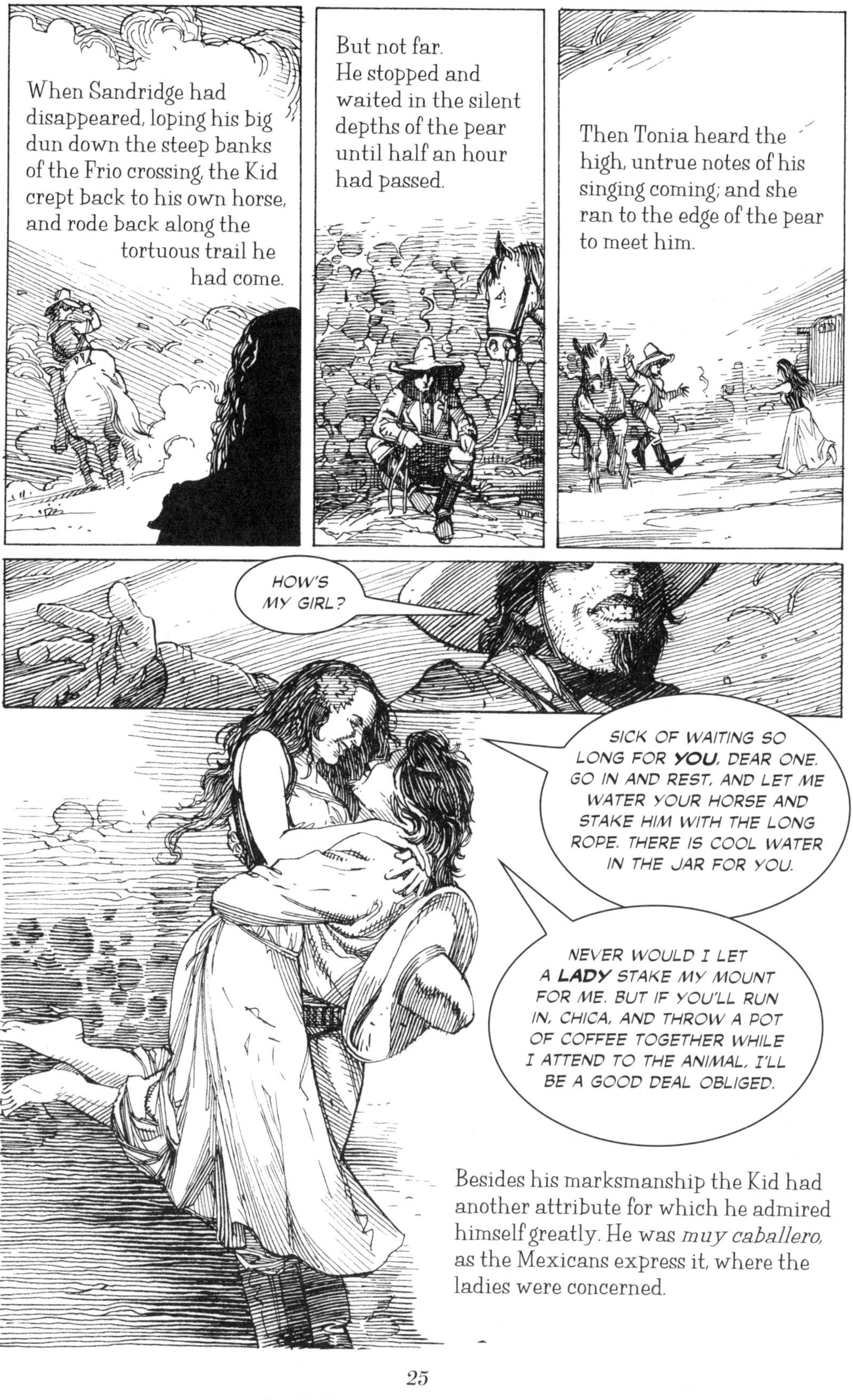
When Sandridge had disappeared, loping his big dun down the steep banks of the Frio crossing, the Kid crept back to his own horse, and rode back along the tortuous trail he had come.
But not far.
He stopped and waited in the silent depths of the pear until half an hour had passed.
Then Tonia heard the high, untrue notes of his singing coming; and she ran to the edge of the pear to meet him.
HOW'S MY GIRL?
SICK OF WAITING SO LONG FOR **YOU**, DEAR ONE. GO IN AND REST, AND LET ME WATER YOUR HORSE AND STAKE HIM WITH THE LONG ROPE. THERE IS COOL WATER IN THE JAR FOR YOU.
NEVER WOULD I LET A **LADY** STAKE MY MOUNT FOR ME. BUT IF YOU'LL RUN IN, CHICA, AND THROW A POT OF COFFEE TOGETHER WHILE I ATTEND TO THE ANIMAL, I'LL BE A GOOD DEAL OBLIGED.
Besides his marksmanship the Kid had another attribute for which he admired himself greatly. He was *muy caballero*, as the Mexicans express it, where the ladies were concerned.

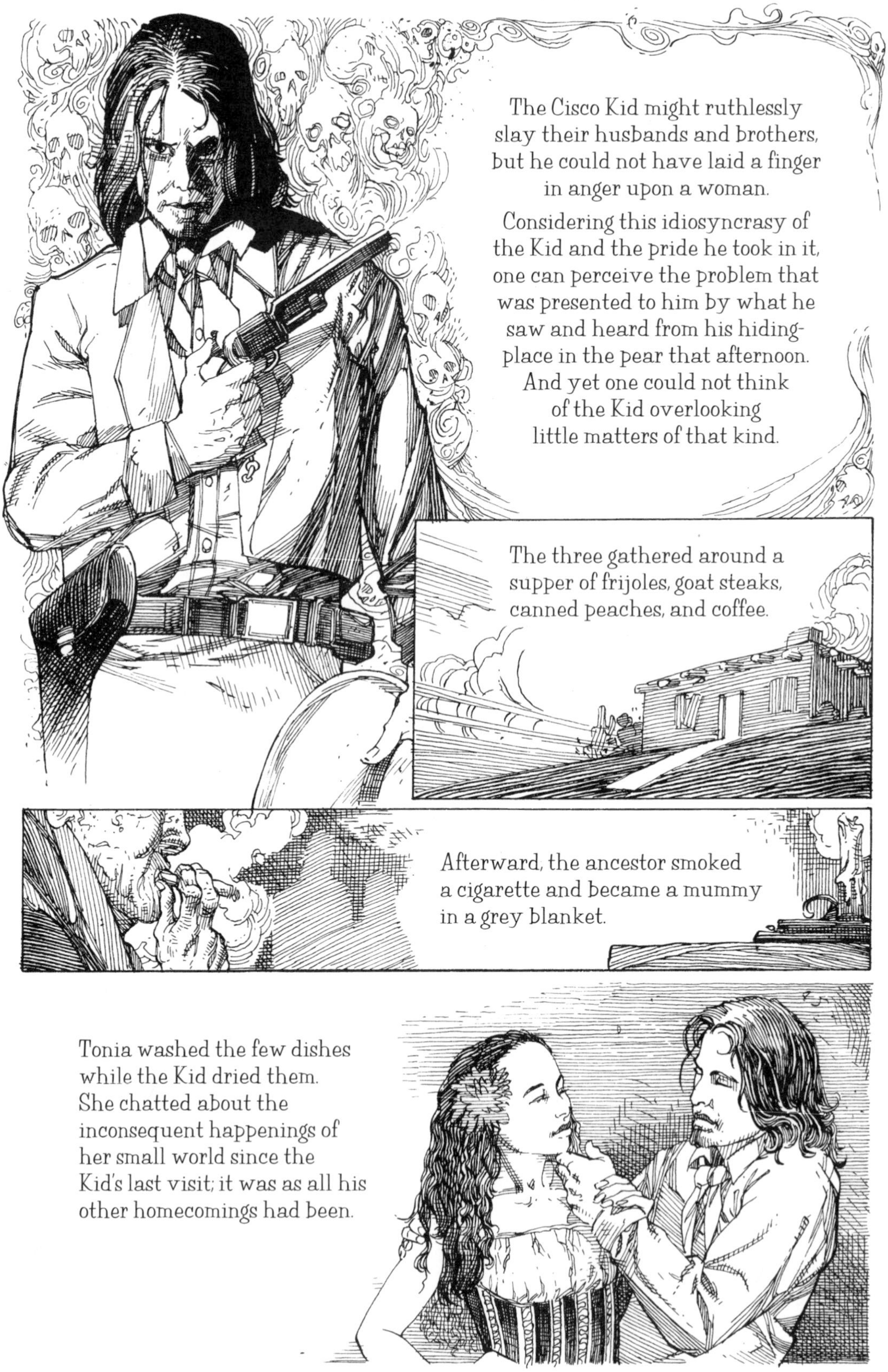
The Cisco Kid might ruthlessly slay their husbands and brothers, but he could not have laid a finger in anger upon a woman.
Considering this idiosyncrasy of the Kid and the pride he took in it, one can perceive the problem that was presented to him by what he saw and heard from his hiding-place in the pear that afternoon. And yet one could not think of the Kid overlooking little matters of that kind.
The three gathered around a supper of frijoles, goat steaks, canned peaches, and coffee.
Afterward, the ancestor smoked a cigarette and became a mummy in a grey blanket.
Tonia washed the few dishes while the Kid dried them. She chatted about the inconsequent happenings of her small world since the Kid's last visit; it was as all his other homecomings had been.

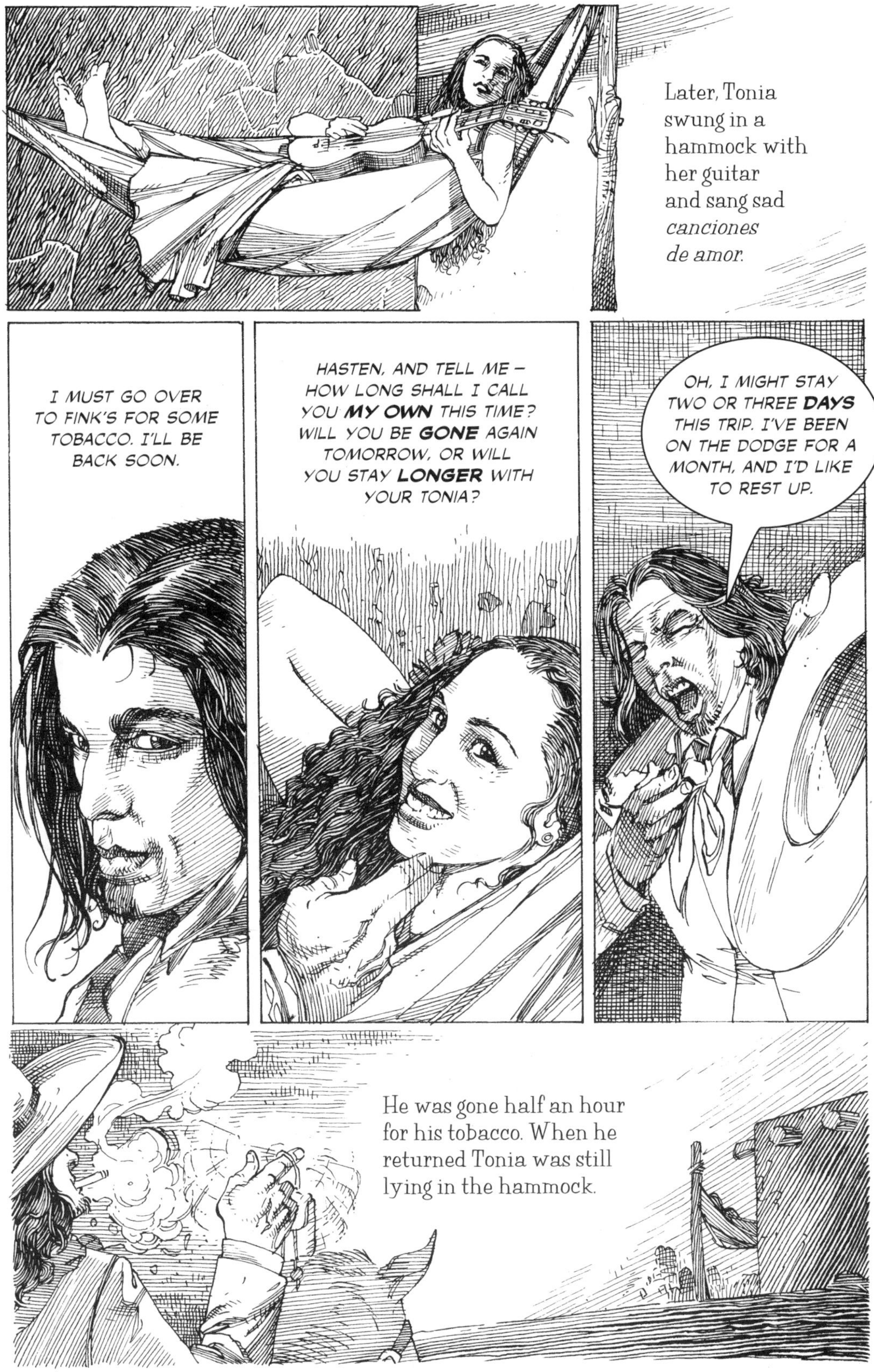
Later, Tonia swung in a hammock with her guitar and sang sad *canciones de amor*.
I MUST GO OVER TO FINK'S FOR SOME TOBACCO. I'LL BE BACK SOON.
HASTEN, AND TELL ME – HOW LONG SHALL I CALL YOU **MY OWN** THIS TIME? WILL YOU BE **GONE** AGAIN TOMORROW, OR WILL YOU STAY **LONGER** WITH YOUR TONIA?
OH, I MIGHT STAY TWO OR THREE **DAYS** THIS TRIP. I'VE BEEN ON THE DODGE FOR A MONTH, AND I'D LIKE TO REST UP.
He was gone half an hour for his tobacco. When he returned Tonia was still lying in the hammock.

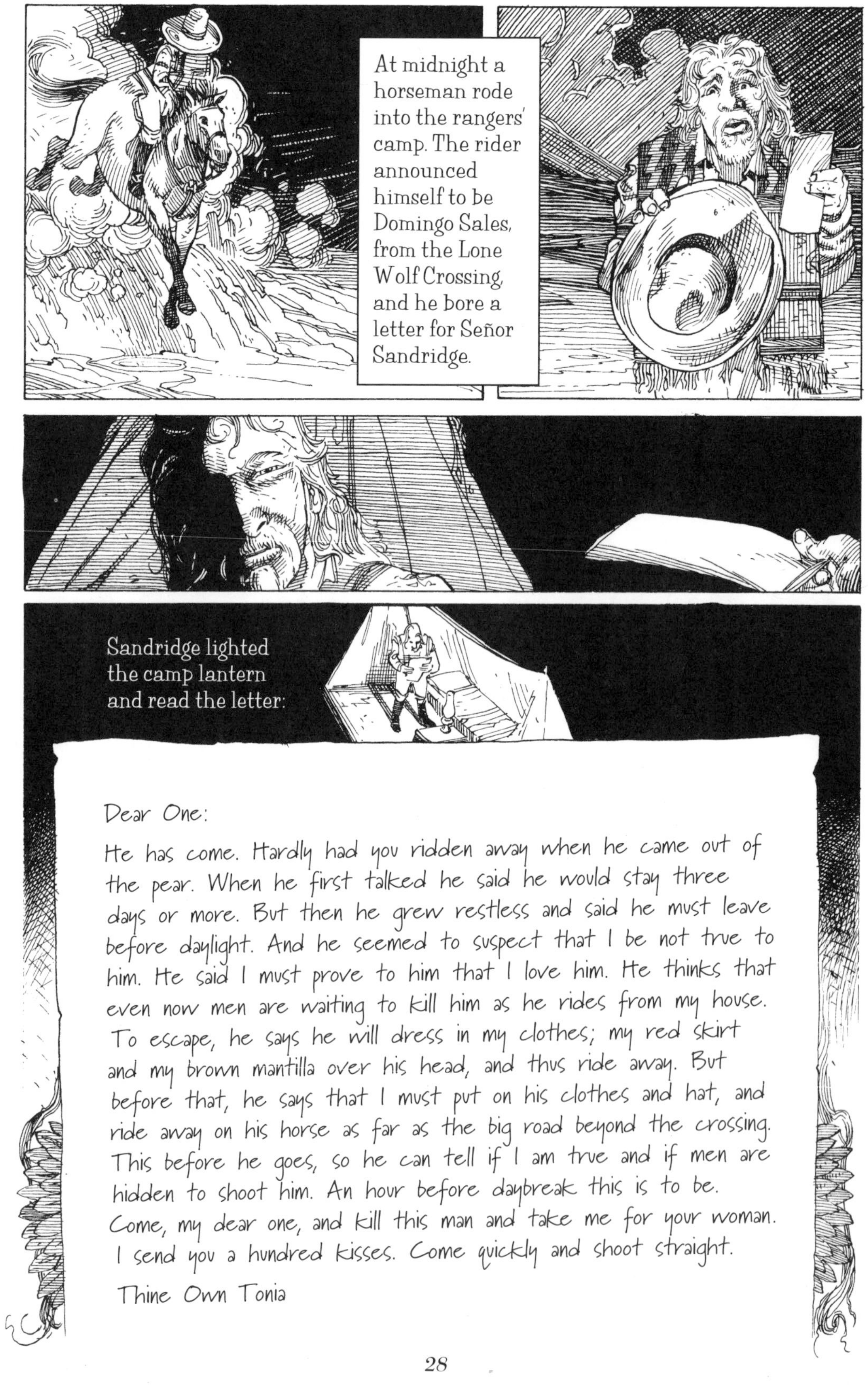
At midnight a horseman rode into the rangers' camp. The rider announced himself to be Domingo Sales, from the Lone Wolf Crossing, and he bore a letter for Señor Sandridge.
Sandridge lighted the camp lantern and read the letter:
Dear One:
He has come. Hardly had you ridden away when he came out of the pear. When he first talked he said he would stay three days or more. But then he grew restless and said he must leave before daylight. And he seemed to suspect that I be not true to him. He said I must prove to him that I love him. He thinks that even now men are waiting to kill him as he rides from my house. To escape, he says he will dress in my clothes; my red skirt and my brown mantilla over his head, and thus ride away. But before that, he says that I must put on his clothes and hat, and ride away on his horse as far as the big road beyond the crossing. This before he goes, so he can tell if I am true and if men are hidden to shoot him. An hour before daybreak this is to be. Come, my dear one, and kill this man and take me for your woman. I send you a hundred kisses. Come quickly and shoot straight.
Thine Own Tonia

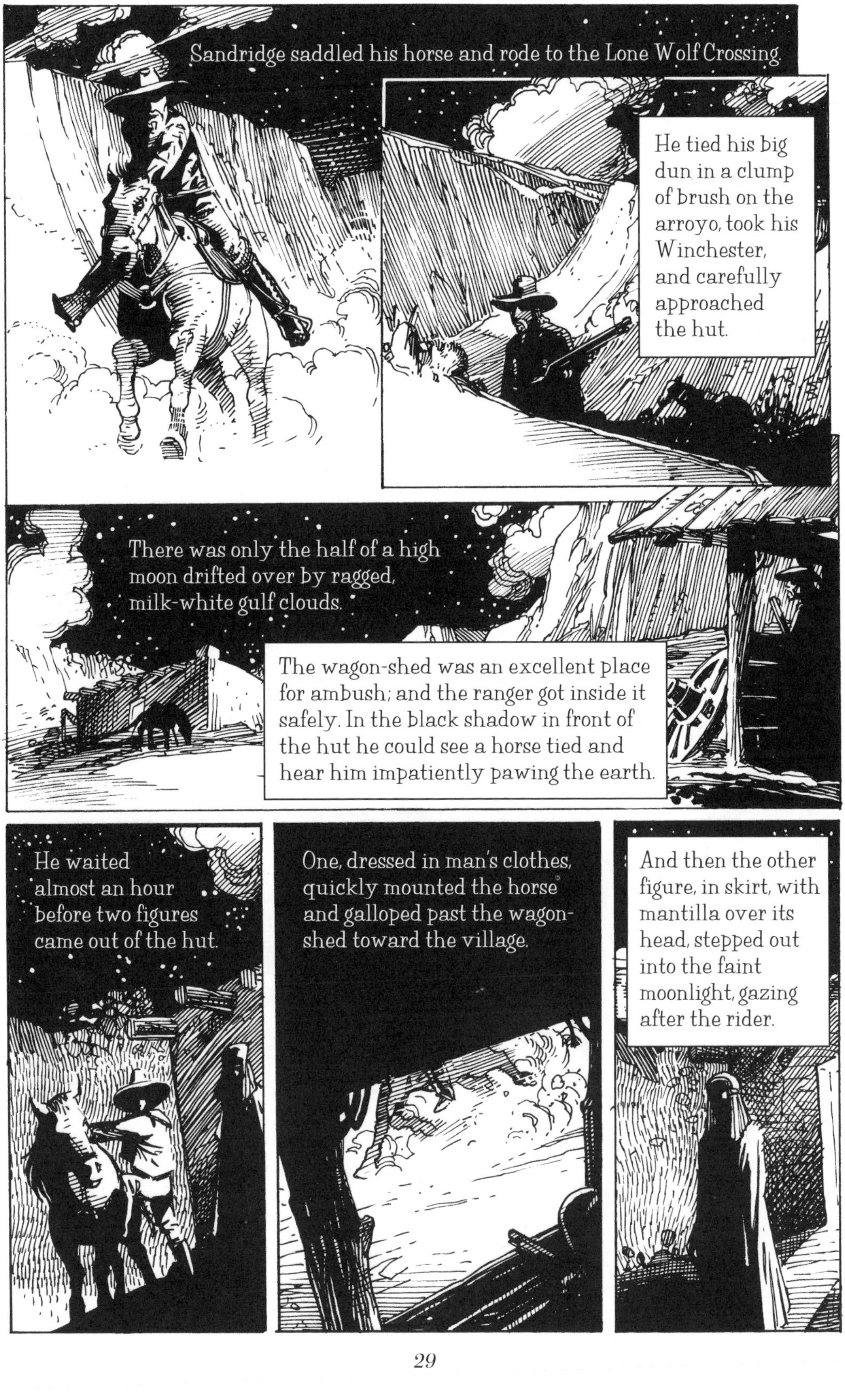
Sandridge saddled his horse and rode to the Lone Wolf Crossing.
He tied his big dun in a clump of brush on the arroyo, took his Winchester, and carefully approached the hut.
There was only the half of a high moon drifted over by ragged, milk-white gulf clouds.
The wagon-shed was an excellent place for ambush; and the ranger got inside it safely. In the black shadow in front of the hut he could see a horse tied and hear him impatiently pawing the earth.
He waited almost an hour before two figures came out of the hut.
One, dressed in man's clothes, quickly mounted the horse and galloped past the wagon-shed toward the village.
And then the other figure, in skirt, with mantilla over its head, stepped out into the faint moonlight, gazing after the rider.

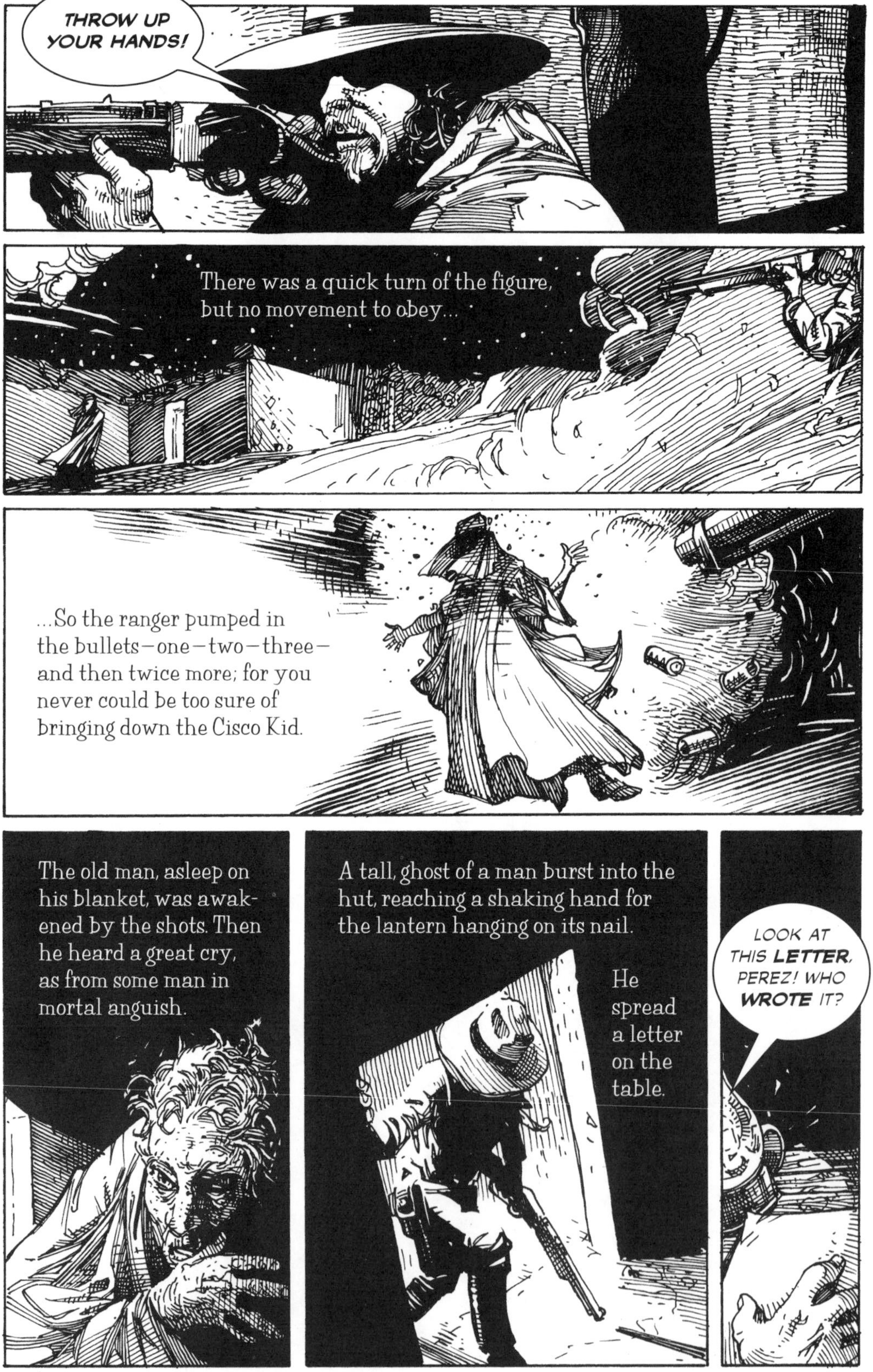
THROW UP YOUR HANDS!
There was a quick turn of the figure, but no movement to obey...
...So the ranger pumped in the bullets—one—two—three—and then twice more; for you never could be too sure of bringing down the Cisco Kid.
The old man, asleep on his blanket, was awakened by the shots. Then he heard a great cry, as from some man in mortal anguish.
A tall, ghost of a man burst into the hut, reaching a shaking hand for the lantern hanging on its nail.
He spread a letter on the table.
LOOK AT THIS LETTER, PEREZ! WHO WROTE IT?

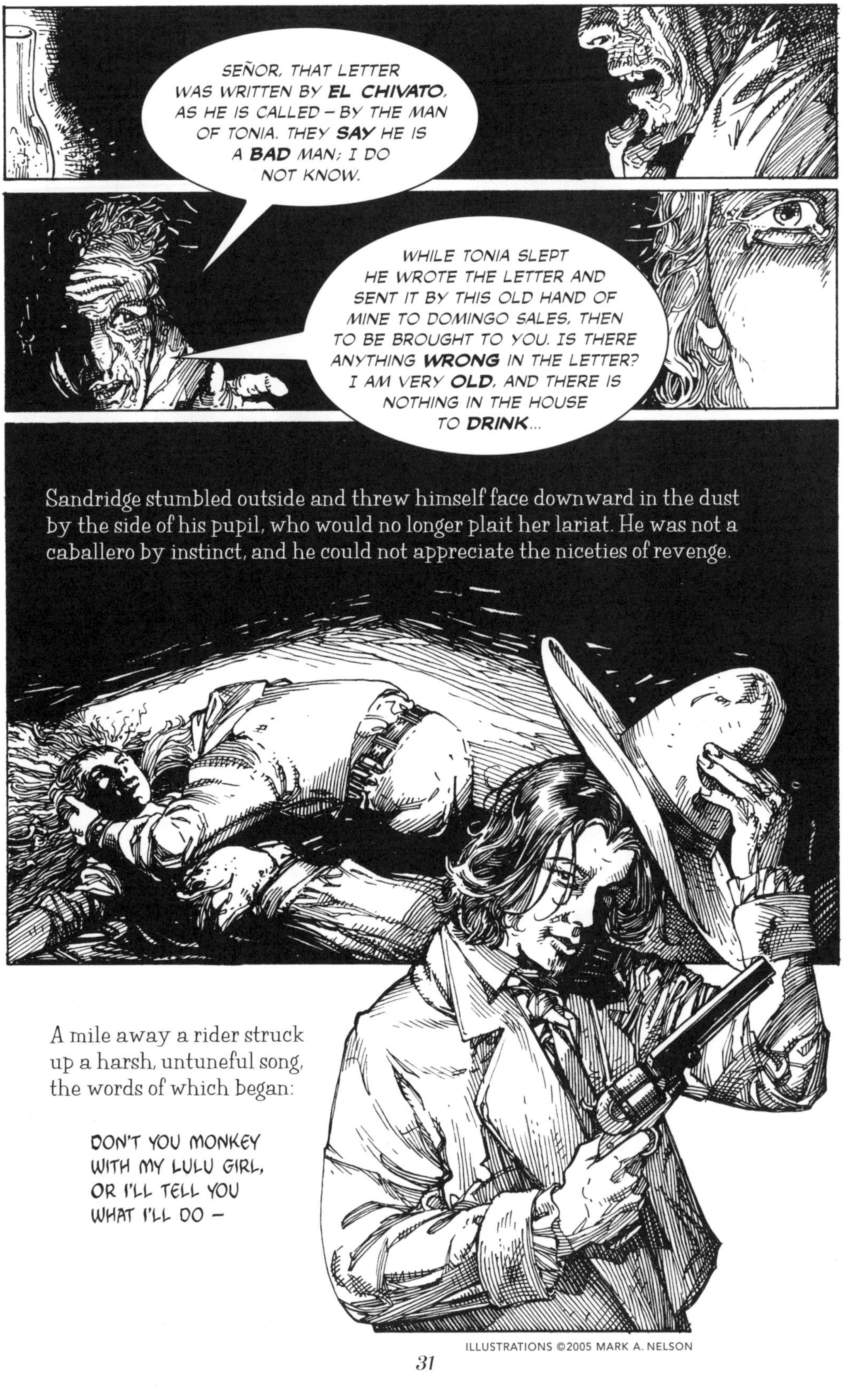
SEÑOR, THAT LETTER WAS WRITTEN BY **EL CHIVATO**, AS HE IS CALLED – BY THE MAN OF TONIA. THEY **SAY** HE IS A **BAD** MAN; I DO NOT KNOW.
WHILE TONIA SLEPT HE WROTE THE LETTER AND SENT IT BY THIS OLD HAND OF MINE TO DOMINGO SALES, THEN TO BE BROUGHT TO YOU. IS THERE ANYTHING **WRONG** IN THE LETTER? I AM VERY **OLD**, AND THERE IS NOTHING IN THE HOUSE TO **DRINK**...
Sandridge stumbled outside and threw himself face downward in the dust by the side of his pupil, who would no longer plait her lariat. He was not a caballero by instinct, and he could not appreciate the niceties of revenge.
DON'T YOU MONKEY WITH MY LULU GIRL, OR I'LL TELL YOU WHAT I'LL DO –

A mile away a rider struck up a harsh, untuneful song, the words of which began:

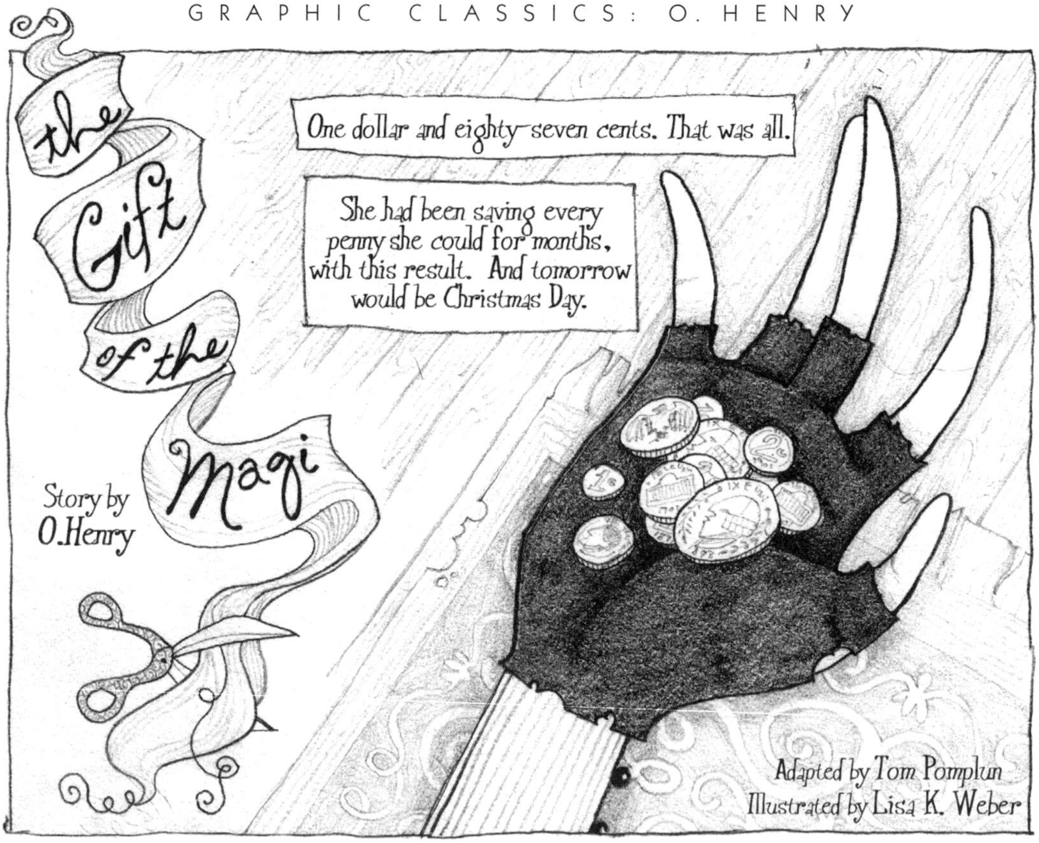
the Gift of the Magi
Story by O.Henry
One dollar and eighty-seven cents. That was all.
She had been saving every penny she could for months, with this result. And tomorrow would be Christmas Day.
Adapted by Tom Pomplun
Illustrated by Lisa K. Weber

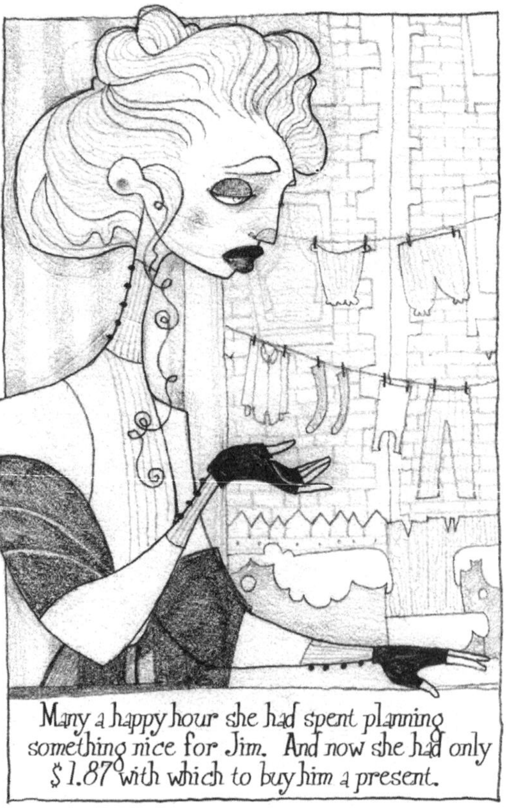
Many a happy hour she had spent planning something nice for Jim. And now she had only $1.87 with which to buy him a present.

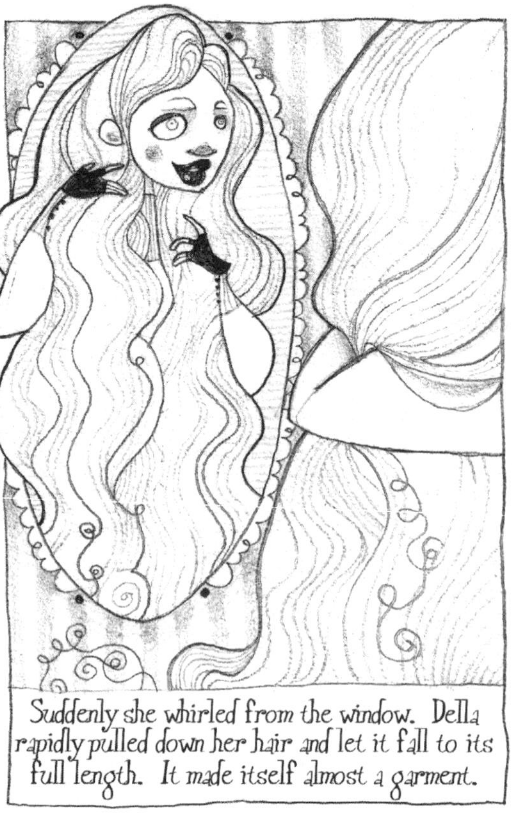
Suddenly she whirled from the window. Della rapidly pulled down her hair and let it fall to its full length. It made itself almost a garment.

There were but two possessions in which Jim and Della took pride.
One was Jim's gold watch that had been his father's and his grandfather's.

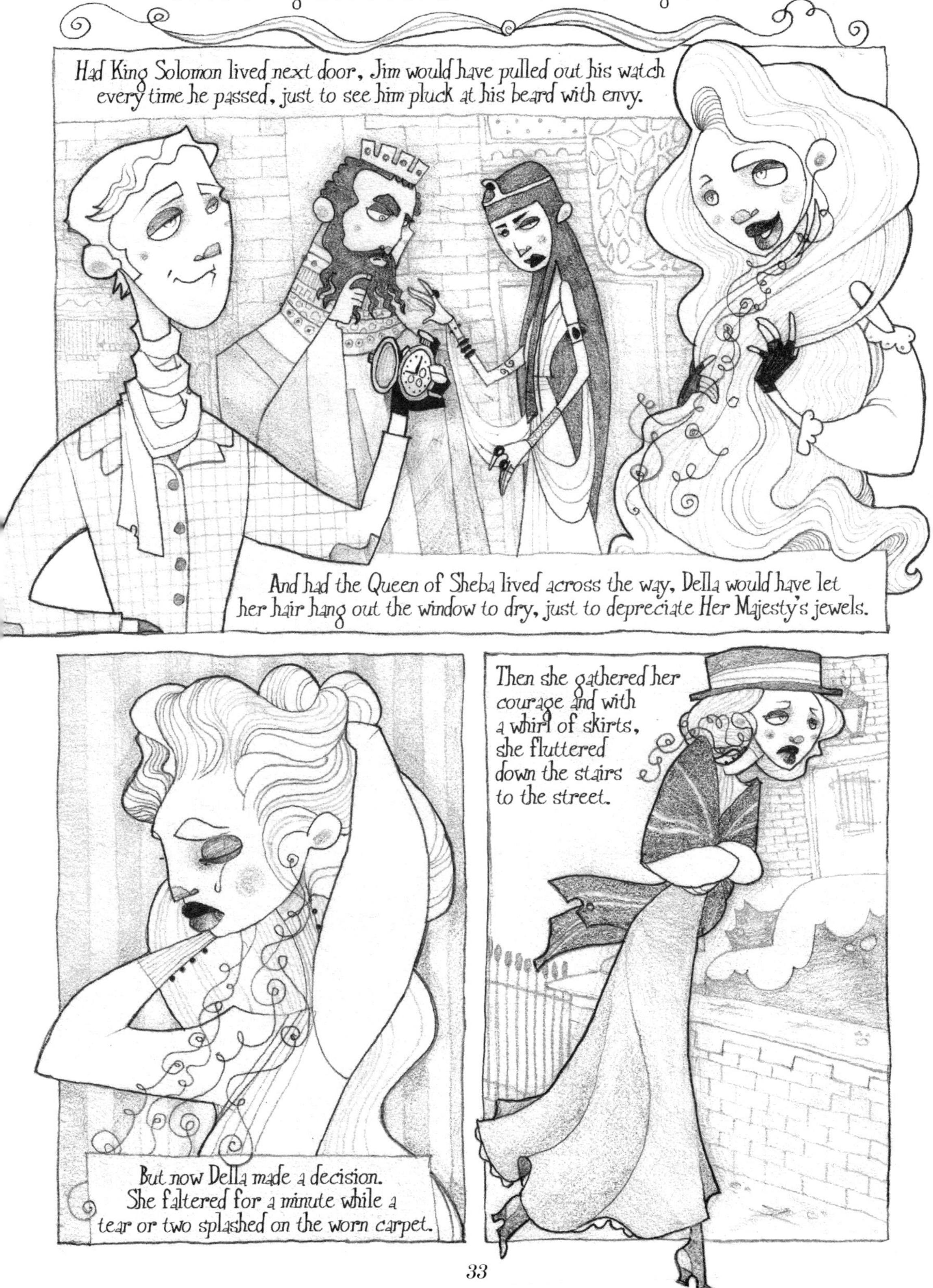
Had King Solomon lived next door, Jim would have pulled out his watch every time he passed, just to see him pluck at his beard with envy.
And had the Queen of Sheba lived across the way, Della would have let her hair hang out the window to dry, just to depreciate Her Majesty's jewels.
But now Della made a decision. She faltered for a minute while a tear or two splashed on the worn carpet.
Then she gathered her courage and with a whirl of skirts, she fluttered down the stairs to the street.

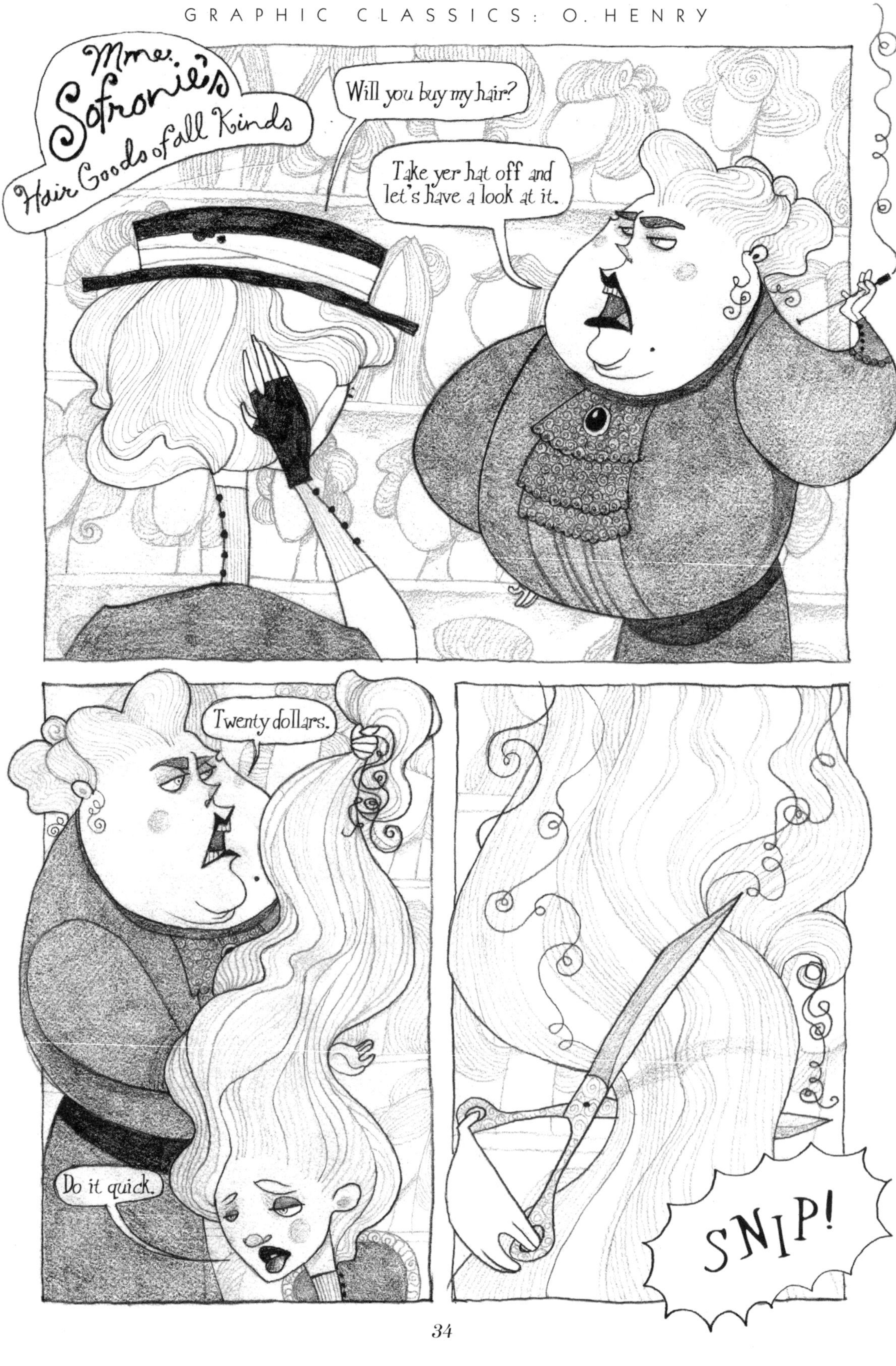
Mme. Sofronie's
Hair Goods of all Kinds
Will you buy my hair?
Take yer hat off and let's have a look at it.
Twenty dollars.
Do it quick.
SNIP!

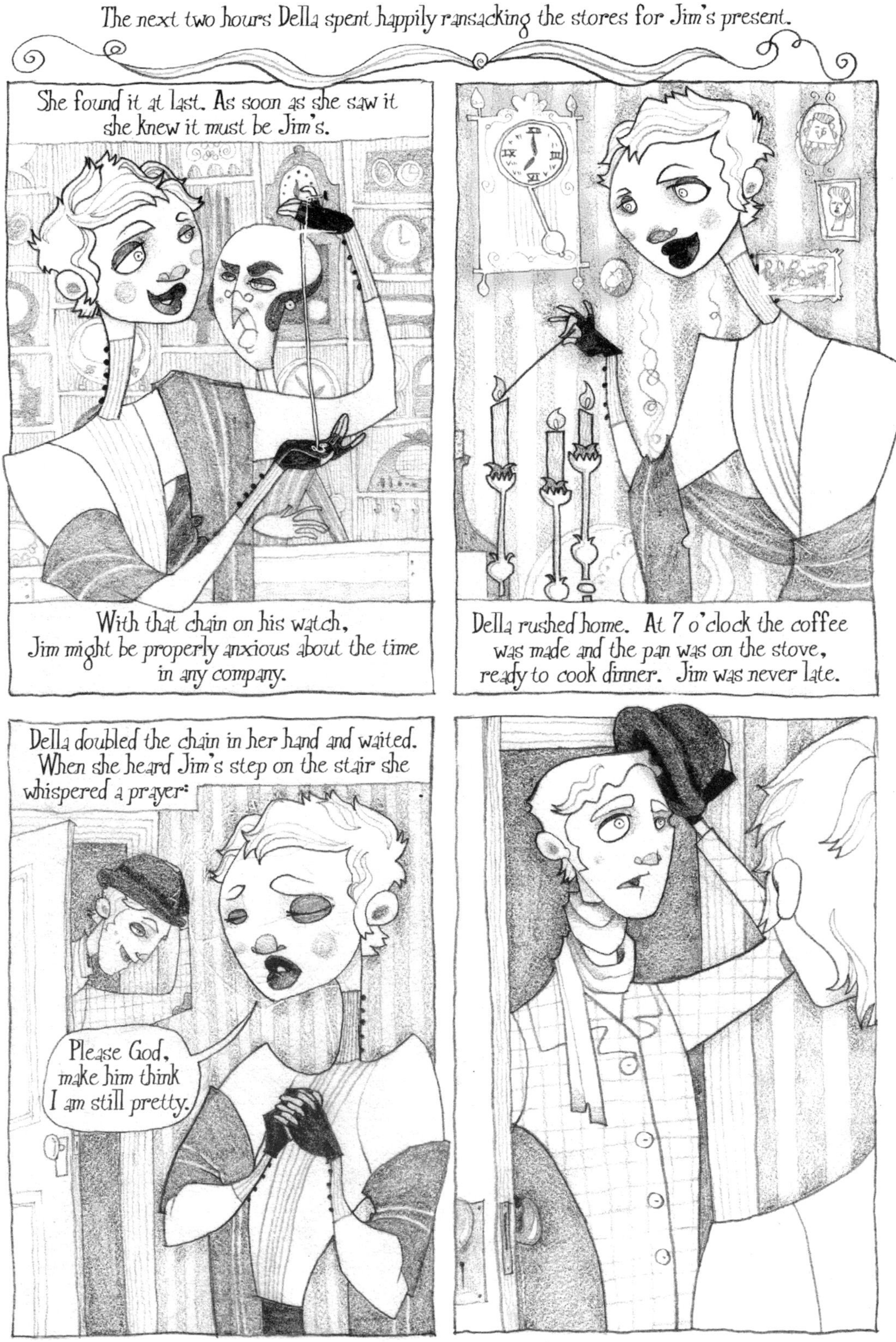
The next two hours Della spent happily ransacking the stores for Jim's present.
She found it at last. As soon as she saw it she knew it must be Jim's.
With that chain on his watch, Jim might be properly anxious about the time in any company.
Della rushed home. At 7 o'clock the coffee was made and the pan was on the stove, ready to cook dinner. Jim was never late.
Della doubled the chain in her hand and waited. When she heard Jim's step on the stair she whispered a prayer:
Please God, make him think I am still pretty.

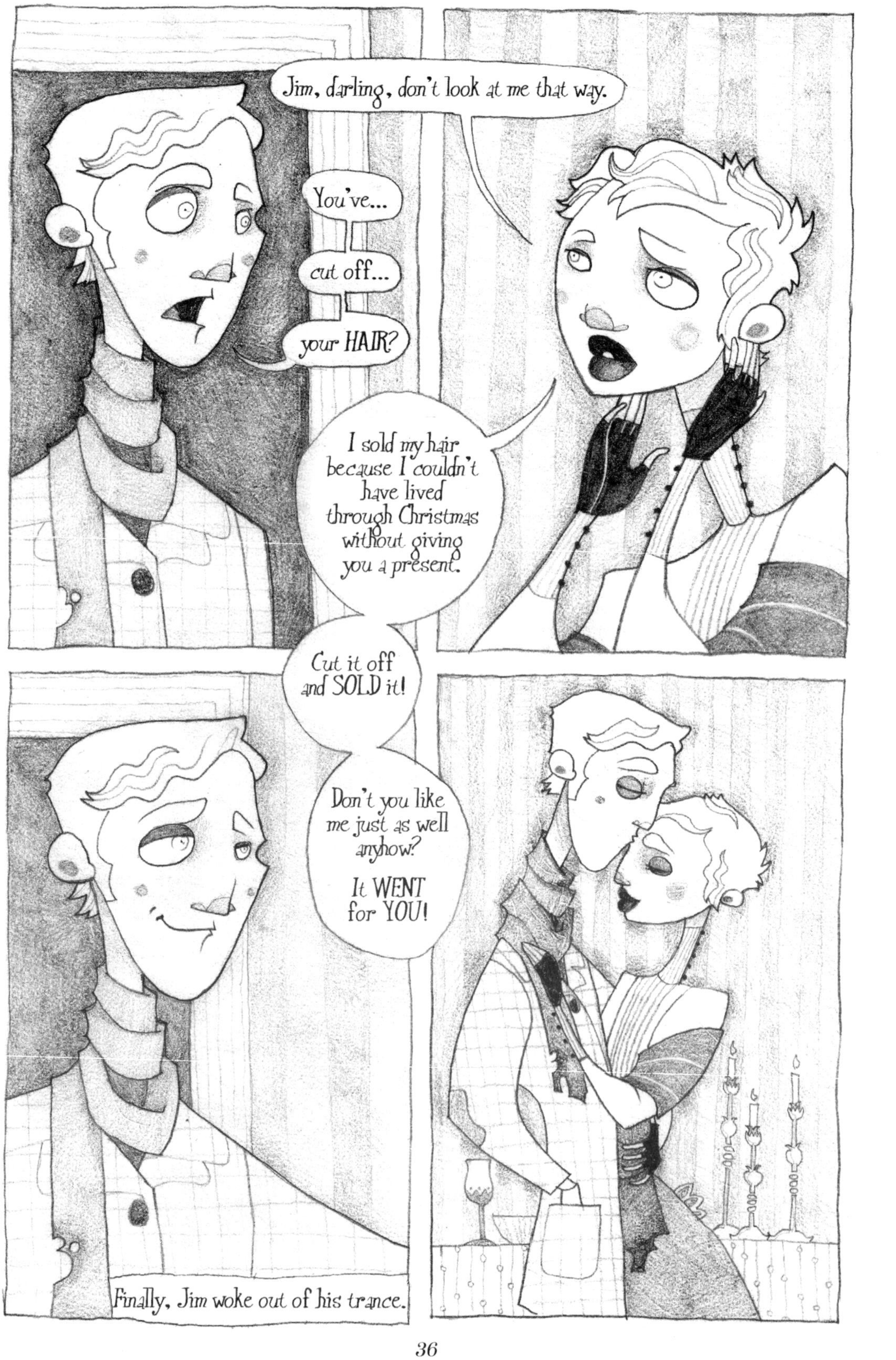

You've...
cut off...
your HAIR?
Jim, darling, don't look at me that way.
I sold my hair because I couldn't have lived through Christmas without giving you a present.
Cut it off and SOLD it!
Don't you like me just as well anyhow?
It WENT for YOU!
Finally, Jim woke out of his trance.

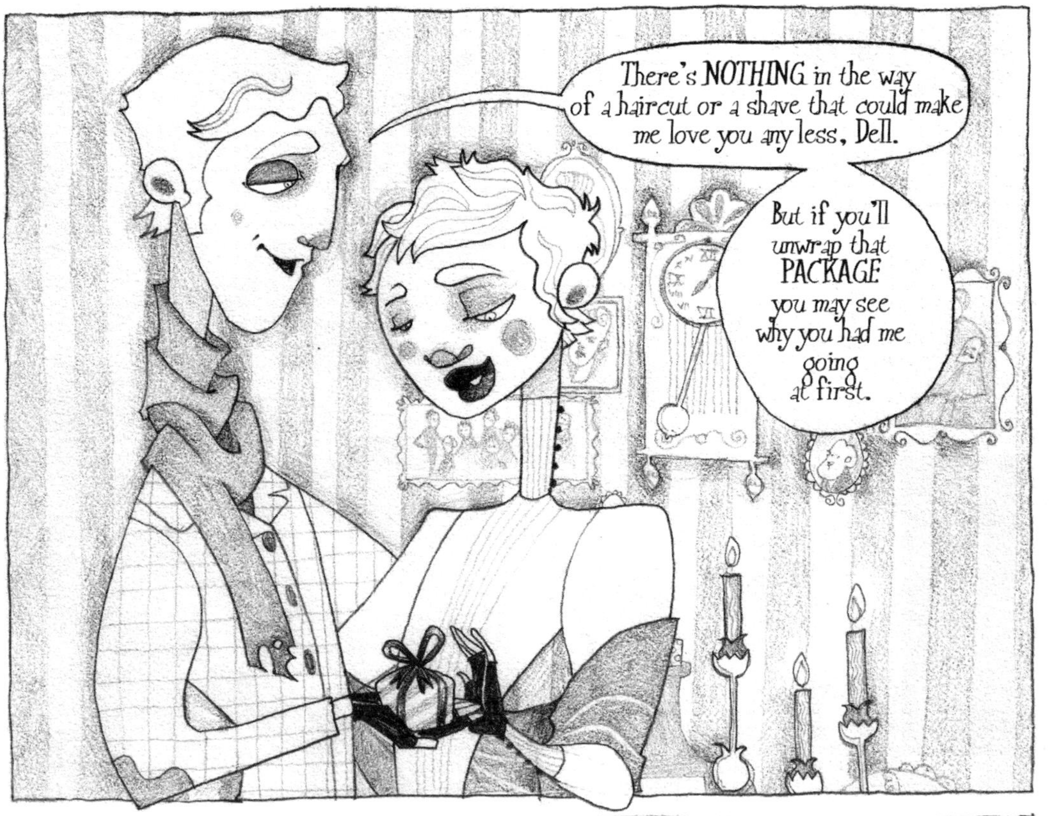
There's NOTHING in the way of a haircut or a shave that could make me love you any less, Dell.
But if you'll unwrap that PACKAGE you may see why you had me going at first.

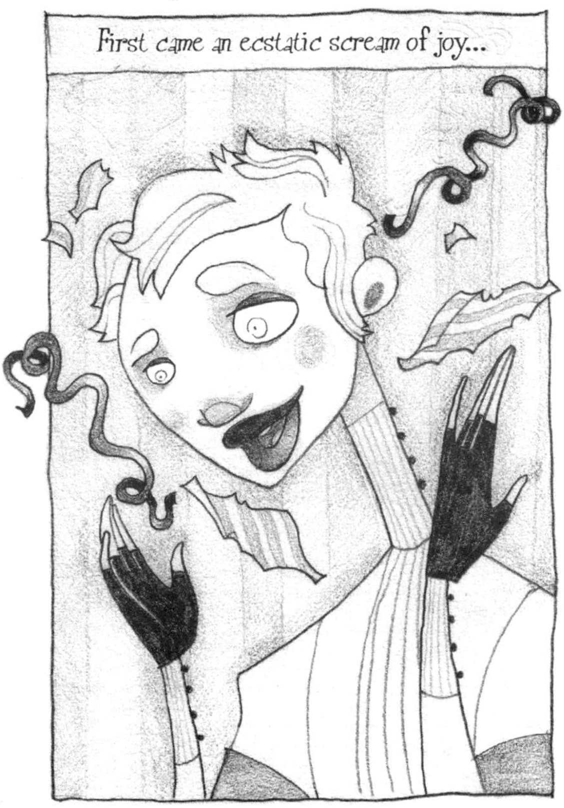
First came an ecstatic scream of joy...

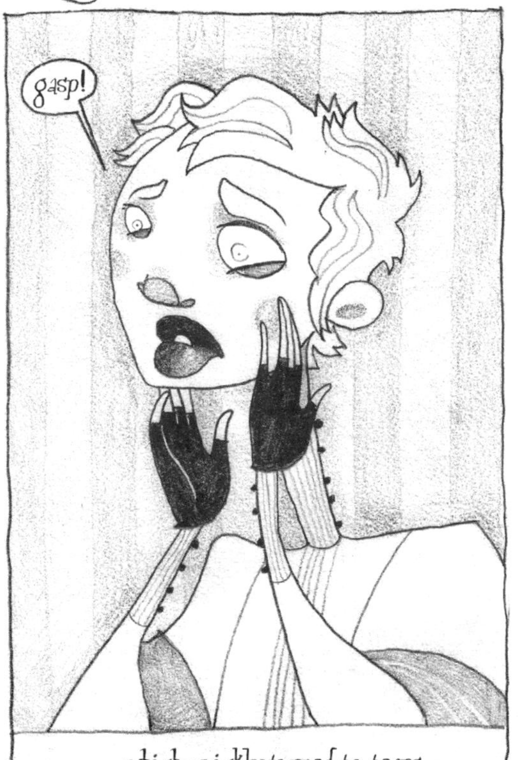
gasp!
...which quickly turned to tears.

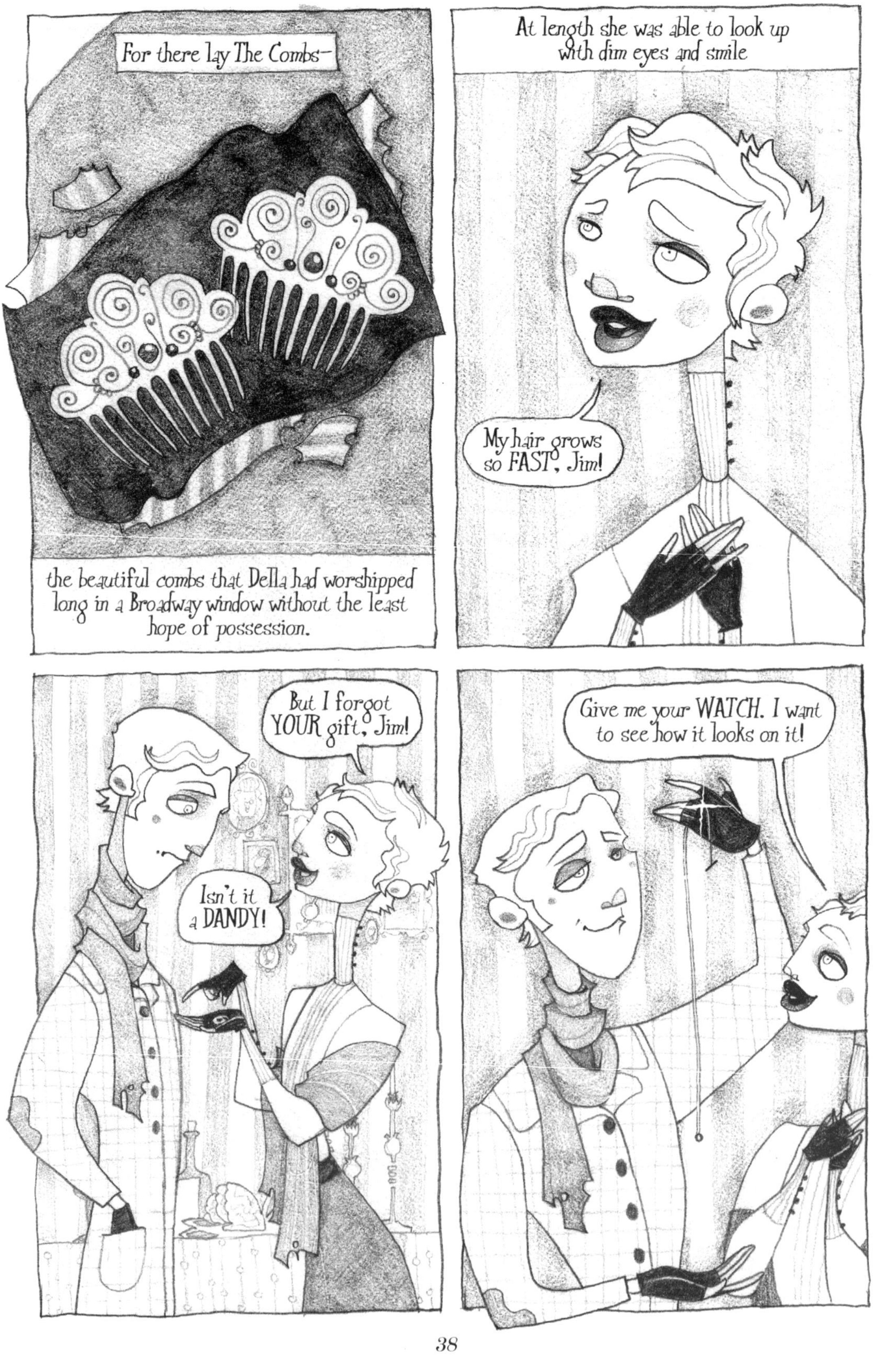
For there lay The Combs–
the beautiful combs that Della had worshipped long in a Broadway window without the least hope of possession.
At length she was able to look up with dim eyes and smile
My hair grows so FAST, Jim!
But I forgot YOUR gift, Jim!
Isn't it a DANDY!
Give me your WATCH. I want to see how it looks on it!

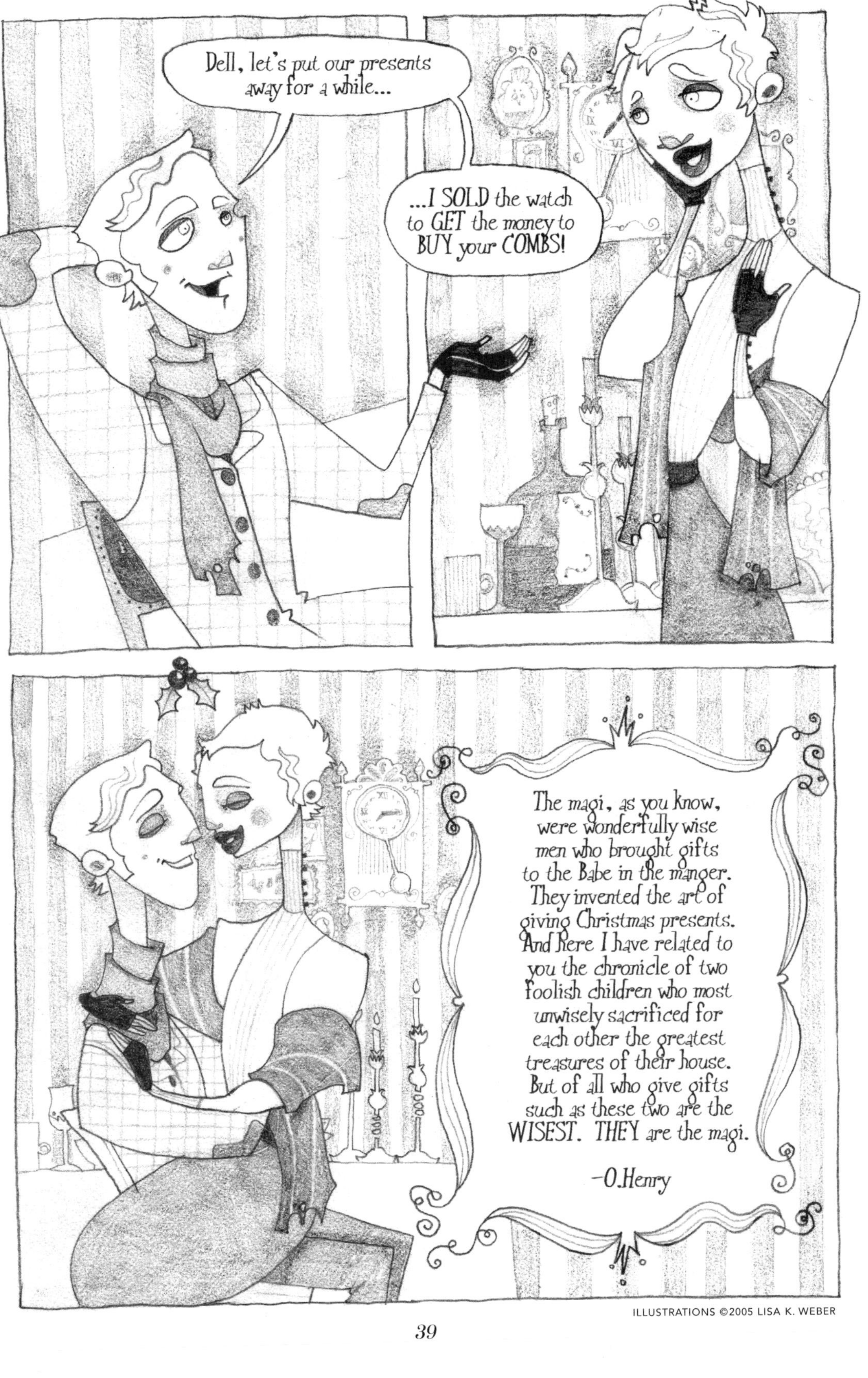
Dell, let's put our presents away for a while...
...I SOLD the watch to GET the money to BUY your COMBS!
The magi, as you know, were wonderfully wise men who brought gifts to the Babe in the manger. They invented the art of giving Christmas presents. And here I have related to you the chronicle of two foolish children who most unwisely sacrificed for each other the greatest treasures of their house. But of all who give gifts such as these two are the WISEST. THEY are the magi.
–O.Henry

O. HENRY'S AFTER 20 YEARS

ILLUSTRATED BY RACHEL MASILAMANI

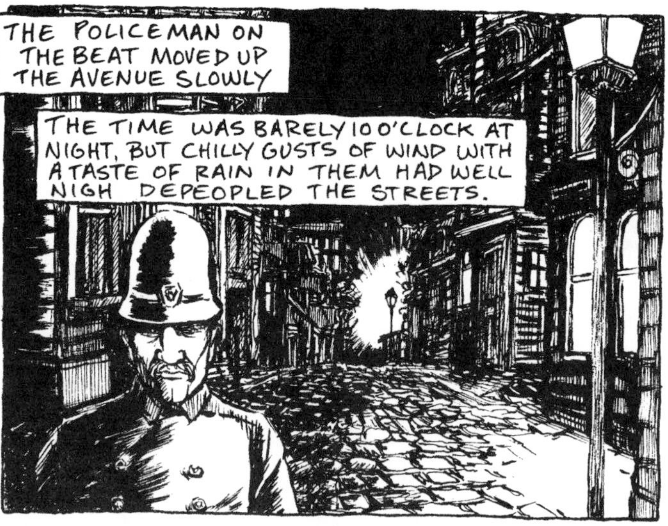
THE POLICEMAN ON THE BEAT MOVED UP THE AVENUE SLOWLY
THE TIME WAS BARELY 10 O'CLOCK AT NIGHT, BUT CHILLY GUSTS OF WIND WITH A TASTE OF RAIN IN THEM HAD WELL NIGH DEPEOPLED THE STREETS.

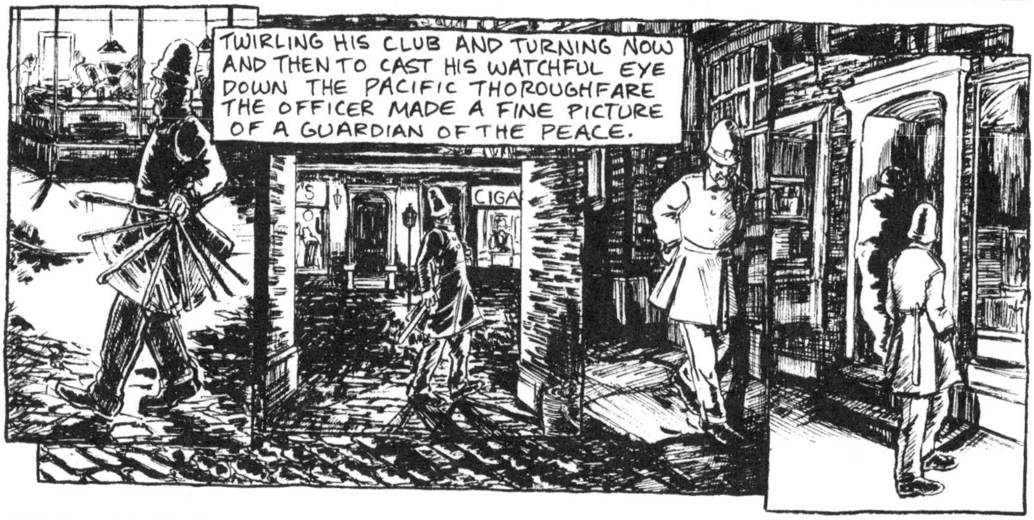
TWIRLING HIS CLUB AND TURNING NOW AND THEN TO CAST HIS WATCHFUL EYE DOWN THE PACIFIC THOROUGHFARE THE OFFICER MADE A FINE PICTURE OF A GUARDIAN OF THE PEACE.
CIGA

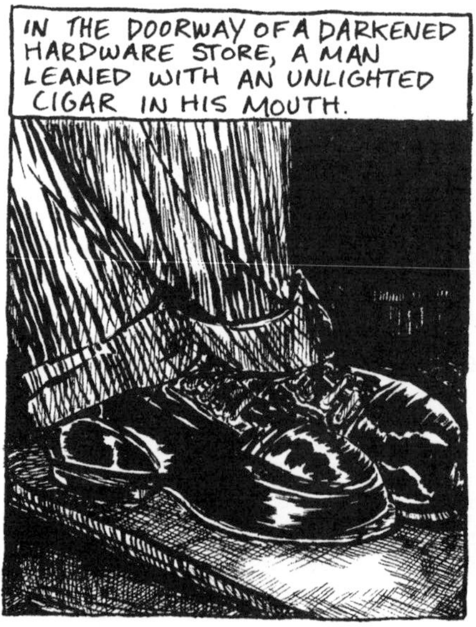
IN THE DOORWAY OF A DARKENED HARDWARE STORE, A MAN LEANED WITH AN UNLIGHTED CIGAR IN HIS MOUTH.

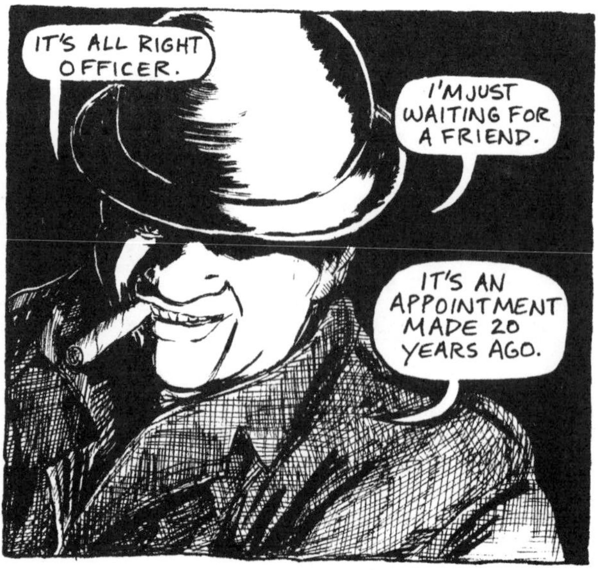
IT'S ALL RIGHT OFFICER.
I'M JUST WAITING FOR A FRIEND.
IT'S AN APPOINTMENT MADE 20 YEARS AGO.

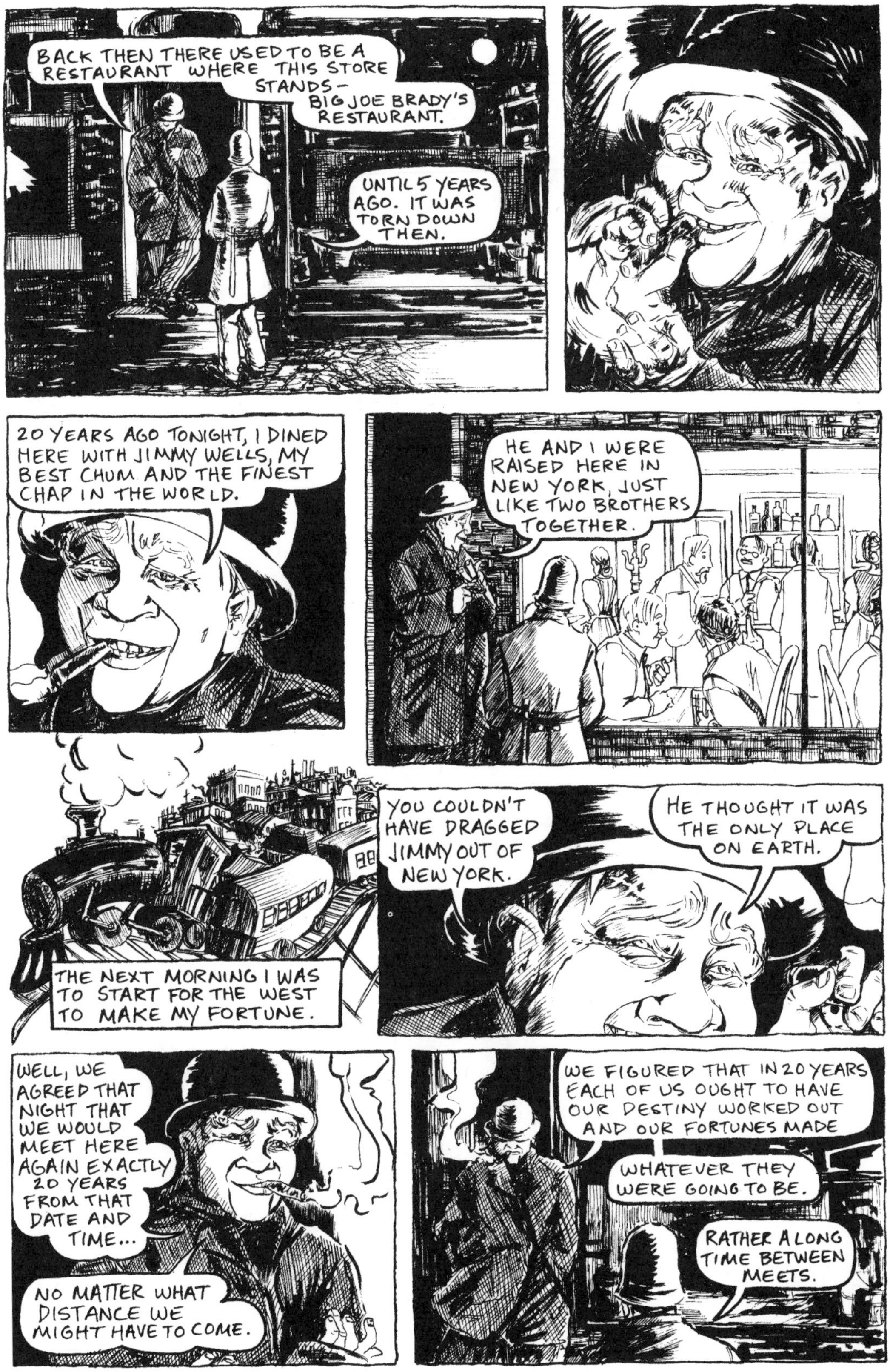
BACK THEN THERE USED TO BE A RESTAURANT WHERE THIS STORE STANDS—
BIG JOE BRADY'S RESTAURANT.
UNTIL 5 YEARS AGO. IT WAS TORN DOWN THEN.
20 YEARS AGO TONIGHT, I DINED HERE WITH JIMMY WELLS, MY BEST CHUM AND THE FINEST CHAP IN THE WORLD.
HE AND I WERE RAISED HERE IN NEW YORK, JUST LIKE TWO BROTHERS TOGETHER.
THE NEXT MORNING I WAS TO START FOR THE WEST TO MAKE MY FORTUNE.
YOU COULDN'T HAVE DRAGGED JIMMY OUT OF NEW YORK.
HE THOUGHT IT WAS THE ONLY PLACE ON EARTH.
WELL, WE AGREED THAT NIGHT THAT WE WOULD MEET HERE AGAIN EXACTLY 20 YEARS FROM THAT DATE AND TIME...
NO MATTER WHAT DISTANCE WE MIGHT HAVE TO COME.
WE FIGURED THAT IN 20 YEARS EACH OF US OUGHT TO HAVE OUR DESTINY WORKED OUT AND OUR FORTUNES MADE
WHATEVER THEY WERE GOING TO BE.
RATHER A LONG TIME BETWEEN MEETS.

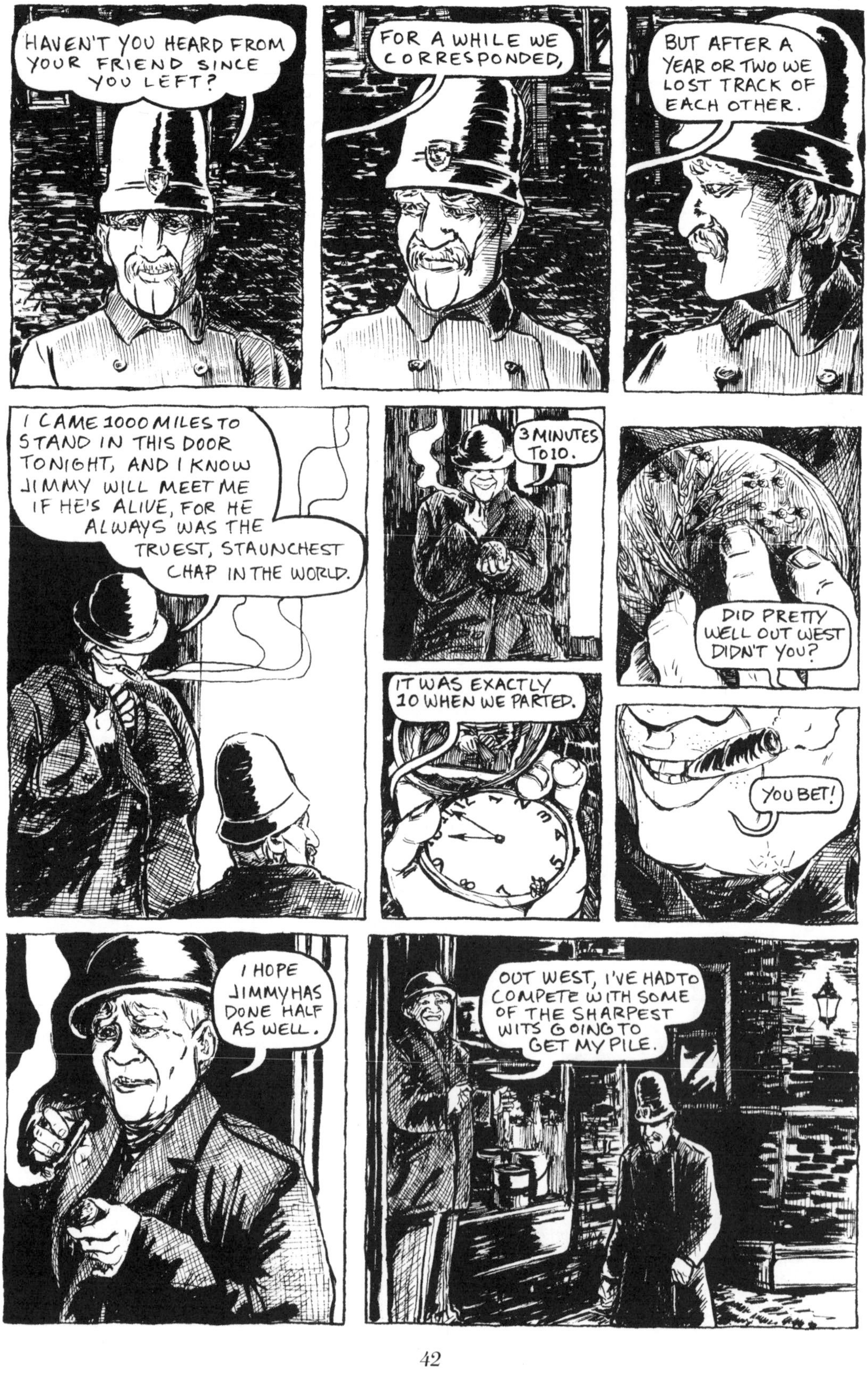
HAVEN'T YOU HEARD FROM YOUR FRIEND SINCE YOU LEFT?
FOR A WHILE WE CORRESPONDED,
BUT AFTER A YEAR OR TWO WE LOST TRACK OF EACH OTHER.
I CAME 1000 MILES TO STAND IN THIS DOOR TONIGHT, AND I KNOW JIMMY WILL MEET ME IF HE'S ALIVE, FOR HE ALWAYS WAS THE TRUEST, STAUNCHEST CHAP IN THE WORLD.
3 MINUTES TO 10.
IT WAS EXACTLY 10 WHEN WE PARTED.
DID PRETTY WELL OUT WEST DIDN'T YOU?
YOU BET!
I HOPE JIMMY HAS DONE HALF AS WELL.
OUT WEST, I'VE HAD TO COMPETE WITH SOME OF THE SHARPEST WITS GOING TO GET MY PILE.

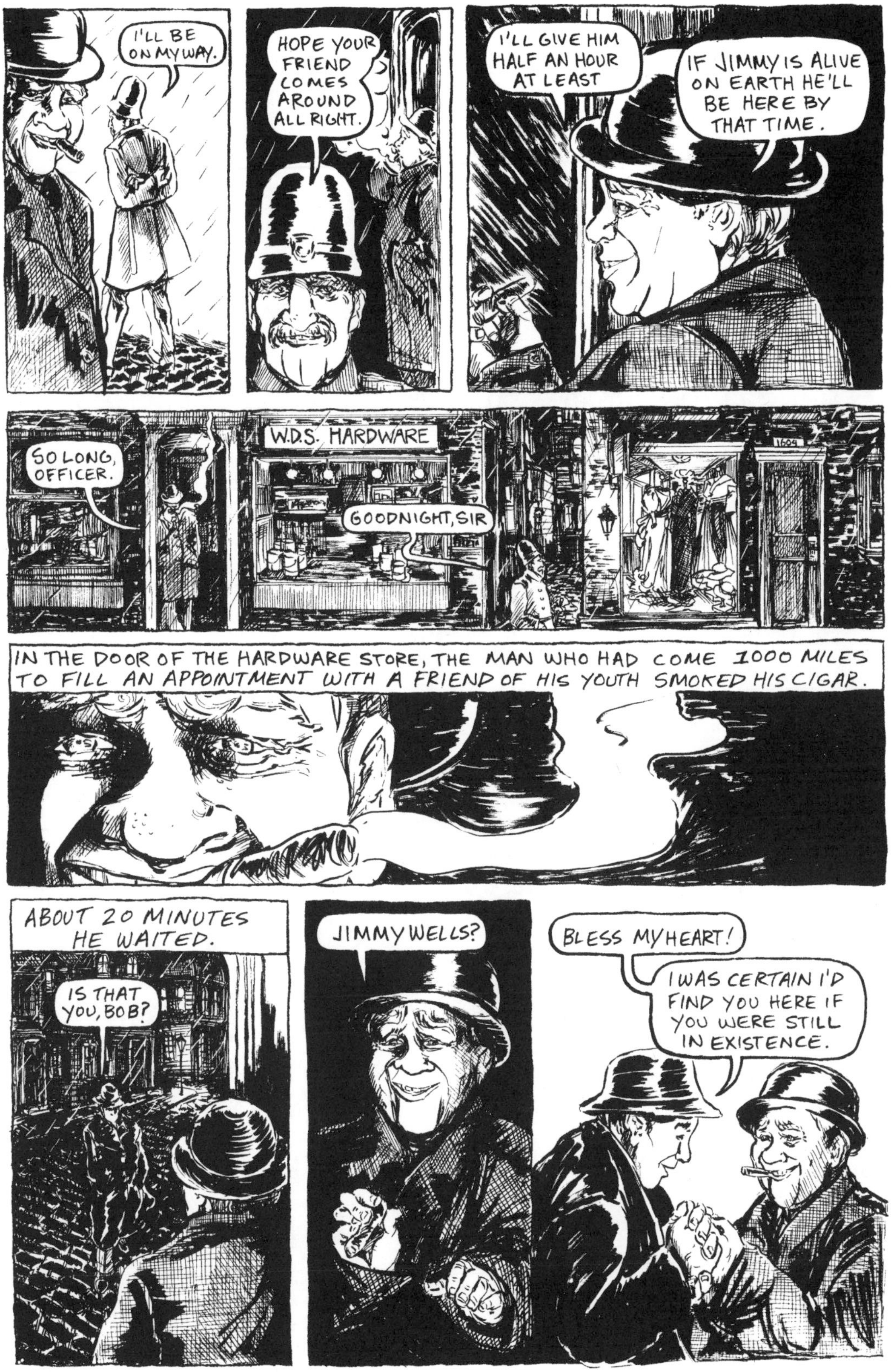
I'LL BE ON MY WAY.
HOPE YOUR FRIEND COMES AROUND ALL RIGHT.
I'LL GIVE HIM HALF AN HOUR AT LEAST
IF JIMMY IS ALIVE ON EARTH HE'LL BE HERE BY THAT TIME.
W.D.S. HARDWARE
SO LONG, OFFICER.
GOODNIGHT, SIR
IN THE DOOR OF THE HARDWARE STORE, THE MAN WHO HAD COME 1000 MILES TO FILL AN APPOINTMENT WITH A FRIEND OF HIS YOUTH SMOKED HIS CIGAR.
ABOUT 20 MINUTES HE WAITED.
IS THAT YOU, BOB?
JIMMY WELLS?
BLESS MY HEART!
I WAS CERTAIN I'D FIND YOU HERE IF YOU WERE STILL IN EXISTENCE.

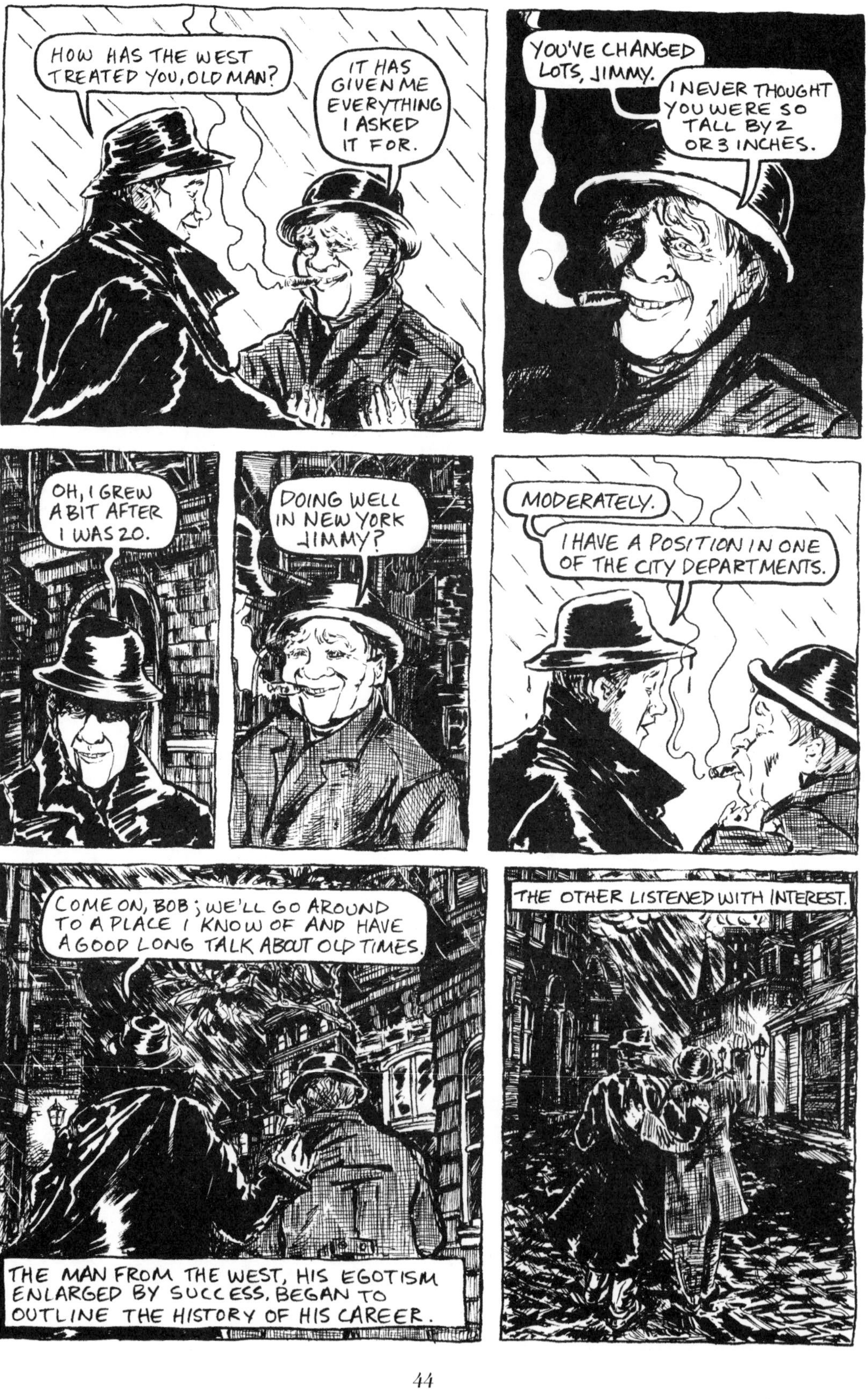
HOW HAS THE WEST TREATED YOU, OLD MAN?
IT HAS GIVEN ME EVERYTHING I ASKED IT FOR.
YOU'VE CHANGED LOTS, JIMMY.
I NEVER THOUGHT YOU WERE SO TALL BY 2 OR 3 INCHES.
OH, I GREW A BIT AFTER I WAS 20.
DOING WELL IN NEW YORK JIMMY?
MODERATELY.
I HAVE A POSITION IN ONE OF THE CITY DEPARTMENTS.
COME ON, BOB; WE'LL GO AROUND TO A PLACE I KNOW OF AND HAVE A GOOD LONG TALK ABOUT OLD TIMES.
THE MAN FROM THE WEST, HIS EGOTISM ENLARGED BY SUCCESS, BEGAN TO OUTLINE THE HISTORY OF HIS CAREER.
THE OTHER LISTENED WITH INTEREST.

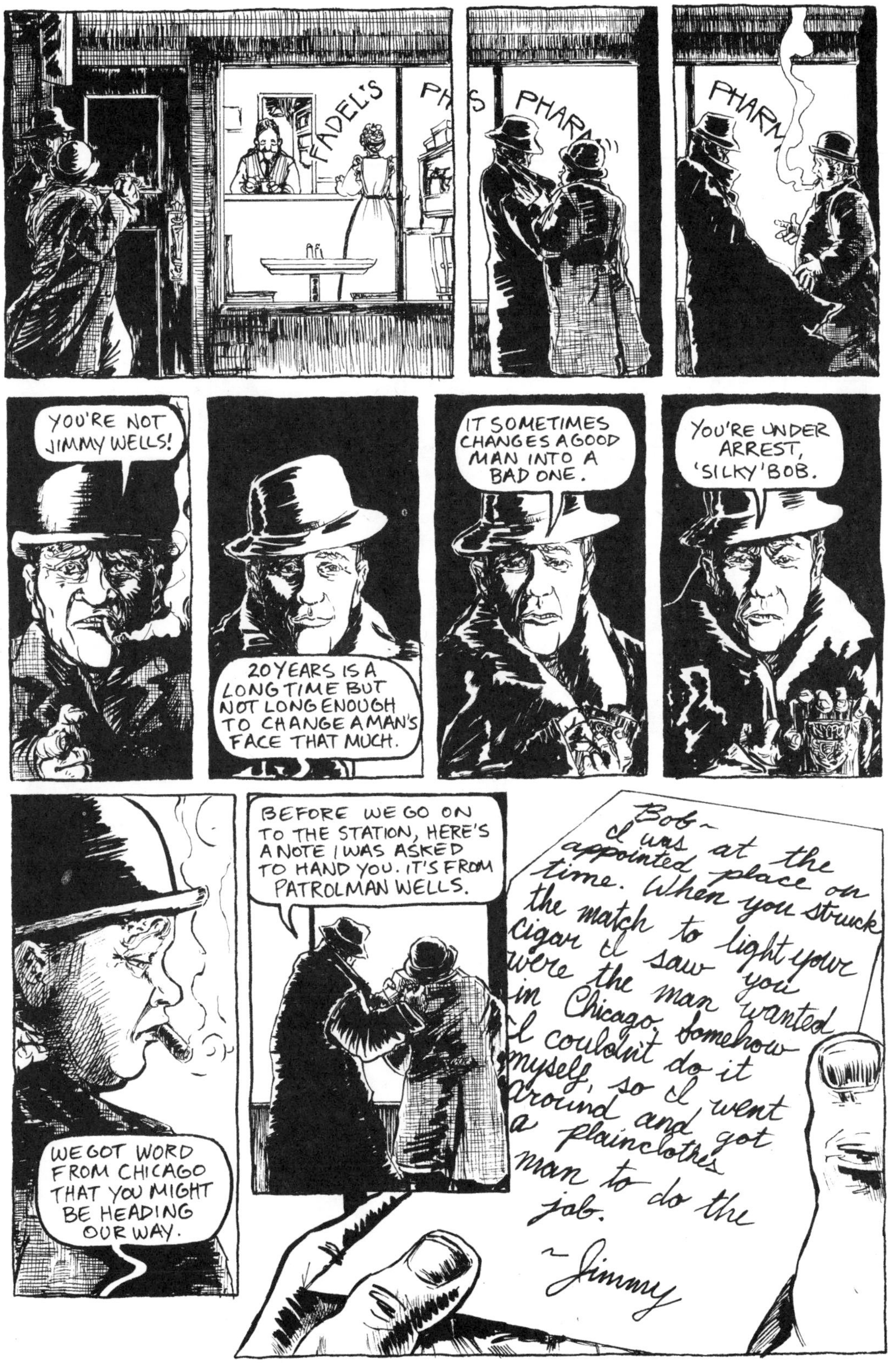
FADEL'S PHARM
PHARM
PHARM
YOU'RE NOT JIMMY WELLS!
20 YEARS IS A LONG TIME BUT NOT LONG ENOUGH TO CHANGE A MAN'S FACE THAT MUCH.
IT SOMETIMES CHANGES A GOOD MAN INTO A BAD ONE.
YOU'RE UNDER ARREST, 'SILKY' BOB.
WE GOT WORD FROM CHICAGO THAT YOU MIGHT BE HEADING OUR WAY.
BEFORE WE GO ON TO THE STATION, HERE'S A NOTE I WAS ASKED TO HAND YOU. IT'S FROM PATROLMAN WELLS.
Bob–
I was at the appointed place on time. When you struck the match to light your cigar I saw you were the man wanted in Chicago. Somehow I couldn't do it myself, so I went around and got a plainclothes man to do the job.
~ Jimmy

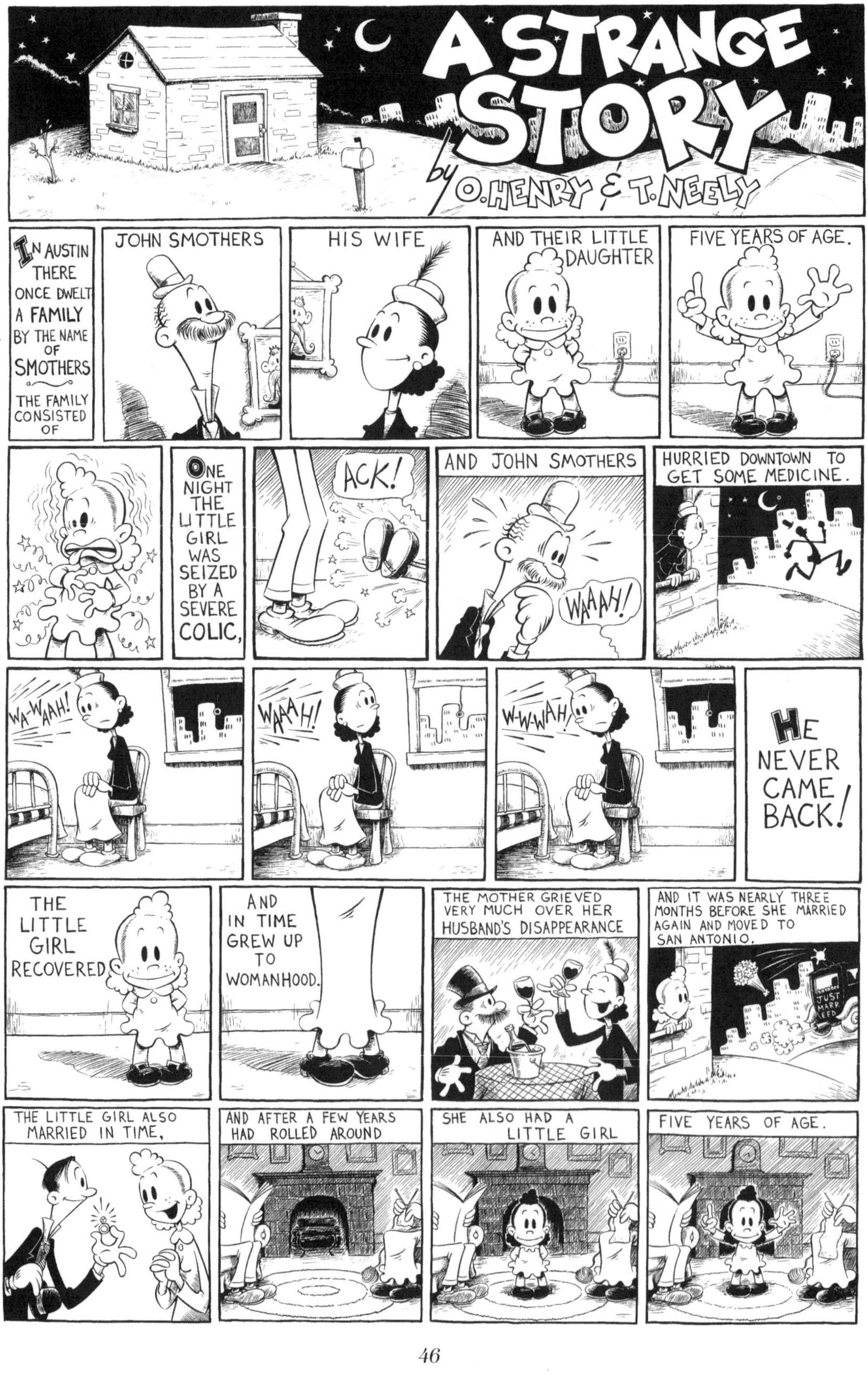
A STRANGE STORY
by O. HENRY & T. NEELY
IN AUSTIN THERE ONCE DWELT A FAMILY BY THE NAME OF SMOTHERS
THE FAMILY CONSISTED OF
JOHN SMOTHERS
HIS WIFE
AND THEIR LITTLE DAUGHTER
FIVE YEARS OF AGE.
ONE NIGHT THE LITTLE GIRL WAS SEIZED BY A SEVERE COLIC,
ACK!
AND JOHN SMOTHERS
WAAAH!
HURRIED DOWNTOWN TO GET SOME MEDICINE.
WA-WAAH!
WAAAH!
W-W-WAAH!
HE NEVER CAME BACK!
THE LITTLE GIRL RECOVERED
AND IN TIME GREW UP TO WOMANHOOD.
THE MOTHER GRIEVED VERY MUCH OVER HER HUSBAND'S DISAPPEARANCE
AND IT WAS NEARLY THREE MONTHS BEFORE SHE MARRIED AGAIN AND MOVED TO SAN ANTONIO.
JUST MARRIED
THE LITTLE GIRL ALSO MARRIED IN TIME,
AND AFTER A FEW YEARS HAD ROLLED AROUND
SHE ALSO HAD A LITTLE GIRL
FIVE YEARS OF AGE.

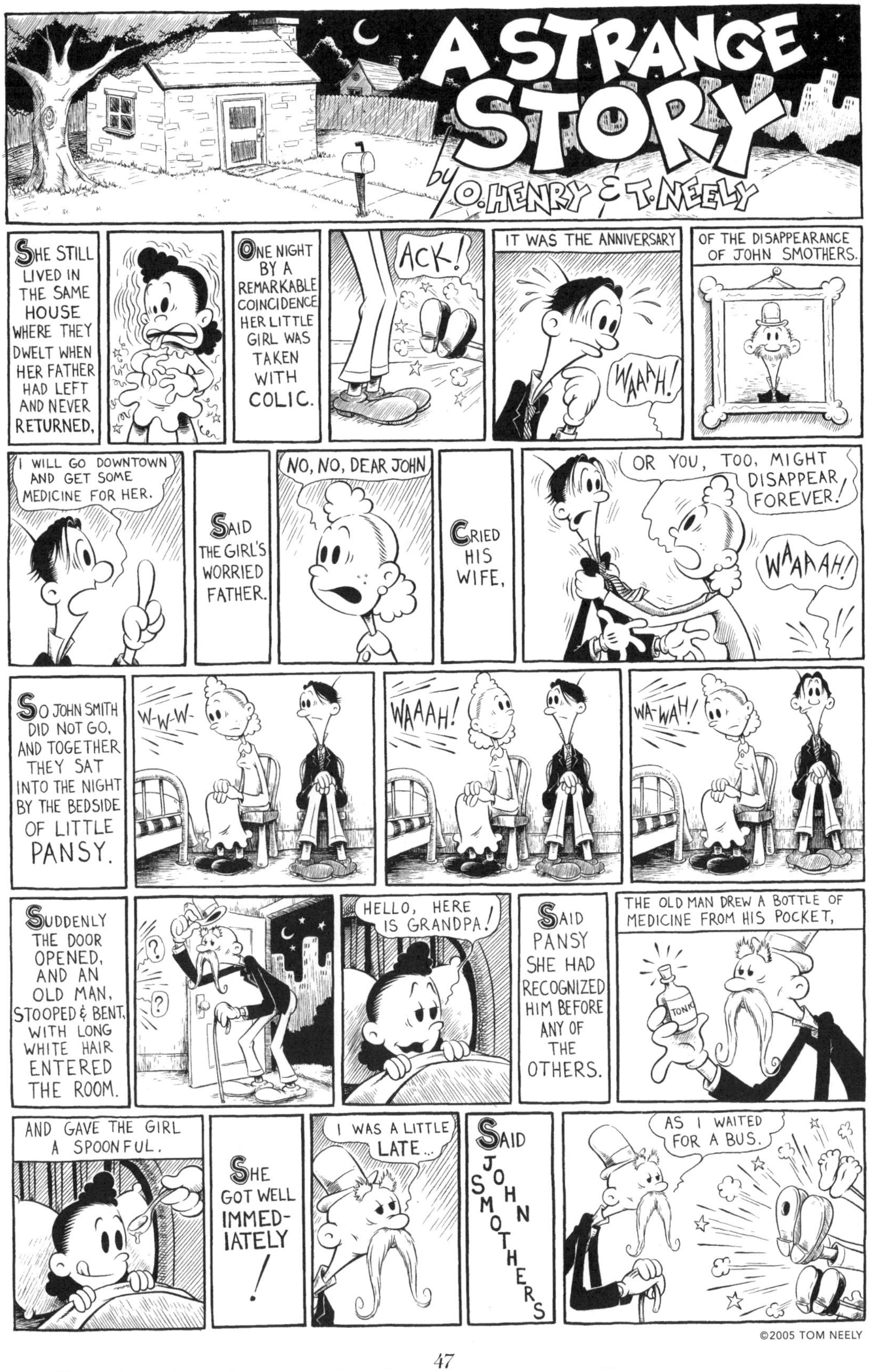
A STRANGE STORY
by O. HENRY & T. NEELY
SHE STILL LIVED IN THE SAME HOUSE WHERE THEY DWELT WHEN HER FATHER HAD LEFT AND NEVER RETURNED,
ONE NIGHT BY A REMARKABLE COINCIDENCE HER LITTLE GIRL WAS TAKEN WITH COLIC.
ACK!
IT WAS THE ANNIVERSARY
WAAAH!
OF THE DISAPPEARANCE OF JOHN SMOTHERS.
I WILL GO DOWNTOWN AND GET SOME MEDICINE FOR HER.
SAID THE GIRL'S WORRIED FATHER.
NO, NO, DEAR JOHN
CRIED HIS WIFE,
OR YOU, TOO, MIGHT DISAPPEAR FOREVER!
WAAAAH!
SO JOHN SMITH DID NOT GO, AND TOGETHER THEY SAT INTO THE NIGHT BY THE BEDSIDE OF LITTLE PANSY.
W-W-W-
WAAAH!
WA-WAH!
SUDDENLY THE DOOR OPENED, AND AN OLD MAN, STOOPED & BENT, WITH LONG WHITE HAIR ENTERED THE ROOM.
?
?
HELLO, HERE IS GRANDPA!
SAID PANSY SHE HAD RECOGNIZED HIM BEFORE ANY OF THE OTHERS.
THE OLD MAN DREW A BOTTLE OF MEDICINE FROM HIS POCKET,
TONIC
AND GAVE THE GIRL A SPOONFUL.
SHE GOT WELL IMMED-IATELY!
I WAS A LITTLE LATE...
SAID JOHN SMOTHERS
AS I WAITED FOR A BUS.

The Marionettes

A tale by **O. HENRY**, adapted
by **ANTONELLA CAPUTO**
illustrated by **RICK GEARY**

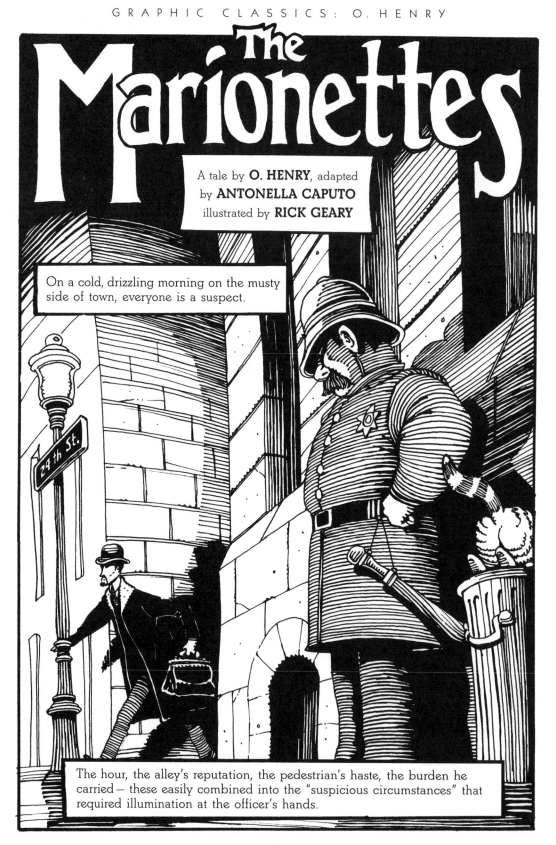

On a cold, drizzling morning on the musty side of town, everyone is a suspect.

The hour, the alley's reputation, the pedestrian's haste, the burden he carried — these easily combined into the "suspicious circumstances" that required illumination at the officer's hands.

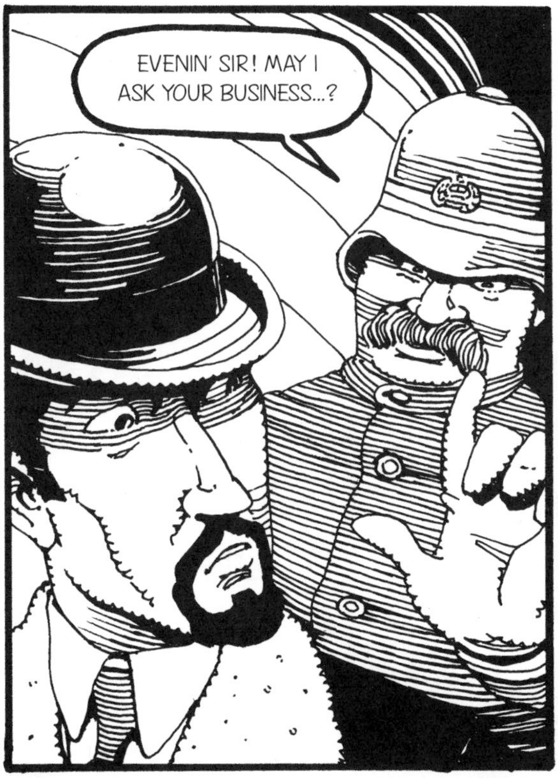
EVENIN' SIR! MAY I ASK YOUR BUSINESS...?

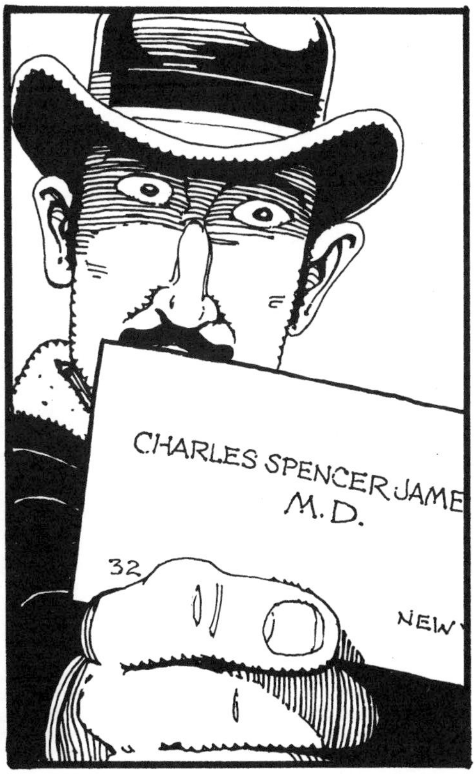
CHARLES SPENCER JAME
M.D.
32
NEW

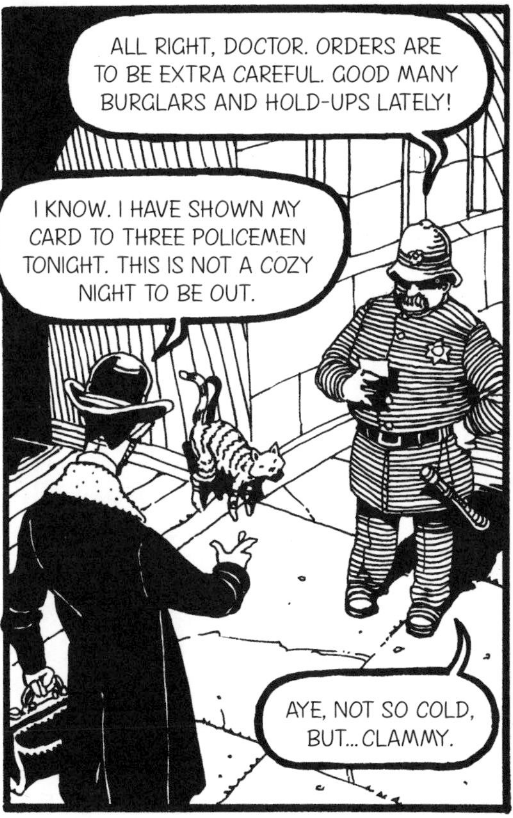
ALL RIGHT, DOCTOR. ORDERS ARE TO BE EXTRA CAREFUL. GOOD MANY BURGLARS AND HOLD-UPS LATELY!
I KNOW. I HAVE SHOWN MY CARD TO THREE POLICEMEN TONIGHT. THIS IS NOT A COZY NIGHT TO BE OUT.
AYE, NOT SO COLD, BUT...CLAMMY.

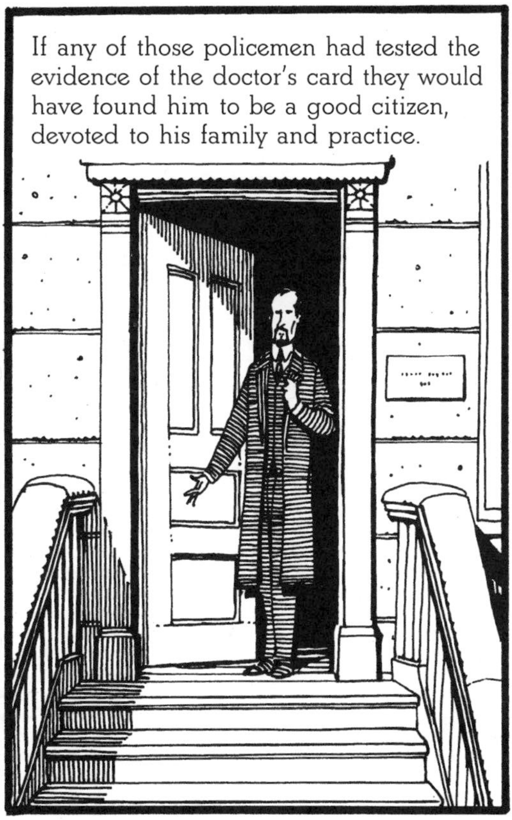
If any of those policemen had tested the evidence of the doctor's card they would have found him to be a good citizen, devoted to his family and practice.

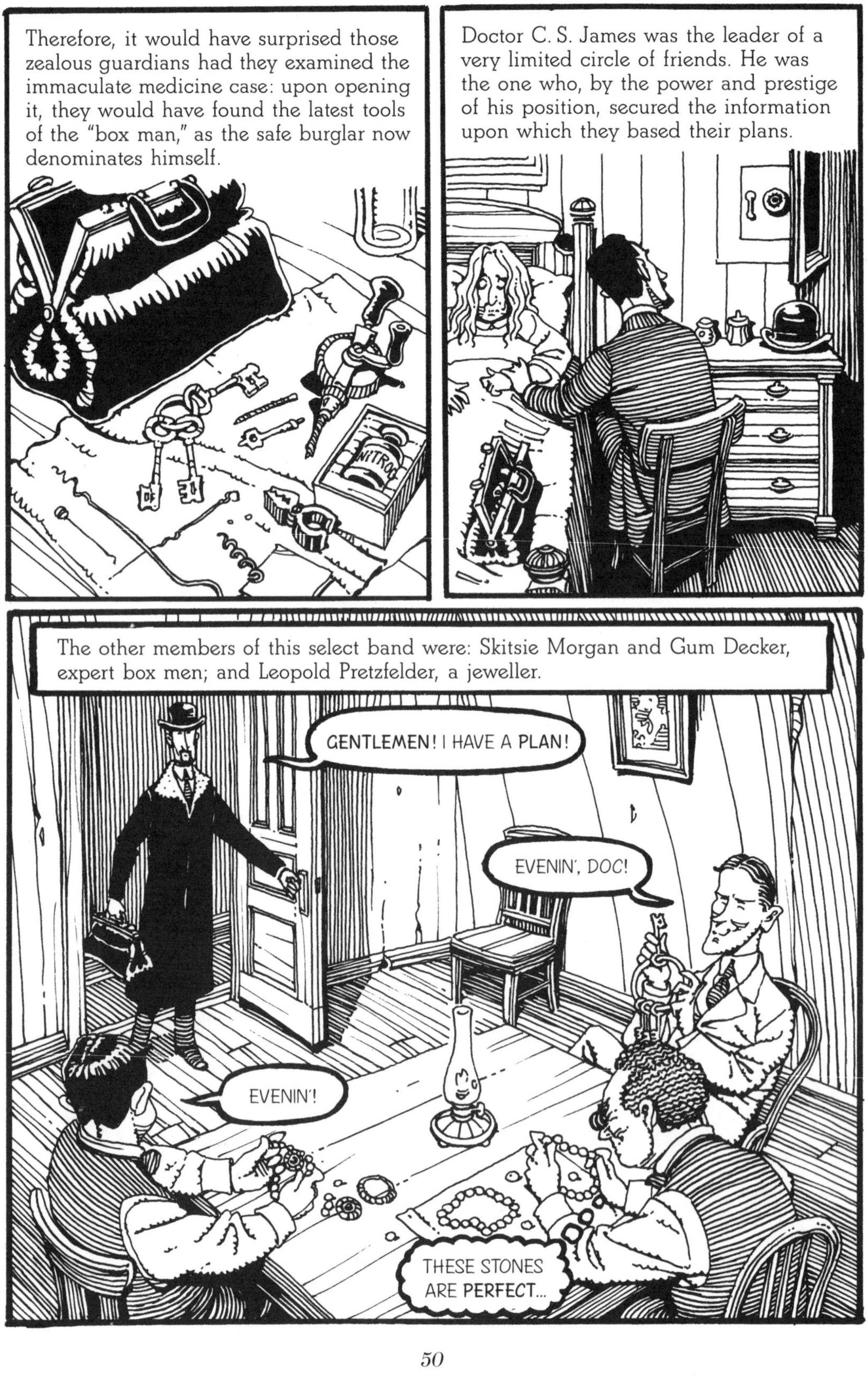
Therefore, it would have surprised those zealous guardians had they examined the immaculate medicine case: upon opening it, they would have found the latest tools of the "box man," as the safe burglar now denominates himself.
Doctor C. S. James was the leader of a very limited circle of friends. He was the one who, by the power and prestige of his position, secured the information upon which they based their plans.
The other members of this select band were: Skitsie Morgan and Gum Decker, expert box men; and Leopold Pretzfelder, a jeweller.
GENTLEMEN! I HAVE A PLAN!
EVENIN', DOC!
EVENIN'!
THESE STONES ARE PERFECT...

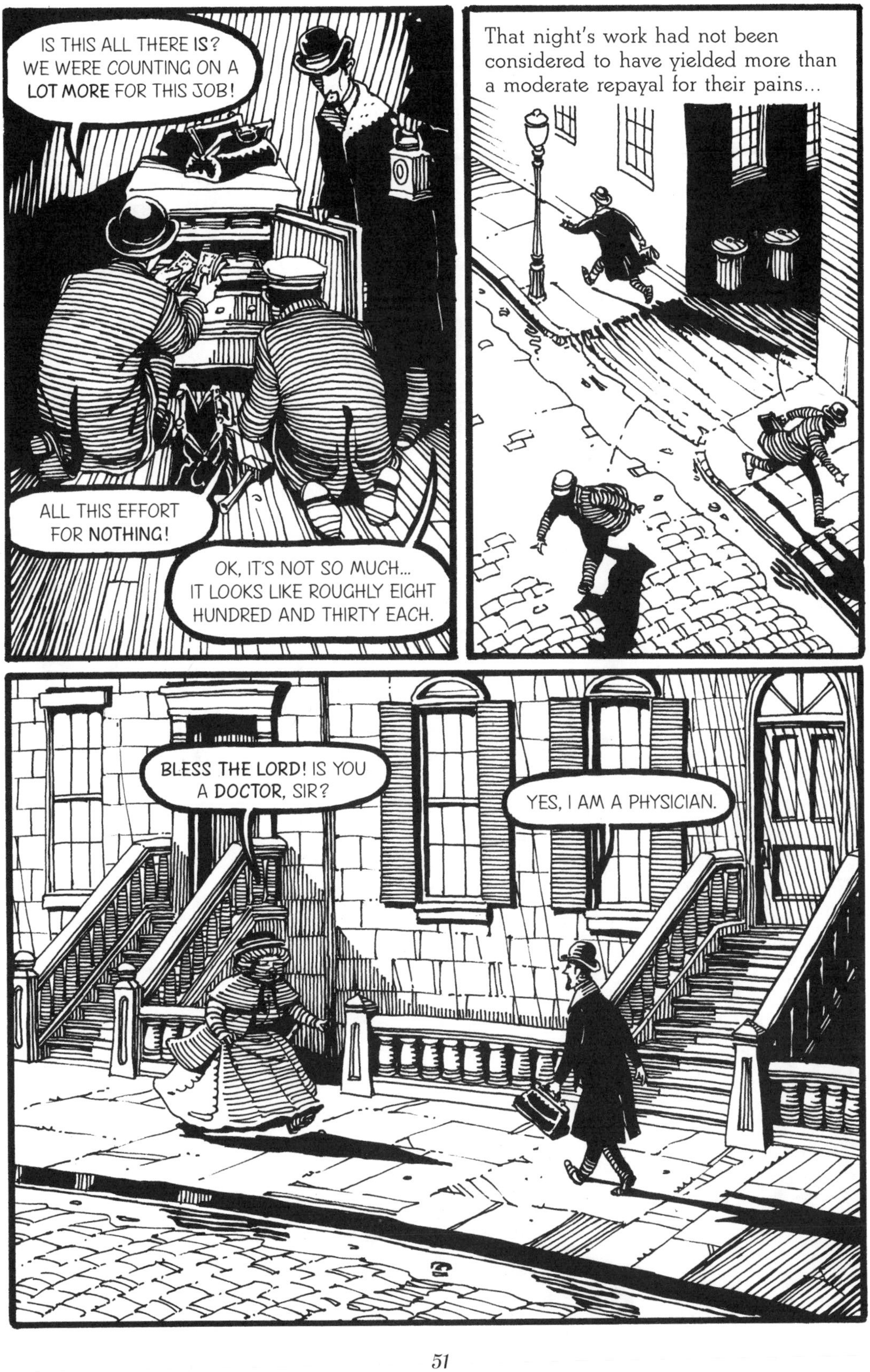
IS THIS ALL THERE IS? WE WERE COUNTING ON A LOT MORE FOR THIS JOB!
ALL THIS EFFORT FOR NOTHING!
OK, IT'S NOT SO MUCH... IT LOOKS LIKE ROUGHLY EIGHT HUNDRED AND THIRTY EACH.
That night's work had not been considered to have yielded more than a moderate repayal for their pains...
BLESS THE LORD! IS YOU A DOCTOR, SIR?
YES, I AM A PHYSICIAN.

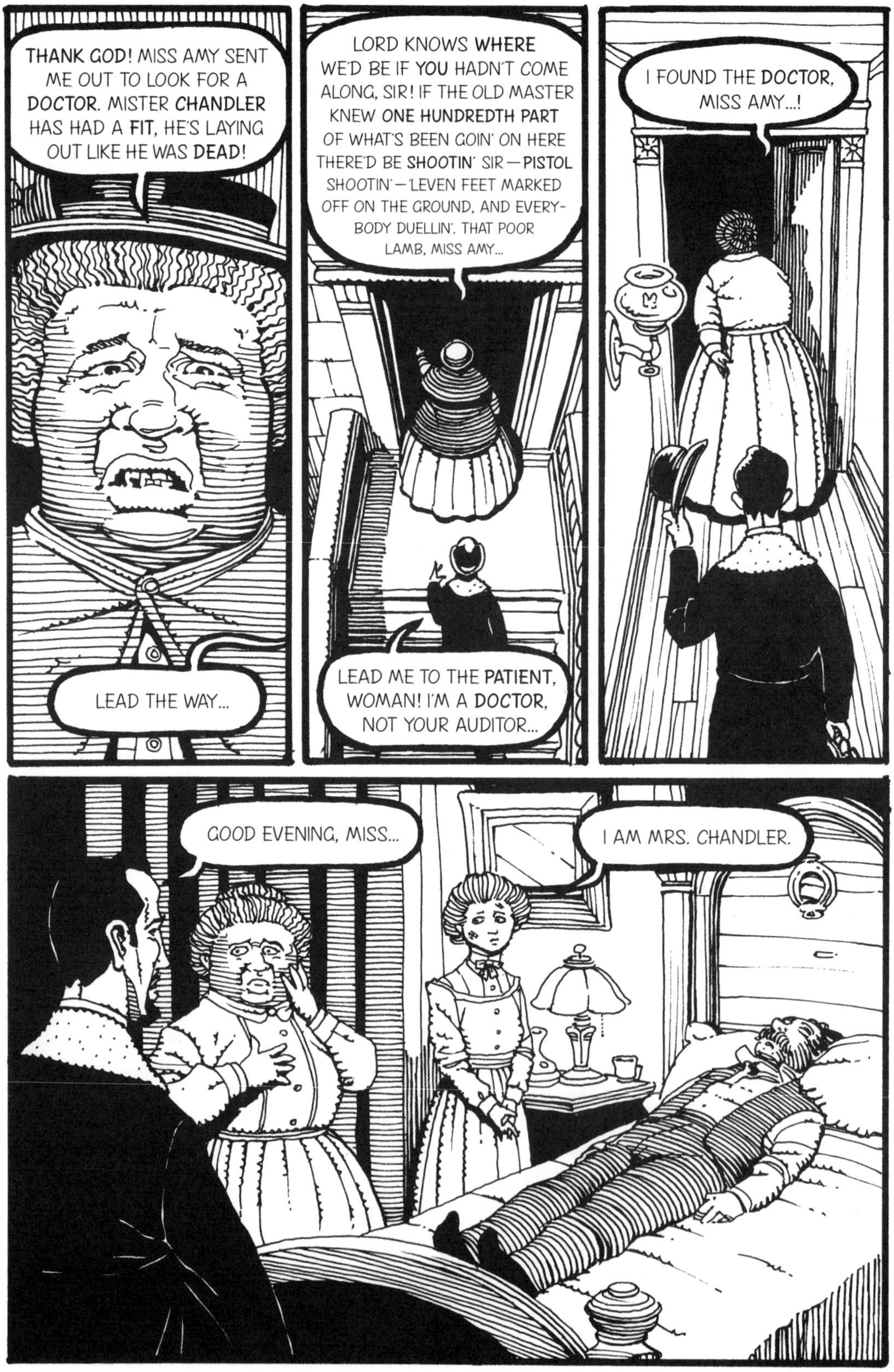
THANK GOD! MISS AMY SENT ME OUT TO LOOK FOR A DOCTOR. MISTER CHANDLER HAS HAD A FIT, HE'S LAYING OUT LIKE HE WAS DEAD!
LEAD THE WAY...
LORD KNOWS WHERE WE'D BE IF YOU HADN'T COME ALONG, SIR! IF THE OLD MASTER KNEW ONE HUNDREDTH PART OF WHAT'S BEEN GOIN' ON HERE THERE'D BE SHOOTIN' SIR—PISTOL SHOOTIN'—'LEVEN FEET MARKED OFF ON THE GROUND, AND EVERY-BODY DUELLIN'. THAT POOR LAMB, MISS AMY...
LEAD ME TO THE PATIENT, WOMAN! I'M A DOCTOR, NOT YOUR AUDITOR...
I FOUND THE DOCTOR, MISS AMY...!
GOOD EVENING, MISS...
I AM MRS. CHANDLER.

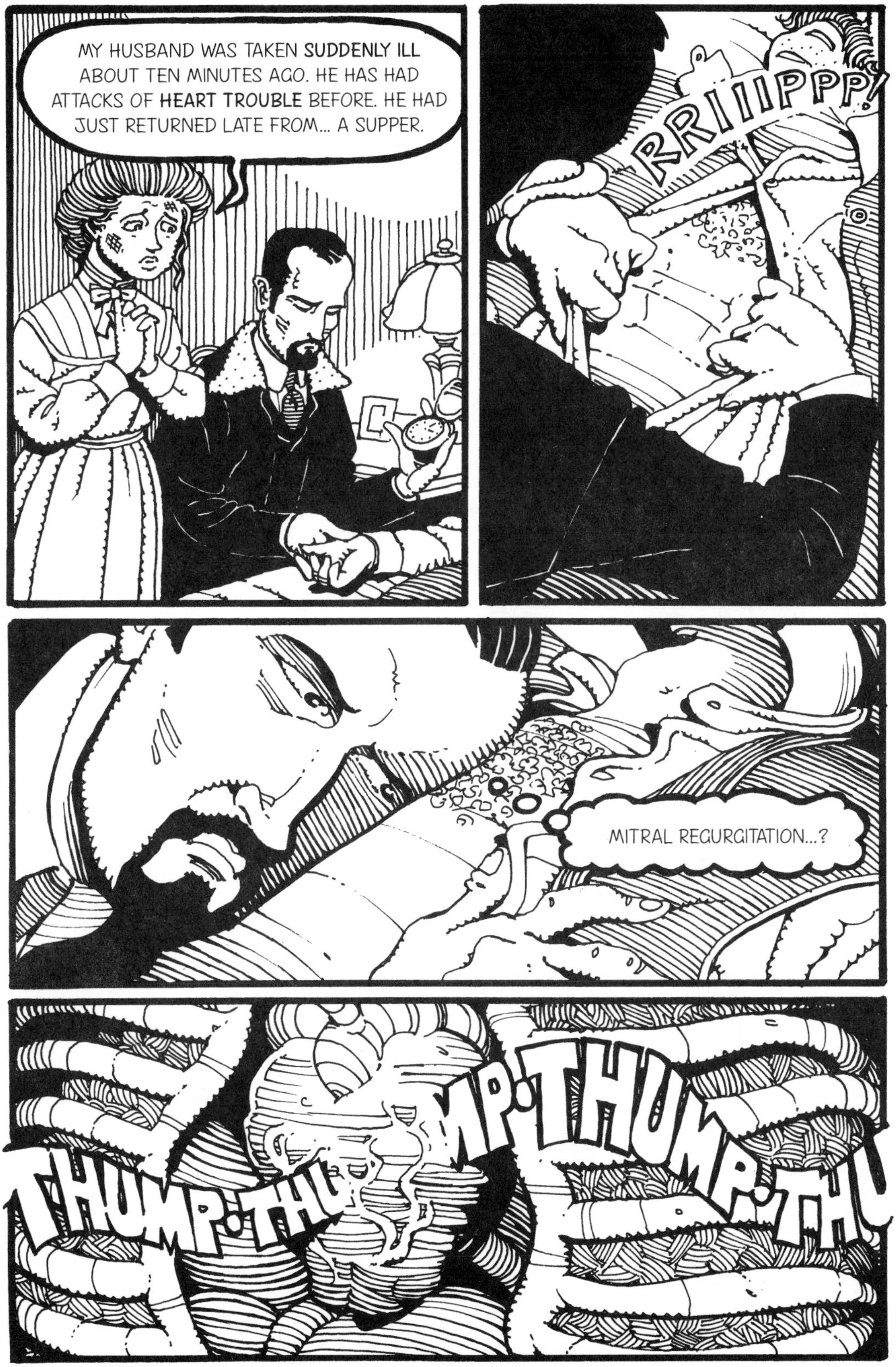
MY HUSBAND WAS TAKEN **SUDDENLY ILL** ABOUT TEN MINUTES AGO. HE HAS HAD ATTACKS OF **HEART TROUBLE** BEFORE. HE HAD JUST RETURNED LATE FROM... A SUPPER.
RRIIIPPP!
MITRAL REGURGITATION...?
THUMP-THUMP-THUMP-THUMP-THU

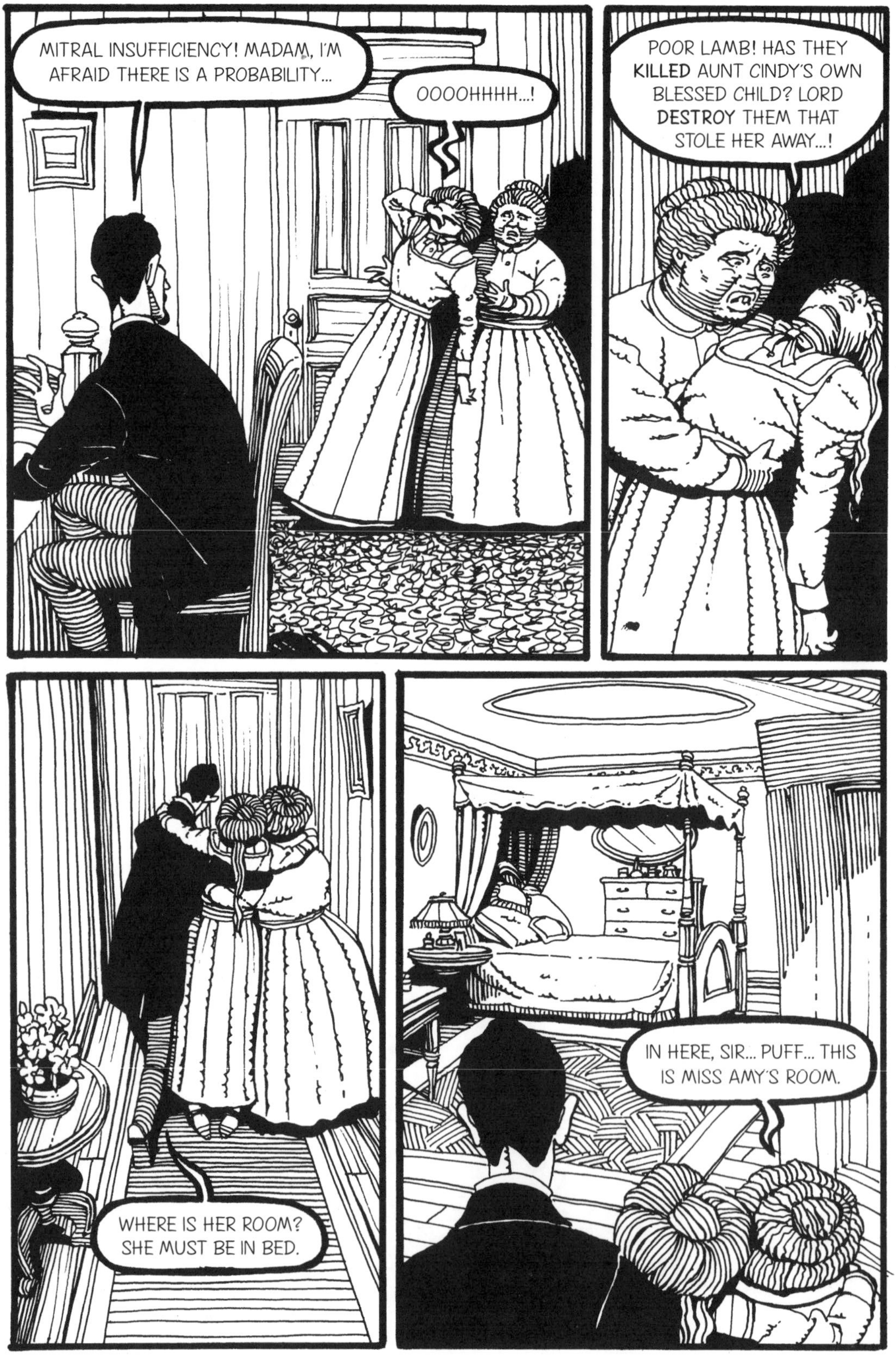
MITRAL INSUFFICIENCY! MADAM, I'M AFRAID THERE IS A PROBABILITY...
OOOOHHHH...!
POOR LAMB! HAS THEY **KILLED** AUNT CINDY'S OWN BLESSED CHILD? LORD **DESTROY** THEM THAT STOLE HER AWAY...!
WHERE IS HER ROOM? SHE MUST BE IN BED.
IN HERE, SIR... PUFF... THIS IS MISS AMY'S ROOM.

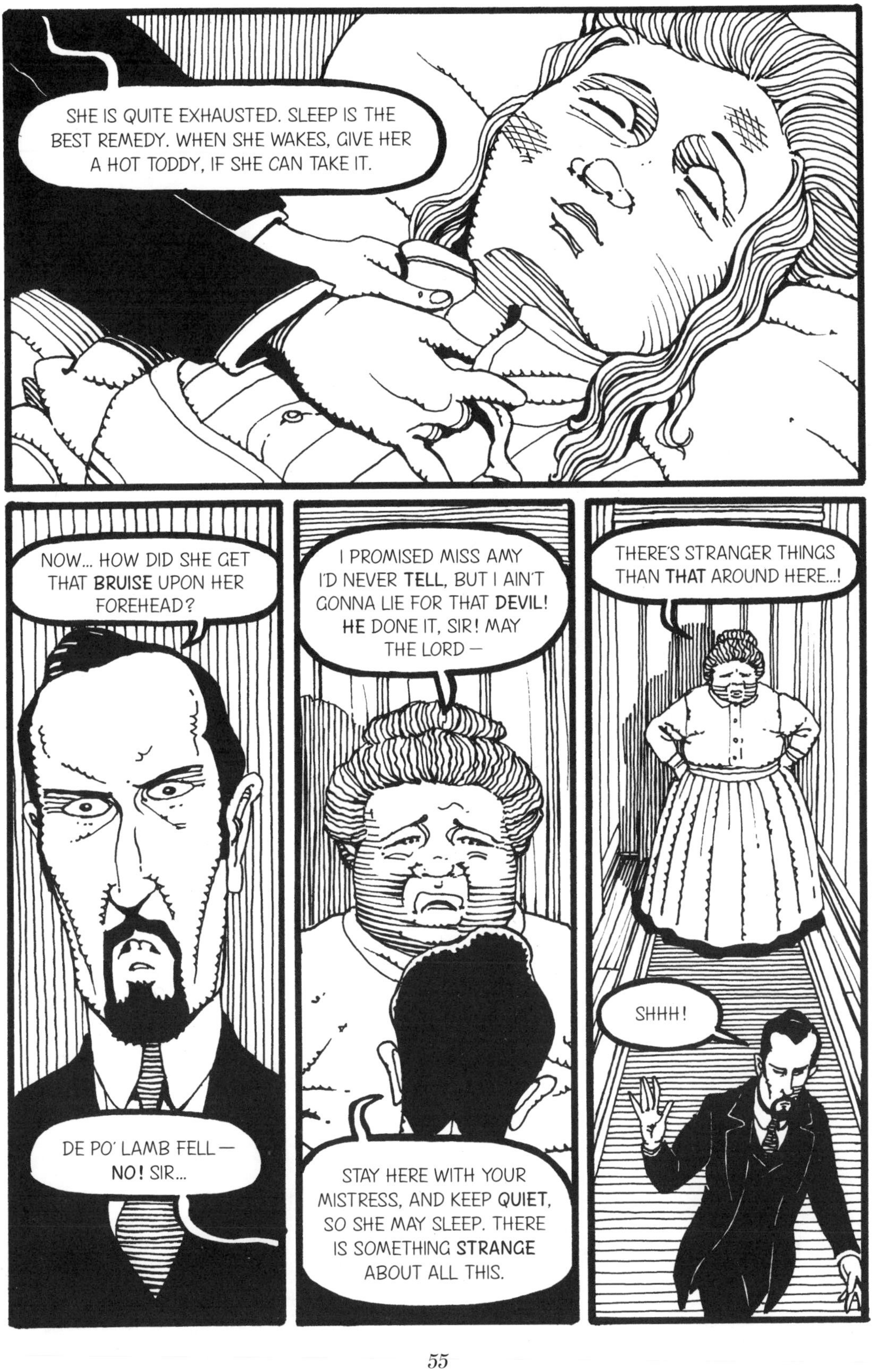
SHE IS QUITE EXHAUSTED. SLEEP IS THE BEST REMEDY. WHEN SHE WAKES, GIVE HER A HOT TODDY, IF SHE CAN TAKE IT.
NOW... HOW DID SHE GET THAT BRUISE UPON HER FOREHEAD?
DE PO' LAMB FELL — NO! SIR...
I PROMISED MISS AMY I'D NEVER TELL, BUT I AIN'T GONNA LIE FOR THAT DEVIL! HE DONE IT, SIR! MAY THE LORD —
STAY HERE WITH YOUR MISTRESS, AND KEEP QUIET, SO SHE MAY SLEEP. THERE IS SOMETHING STRANGE ABOUT ALL THIS.
THERE'S STRANGER THINGS THAN THAT AROUND HERE...!
SHHH!

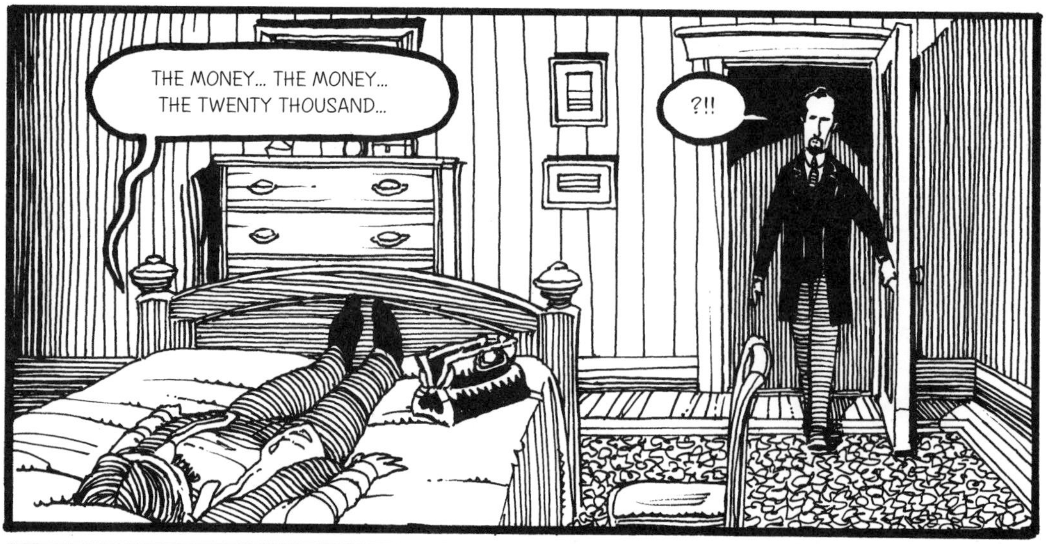
THE MONEY... THE MONEY... THE TWENTY THOUSAND...
?!!

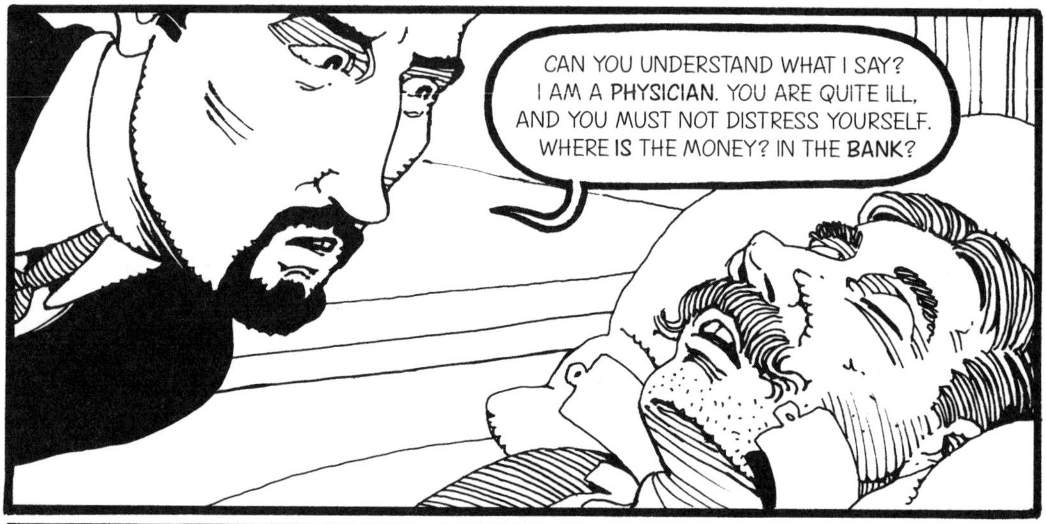
CAN YOU UNDERSTAND WHAT I SAY? I AM A **PHYSICIAN.** YOU ARE QUITE ILL, AND YOU MUST NOT DISTRESS YOURSELF. WHERE **IS** THE MONEY? IN THE **BANK**?

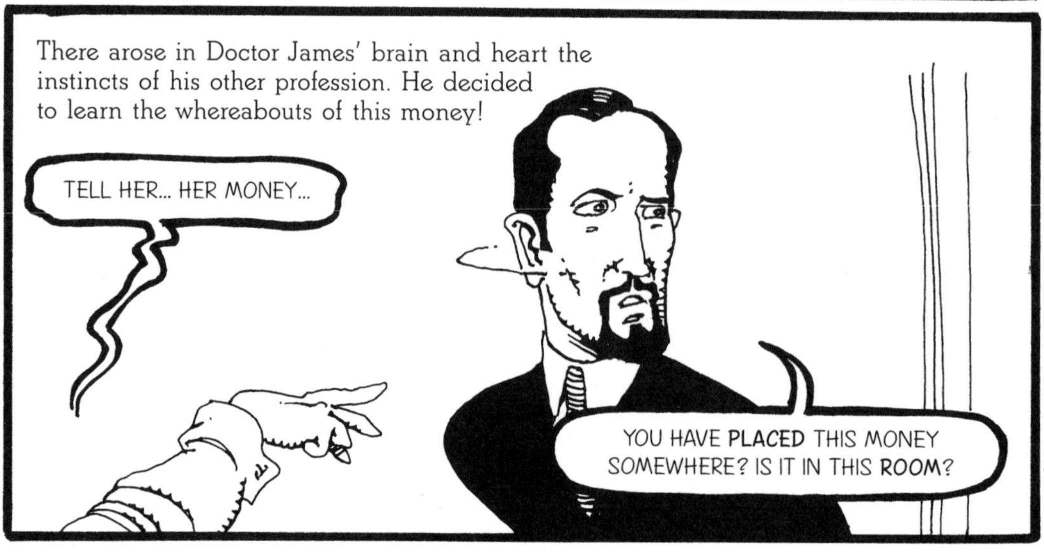
There arose in Doctor James' brain and heart the instincts of his other profession. He decided to learn the whereabouts of this money!
TELL HER... HER MONEY...
YOU HAVE **PLACED** THIS MONEY SOMEWHERE? IS IT IN THIS **ROOM**?

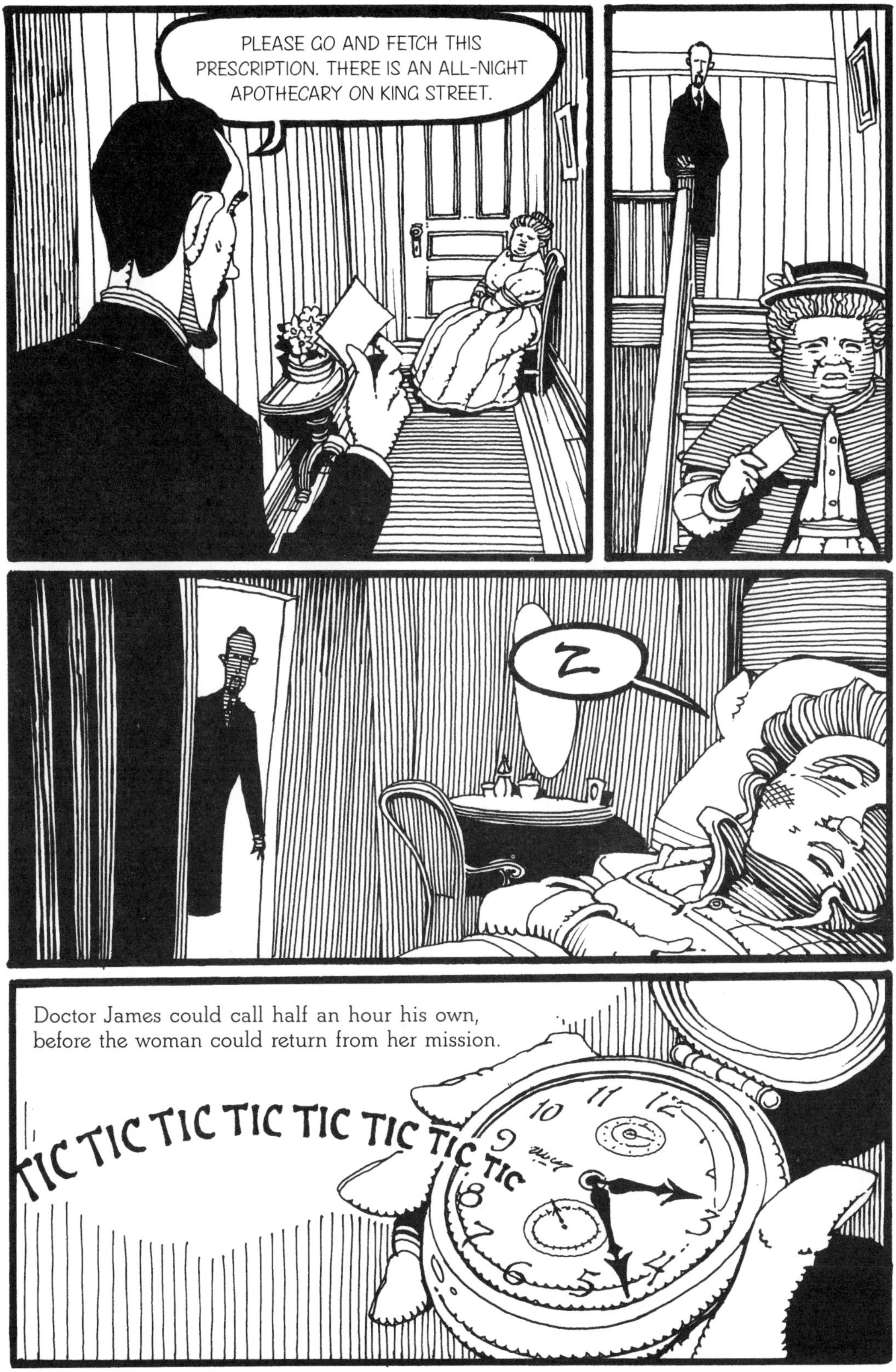
PLEASE GO AND FETCH THIS PRESCRIPTION. THERE IS AN ALL-NIGHT APOTHECARY ON KING STREET.
Z
Doctor James could call half an hour his own, before the woman could return from her mission.
TIC TIC TIC TIC TIC TIC TIC TIC TIC

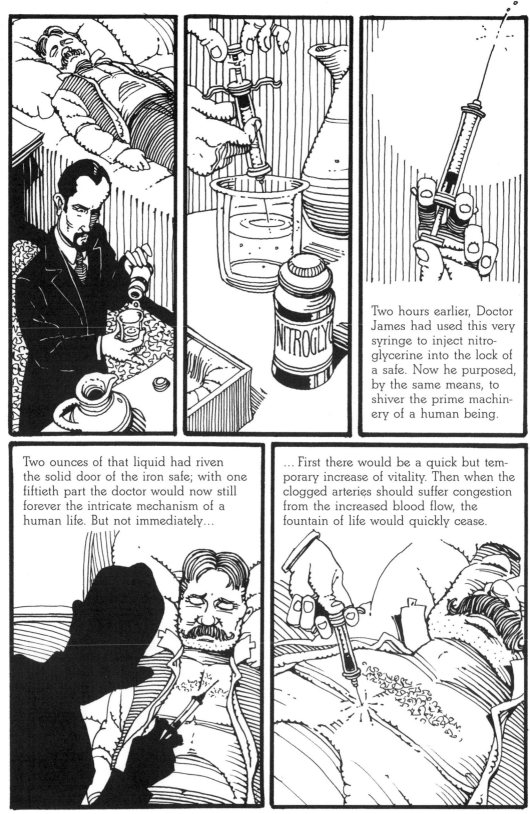

Two hours earlier, Doctor James had used this very syringe to inject nitro-glycerine into the lock of a safe. Now he purposed, by the same means, to shiver the prime machin-ery of a human being.

Two ounces of that liquid had riven the solid door of the iron safe; with one fiftieth part the doctor would now still forever the intricate mechanism of a human life. But not immediately...

... First there would be a quick but tem-porary increase of vitality. Then when the clogged arteries should suffer congestion from the increased blood flow, the fountain of life would quickly cease.

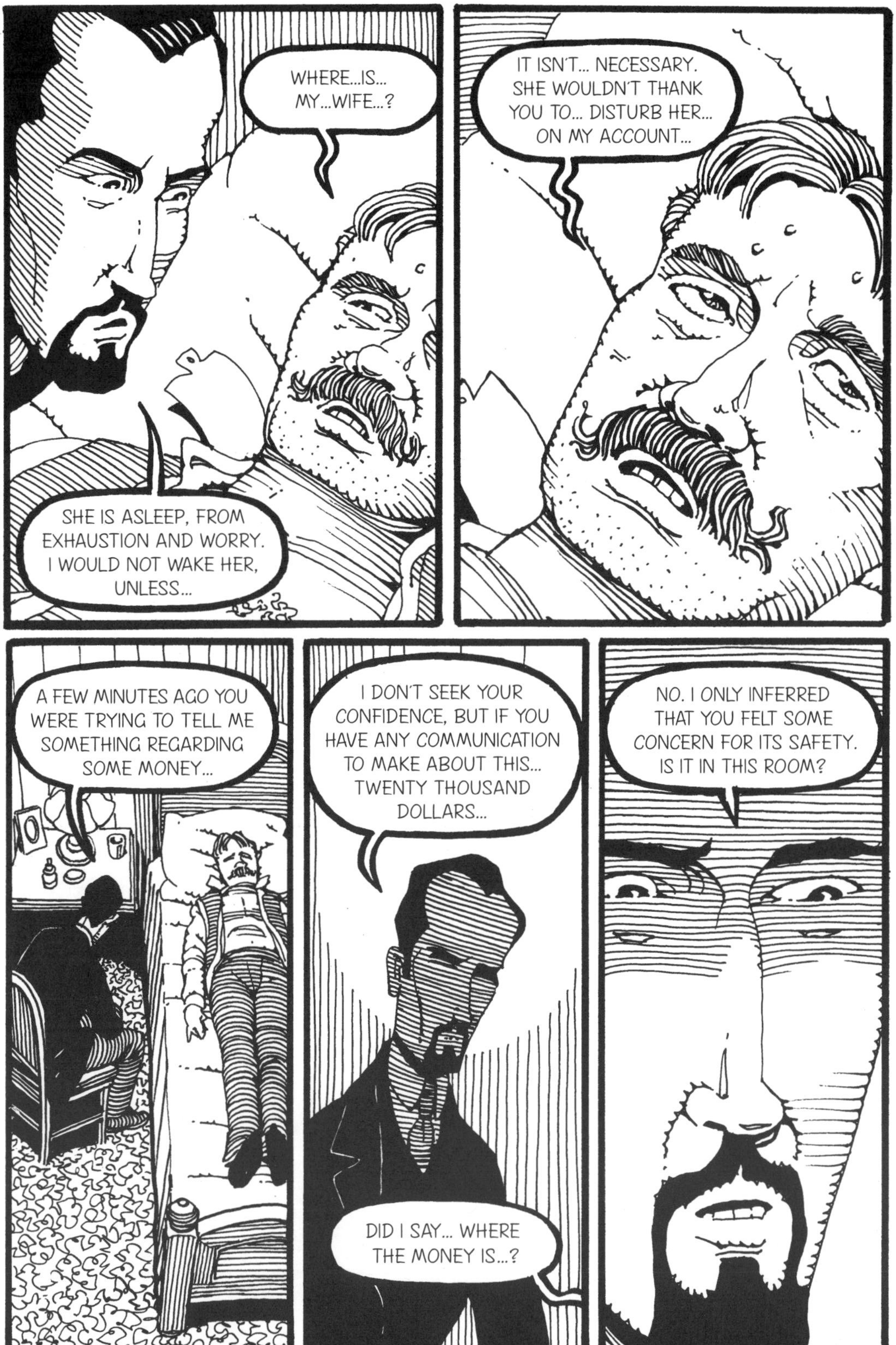
WHERE...IS... MY...WIFE...?
SHE IS ASLEEP, FROM EXHAUSTION AND WORRY. I WOULD NOT WAKE HER, UNLESS...
IT ISN'T... NECESSARY. SHE WOULDN'T THANK YOU TO... DISTURB HER... ON MY ACCOUNT...
A FEW MINUTES AGO YOU WERE TRYING TO TELL ME SOMETHING REGARDING SOME MONEY...
I DON'T SEEK YOUR CONFIDENCE, BUT IF YOU HAVE ANY COMMUNICATION TO MAKE ABOUT THIS... TWENTY THOUSAND DOLLARS...
DID I SAY... WHERE THE MONEY IS...?
NO. I ONLY INFERRED THAT YOU FELT SOME CONCERN FOR ITS SAFETY. IS IT IN THIS ROOM?

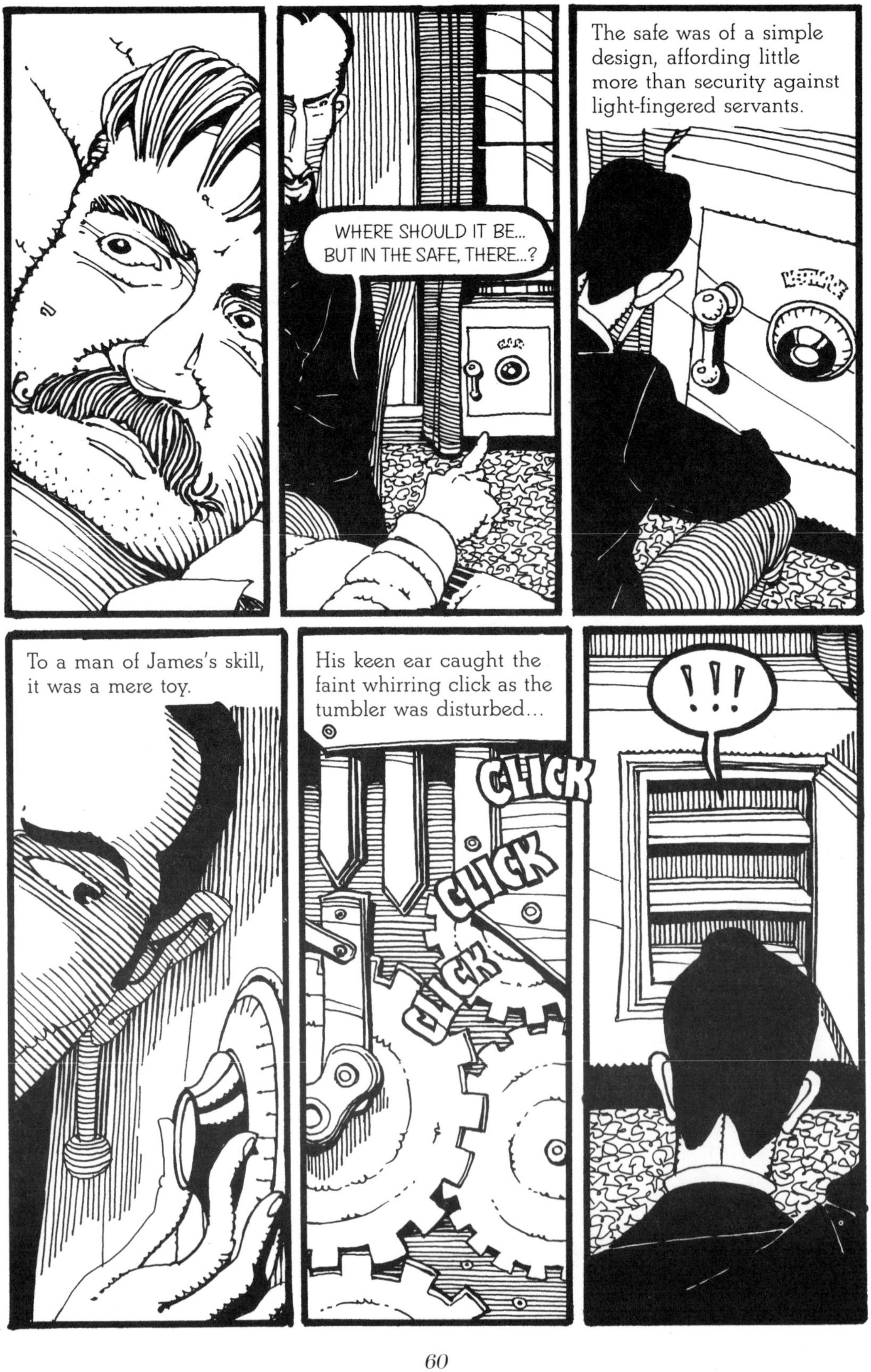
WHERE SHOULD IT BE...
BUT IN THE SAFE, THERE...?
The safe was of a simple design, affording little more than security against light-fingered servants.
To a man of James's skill, it was a mere toy.
His keen ear caught the faint whirring click as the tumbler was disturbed...
CLICK
CLICK
CLICK
!!!

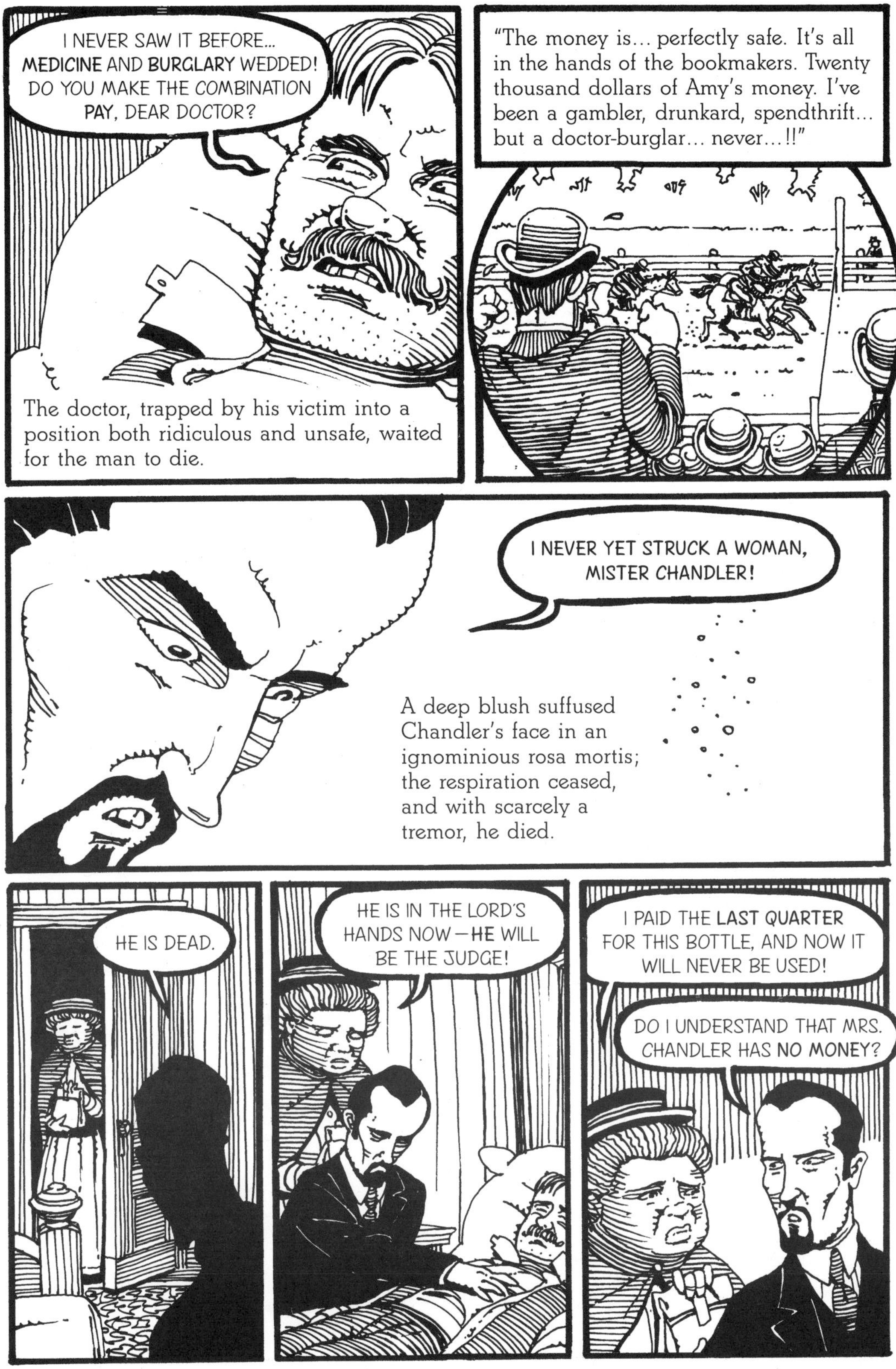

I NEVER SAW IT BEFORE... MEDICINE AND BURGLARY WEDDED! DO YOU MAKE THE COMBINATION PAY, DEAR DOCTOR?
The doctor, trapped by his victim into a position both ridiculous and unsafe, waited for the man to die.
"The money is... perfectly safe. It's all in the hands of the bookmakers. Twenty thousand dollars of Amy's money. I've been a gambler, drunkard, spendthrift... but a doctor-burglar... never...!!"
I NEVER YET STRUCK A WOMAN, MISTER CHANDLER!
A deep blush suffused Chandler's face in an ignominious rosa mortis; the respiration ceased, and with scarcely a tremor, he died.
HE IS DEAD.
HE IS IN THE LORD'S HANDS NOW—HE WILL BE THE JUDGE!
I PAID THE LAST QUARTER FOR THIS BOTTLE, AND NOW IT WILL NEVER BE USED!
DO I UNDERSTAND THAT MRS. CHANDLER HAS NO MONEY?

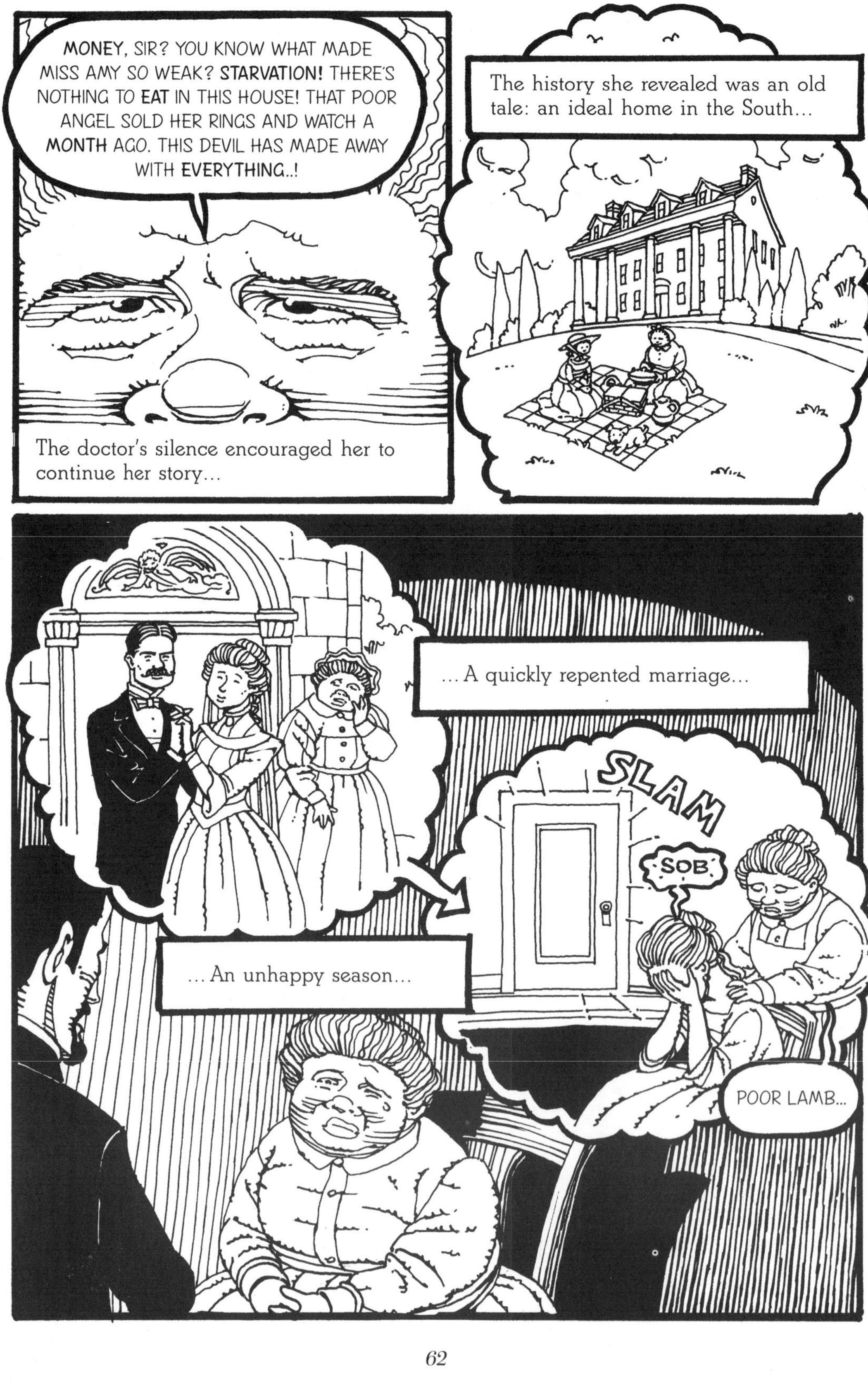

MONEY, SIR? YOU KNOW WHAT MADE MISS AMY SO WEAK? STARVATION! THERE'S NOTHING TO EAT IN THIS HOUSE! THAT POOR ANGEL SOLD HER RINGS AND WATCH A MONTH AGO. THIS DEVIL HAS MADE AWAY WITH EVERYTHING..!
The doctor's silence encouraged her to continue her story...
The history she revealed was an old tale: an ideal home in the South...
...A quickly repented marriage...
SLAM
SOB
...An unhappy season...
POOR LAMB...

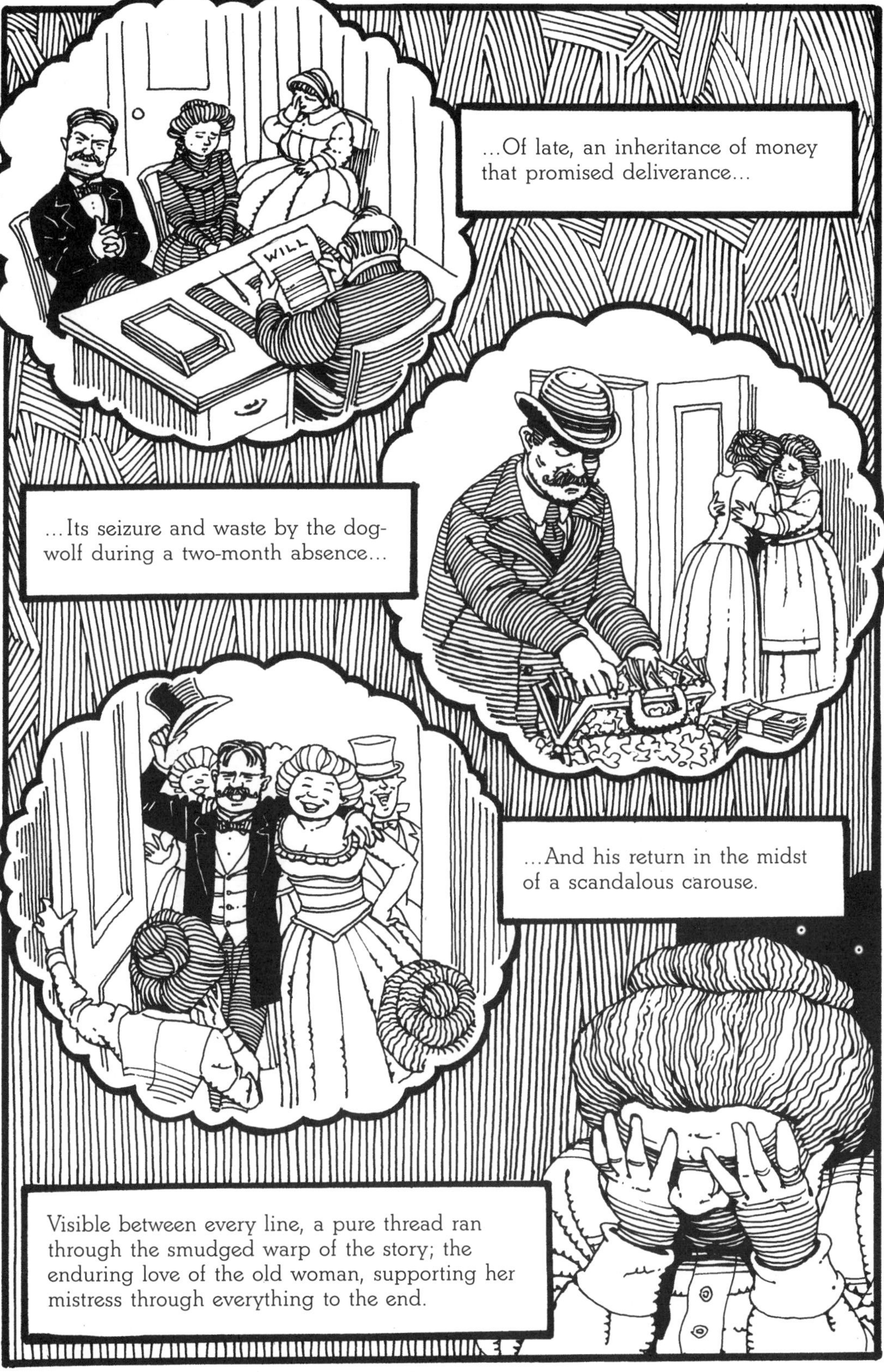
...Of late, an inheritance of money that promised deliverance...
WILL
...Its seizure and waste by the dog-wolf during a two-month absence...
...And his return in the midst of a scandalous carouse.
Visible between every line, a pure thread ran through the smudged warp of the story; the enduring love of the old woman, supporting her mistress through everything to the end.

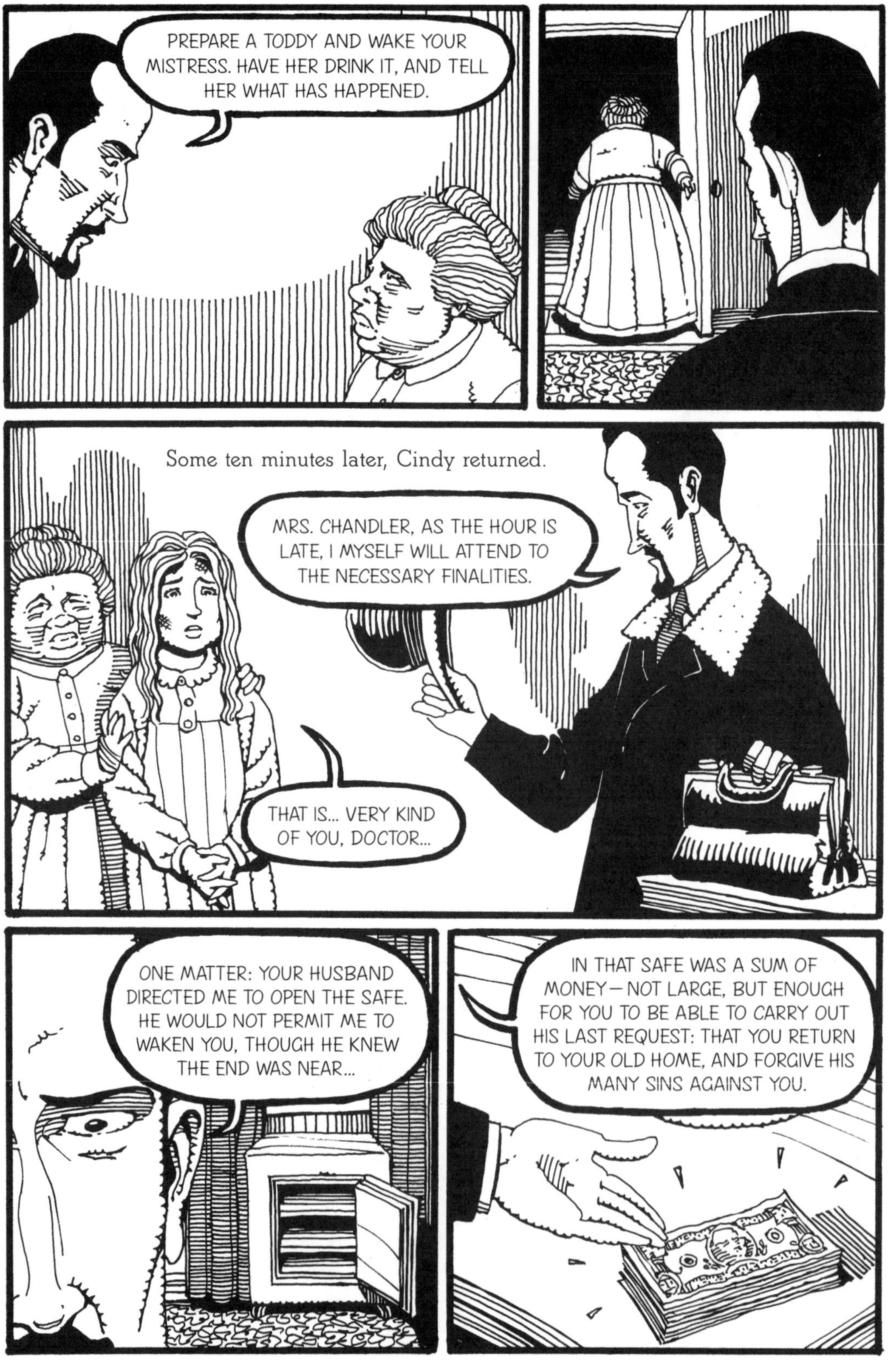
PREPARE A TODDY AND WAKE YOUR MISTRESS. HAVE HER DRINK IT, AND TELL HER WHAT HAS HAPPENED.
Some ten minutes later, Cindy returned.
MRS. CHANDLER, AS THE HOUR IS LATE, I MYSELF WILL ATTEND TO THE NECESSARY FINALITIES.
THAT IS... VERY KIND OF YOU, DOCTOR...
ONE MATTER: YOUR HUSBAND DIRECTED ME TO OPEN THE SAFE. HE WOULD NOT PERMIT ME TO WAKEN YOU, THOUGH HE KNEW THE END WAS NEAR...
IN THAT SAFE WAS A SUM OF MONEY—NOT LARGE, BUT ENOUGH FOR YOU TO BE ABLE TO CARRY OUT HIS LAST REQUEST: THAT YOU RETURN TO YOUR OLD HOME, AND FORGIVE HIS MANY SINS AGAINST YOU.

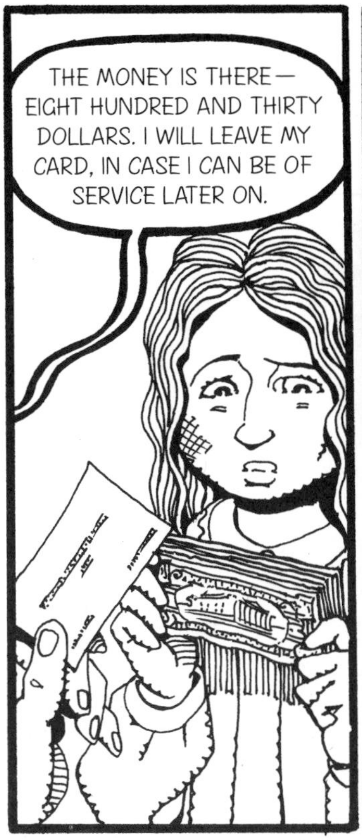
THE MONEY IS THERE— EIGHT HUNDRED AND THIRTY DOLLARS. I WILL LEAVE MY CARD, IN CASE I CAN BE OF SERVICE LATER ON.

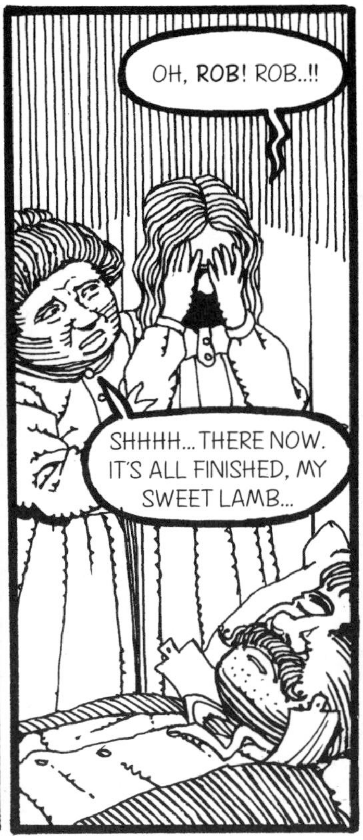
OH, ROB! ROB..!!
SHHHH... THERE NOW. IT'S ALL FINISHED, MY SWEET LAMB...

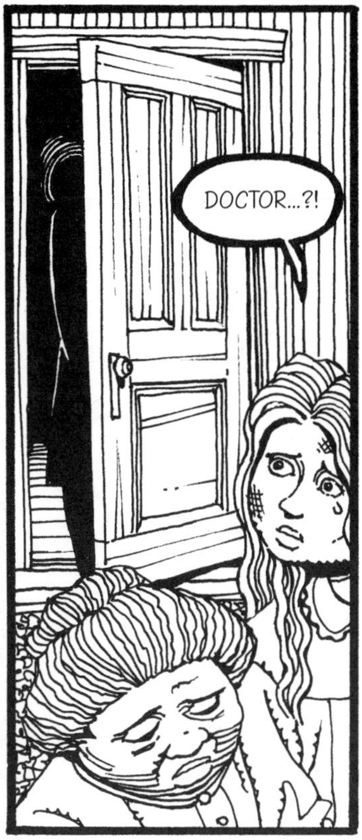
DOCTOR...?!

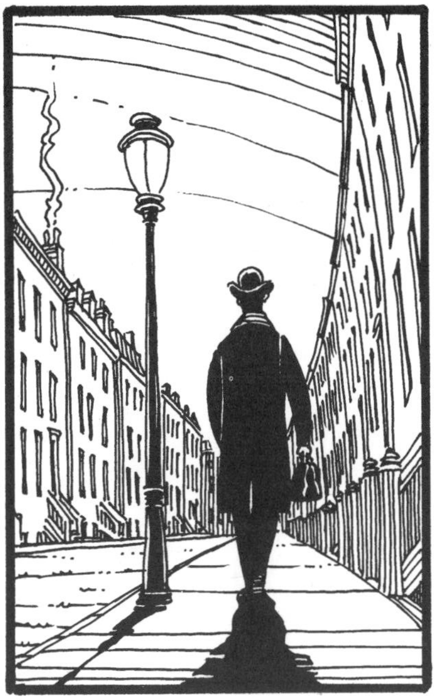

It would be vain to attempt to understand such men. We know only that they exist, and that we can observe them and tell of their performances, as children watch and speak of marionettes. — O. Henry

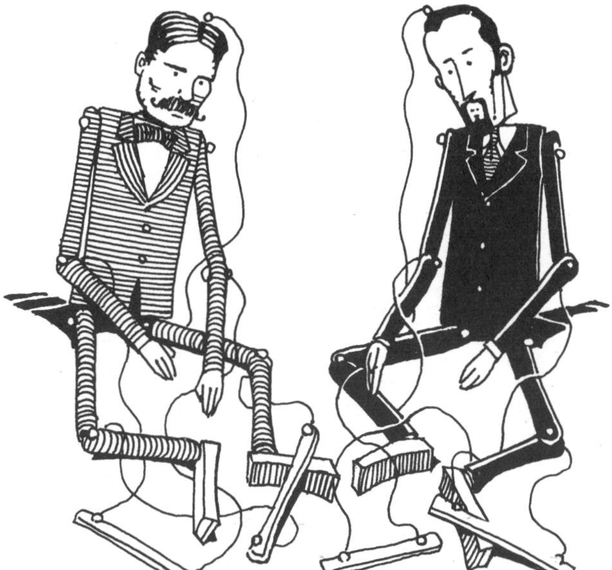

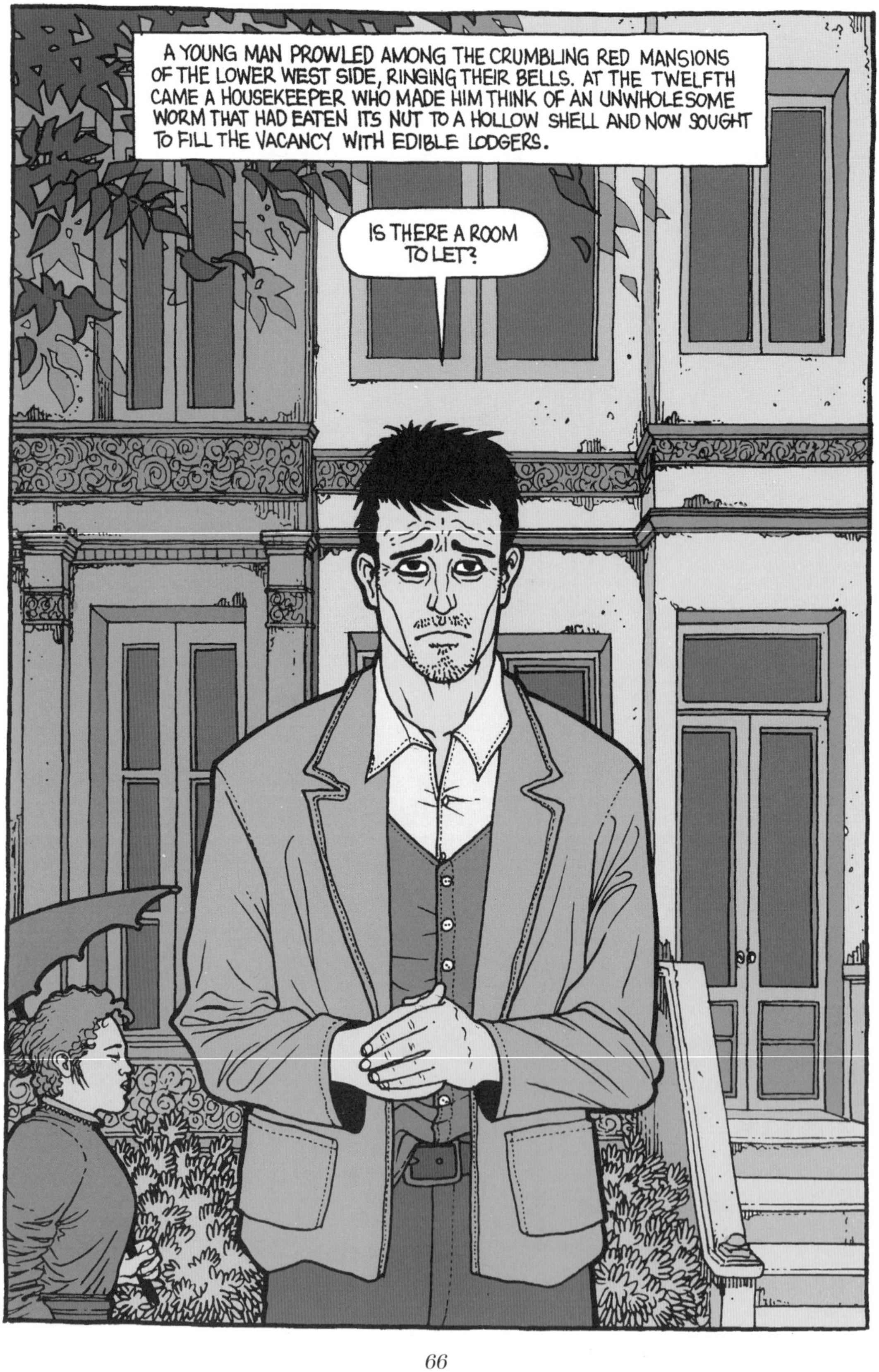
A YOUNG MAN PROWLED AMONG THE CRUMBLING RED MANSIONS OF THE LOWER WEST SIDE, RINGING THEIR BELLS. AT THE TWELFTH CAME A HOUSEKEEPER WHO MADE HIM THINK OF AN UNWHOLESOME WORM THAT HAD EATEN ITS NUT TO A HOLLOW SHELL AND NOW SOUGHT TO FILL THE VACANCY WITH EDIBLE LODGERS.
IS THERE A ROOM TO LET?

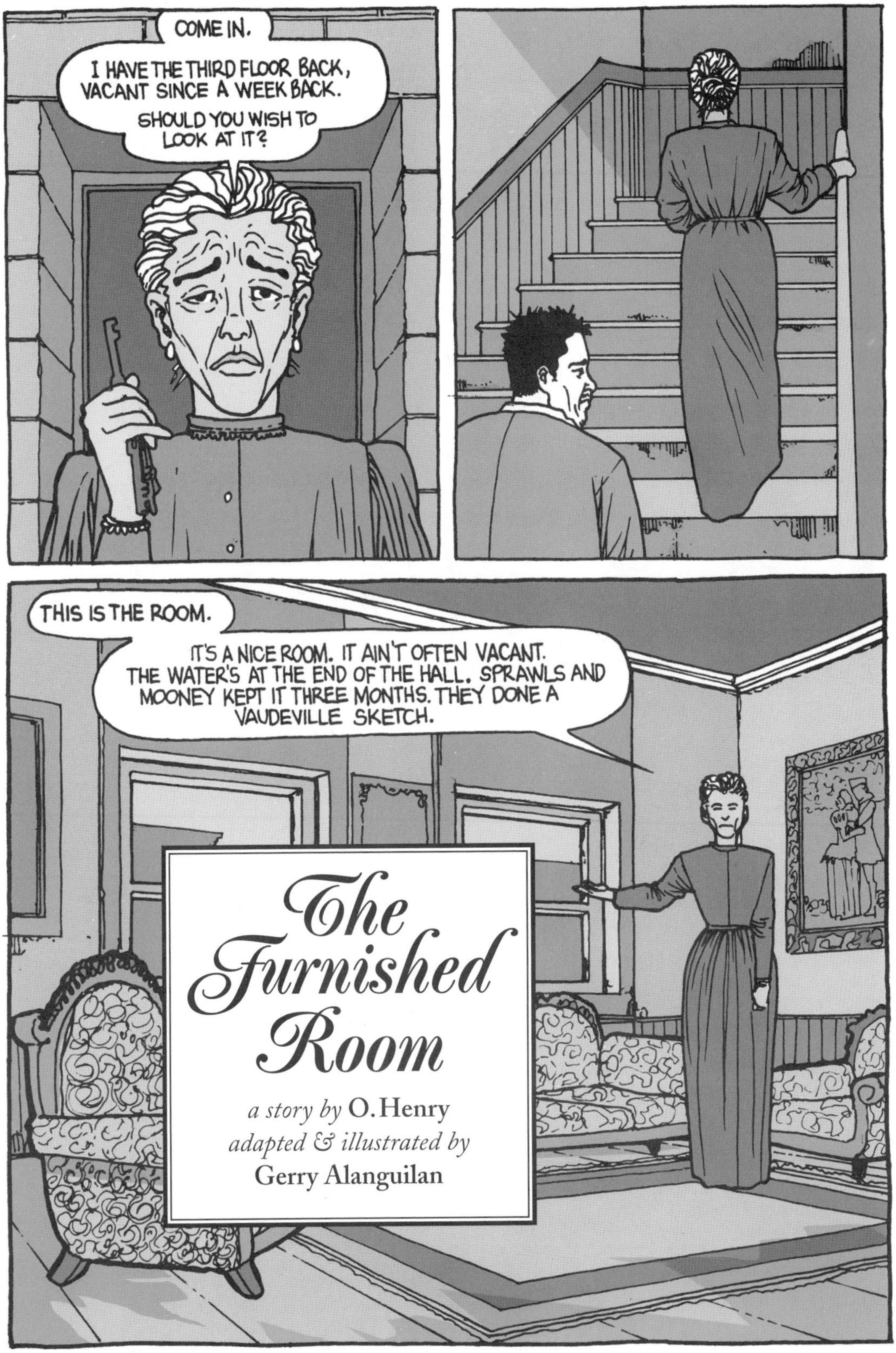
COME IN.
I HAVE THE THIRD FLOOR BACK, VACANT SINCE A WEEK BACK.
SHOULD YOU WISH TO LOOK AT IT?
THIS IS THE ROOM.
IT'S A NICE ROOM. IT AIN'T OFTEN VACANT. THE WATER'S AT THE END OF THE HALL. SPRAWLS AND MOONEY KEPT IT THREE MONTHS. THEY DONE A VAUDEVILLE SKETCH.
The Furnished Room
a story by O.Henry
adapted & illustrated by
Gerry Alanguilan

MISS B'RETTA SPROWLS - YOU MAY HAVE HEARD OF HER - OH, THAT WAS JUST THE STAGE NAMES - RIGHT THERE OVER THE DRESSER IS WHERE THE MARRIAGE CERTIFICATE HUNG, FRAMED.

DO YOU HAVE MANY THEATRICAL PEOPLE ROOMING HERE?

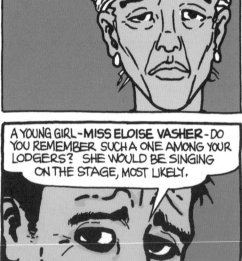

YES, SIR, THIS IS THE THEATRICAL DISTRICT. ACTOR PEOPLE NEVER STAYS LONG ANYWHERE. THEY COMES AND THEY GOES.

HE ENGAGED THE ROOM, PAYING FOR A WEEK IN ADVANCE. AS THE HOUSEKEEPER MOVED AWAY HE PUT, FOR THE THOUSANDTH TIME, THE QUESTION THAT HE CARRIED AT THE END OF HIS TONGUE.

A YOUNG GIRL - MISS ELOISE VASHER - DO YOU REMEMBER SUCH A ONE AMONG YOUR LODGERS? SHE WOULD BE SINGING ON THE STAGE, MOST LIKELY.

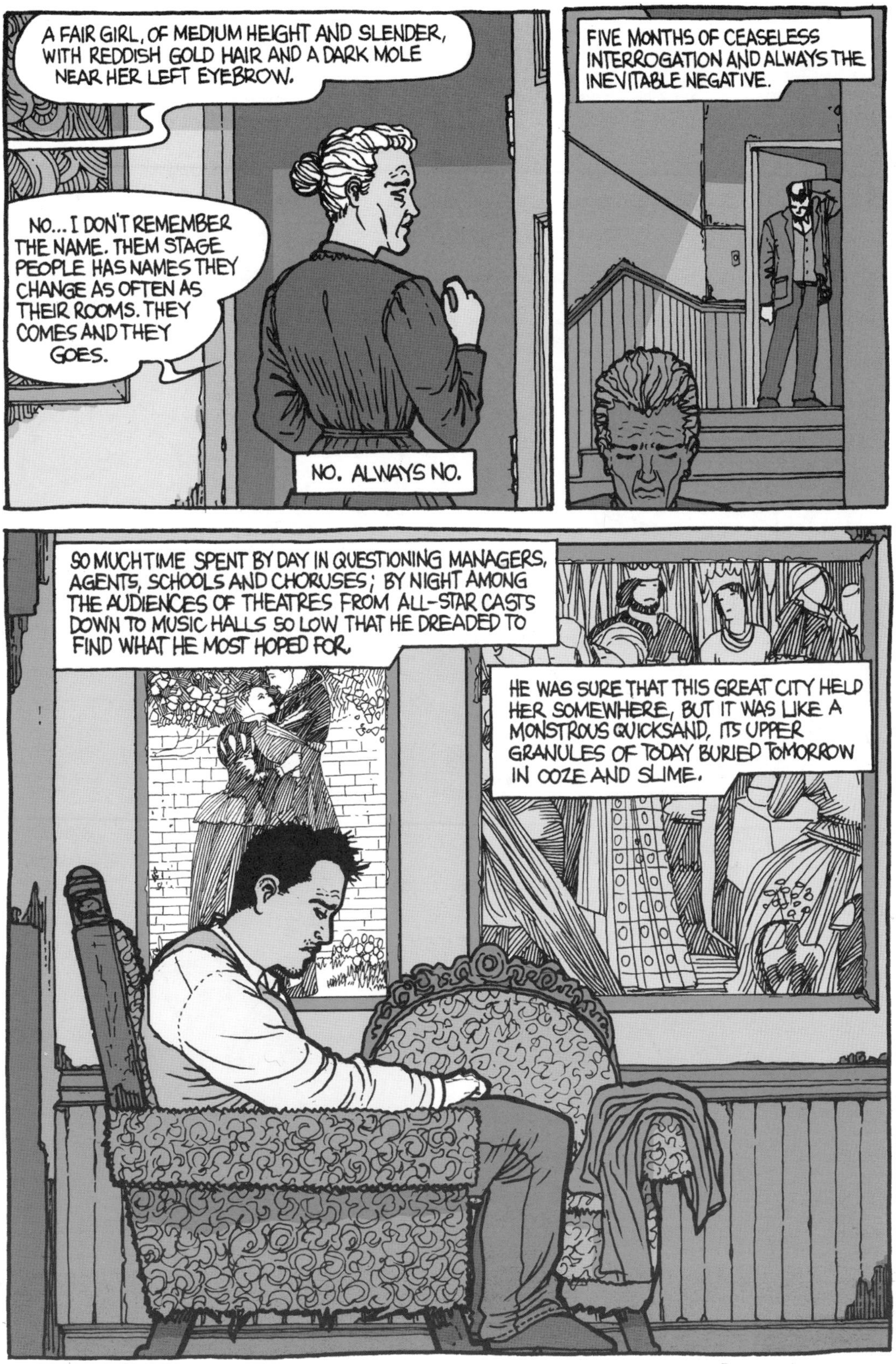
A FAIR GIRL, OF MEDIUM HEIGHT AND SLENDER, WITH REDDISH GOLD HAIR AND A DARK MOLE NEAR HER LEFT EYEBROW.
NO... I DON'T REMEMBER THE NAME. THEM STAGE PEOPLE HAS NAMES THEY CHANGE AS OFTEN AS THEIR ROOMS. THEY COMES AND THEY GOES.
NO. ALWAYS NO.
FIVE MONTHS OF CEASELESS INTERROGATION AND ALWAYS THE INEVITABLE NEGATIVE.
SO MUCH TIME SPENT BY DAY IN QUESTIONING MANAGERS, AGENTS, SCHOOLS AND CHORUSES; BY NIGHT AMONG THE AUDIENCES OF THEATRES FROM ALL-STAR CASTS DOWN TO MUSIC HALLS SO LOW THAT HE DREADED TO FIND WHAT HE MOST HOPED FOR.
HE WAS SURE THAT THIS GREAT CITY HELD HER SOMEWHERE, BUT IT WAS LIKE A MONSTROUS QUICKSAND, ITS UPPER GRANULES OF TODAY BURIED TOMORROW IN OOZE AND SLIME.

THE FURNISHED ROOM RECEIVED ITS LATEST GUEST WITH A HAGGARD, PERFUNCTORY WELCOME, AS IT TRIED TO DISCOURSE TO HIM OF ITS DIVERS TENANTRY. ONE BY ONE, AS THE CHARACTERS OF A CRYPTOGRAPH BECOME EXPLICIT, THE LITTLE SIGNS LEFT BY THE FURNISHED ROOM'S PROCESSION OF GUESTS DEVELOPED A SIGNIFICANCE.

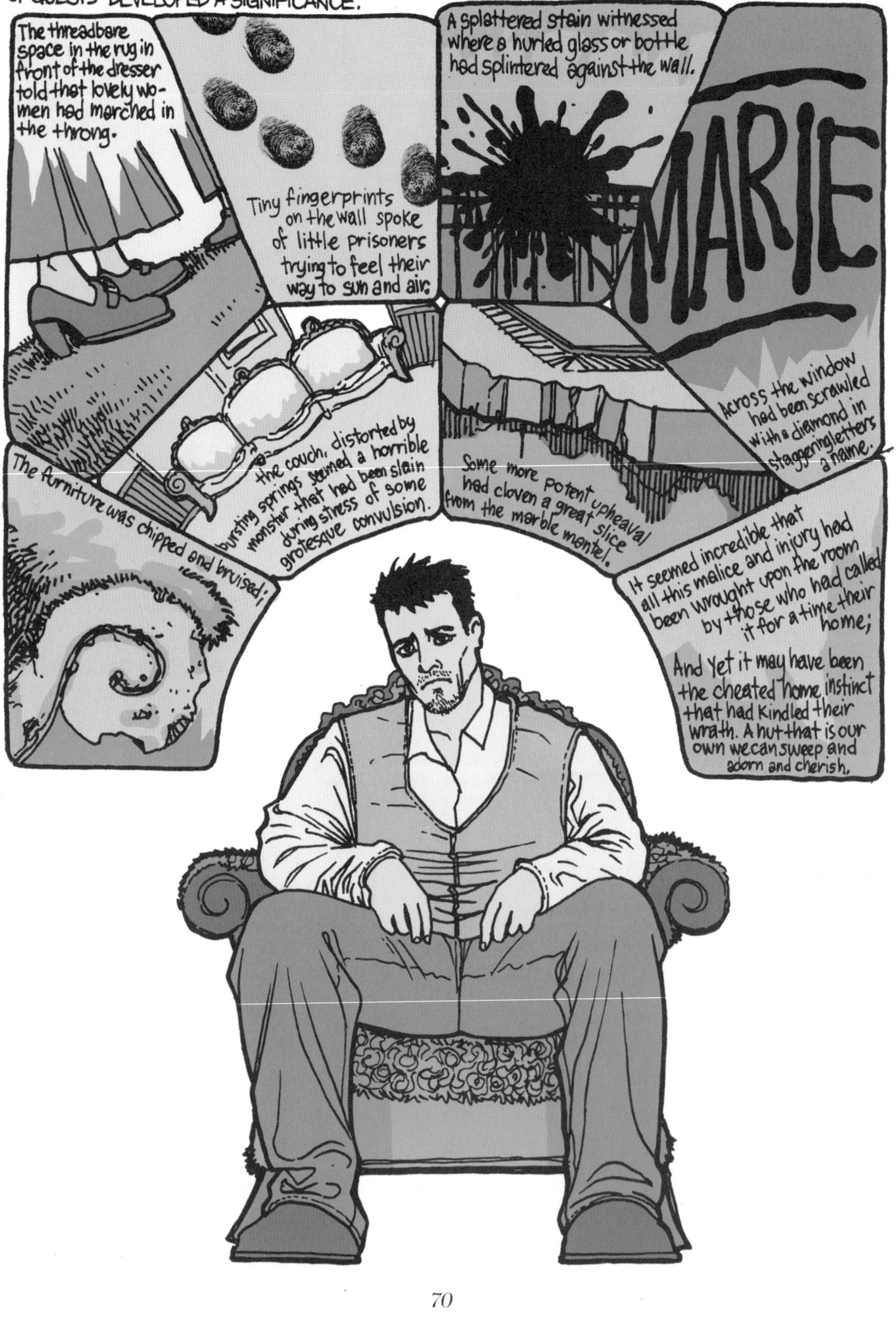
The threadbare space in the rug in front of the dresser told that lovely women had marched in the throng.
Tiny fingerprints on the wall spoke of little prisoners trying to feel their way to sun and air.
A splattered stain witnessed where a hurled glass or bottle had splintered against the wall.
MARIE
Across the window had been scrawled with a diamond in staggering letters a name.
The furniture was chipped and bruised;
the couch, distorted by bursting springs, seemed a horrible monster that had been slain during stress of some grotesque convulsion.
Some more potent upheaval had cloven a great slice from the marble mantel.
It seemed incredible that all this malice and injury had been wrought upon the room by those who had called it for a time their home;
And yet it may have been the cheated home instinct that had kindled their wrath. A hut that is our own we can sweep and adorn and cherish.

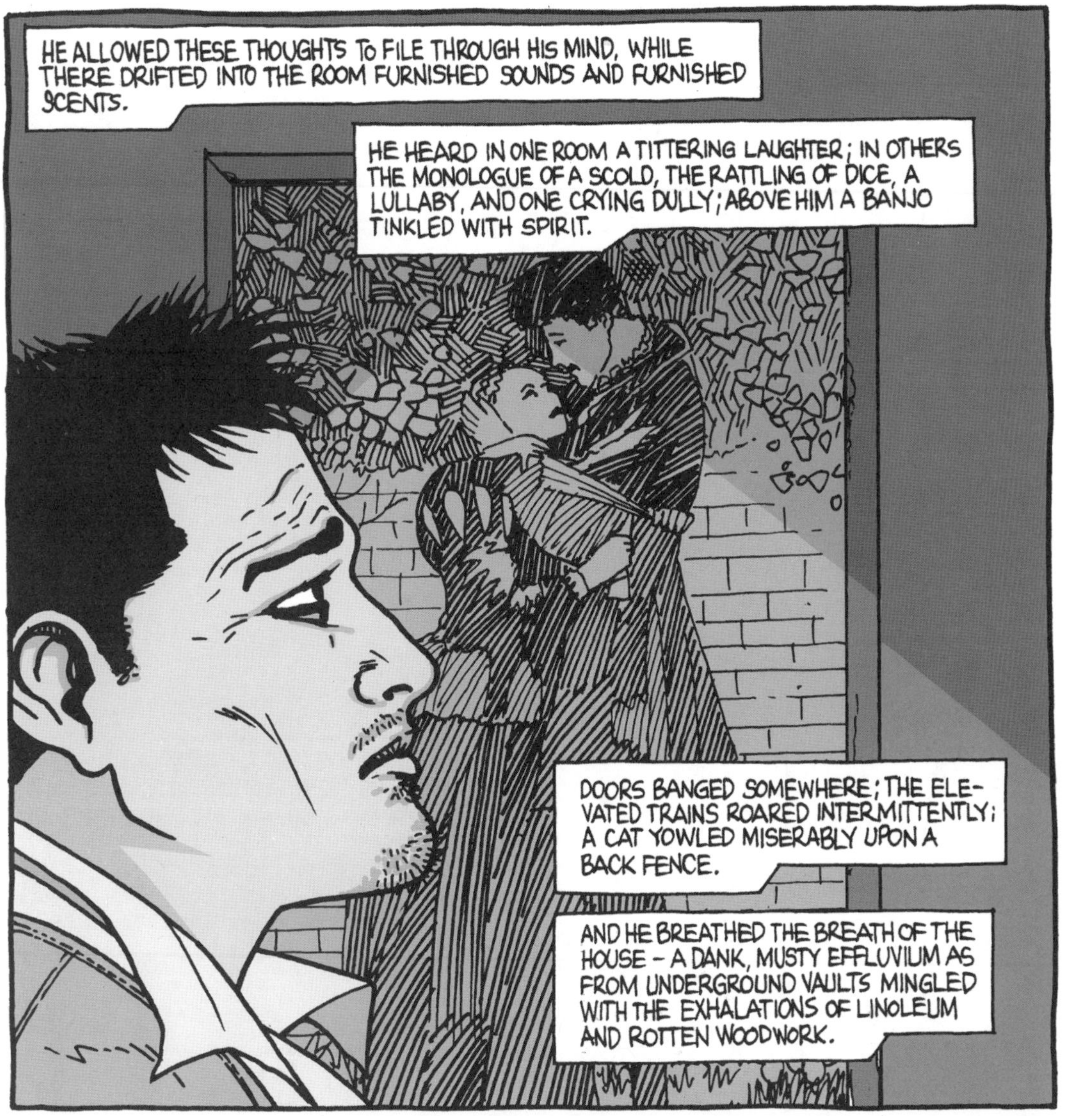
HE ALLOWED THESE THOUGHTS TO FILE THROUGH HIS MIND, WHILE THERE DRIFTED INTO THE ROOM FURNISHED SOUNDS AND FURNISHED SCENTS.
HE HEARD IN ONE ROOM A TITTERING LAUGHTER; IN OTHERS THE MONOLOGUE OF A SCOLD, THE RATTLING OF DICE, A LULLABY, AND ONE CRYING DULLY; ABOVE HIM A BANJO TINKLED WITH SPIRIT.
DOORS BANGED SOMEWHERE; THE ELEVATED TRAINS ROARED INTERMITTENTLY; A CAT YOWLED MISERABLY UPON A BACK FENCE.
AND HE BREATHED THE BREATH OF THE HOUSE - A DANK, MUSTY EFFLUVIUM AS FROM UNDERGROUND VAULTS MINGLED WITH THE EXHALATIONS OF LINOLEUM AND ROTTEN WOODWORK.

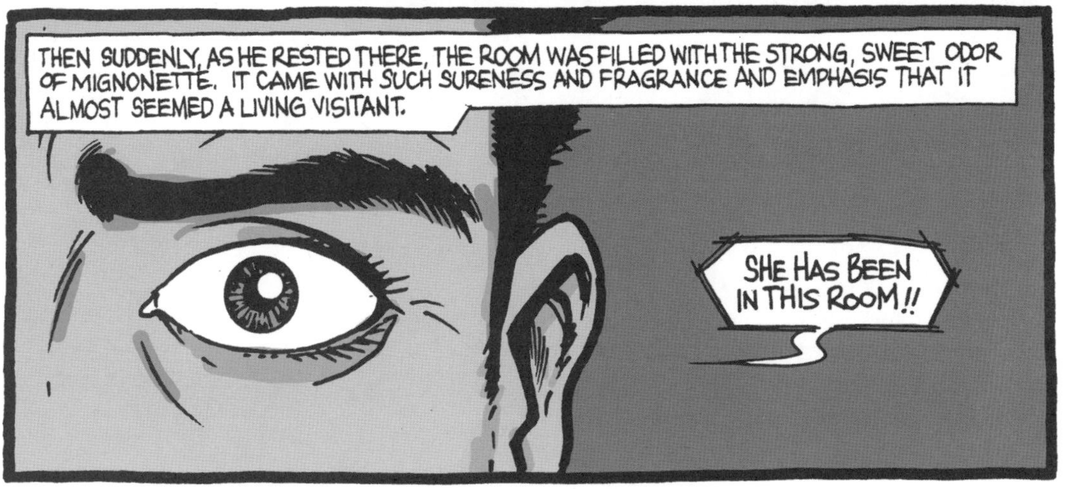
THEN SUDDENLY, AS HE RESTED THERE, THE ROOM WAS FILLED WITH THE STRONG, SWEET ODOR OF MIGNONETTE. IT CAME WITH SUCH SURENESS AND FRAGRANCE AND EMPHASIS THAT IT ALMOST SEEMED A LIVING VISITANT.
SHE HAS BEEN IN THIS ROOM!!

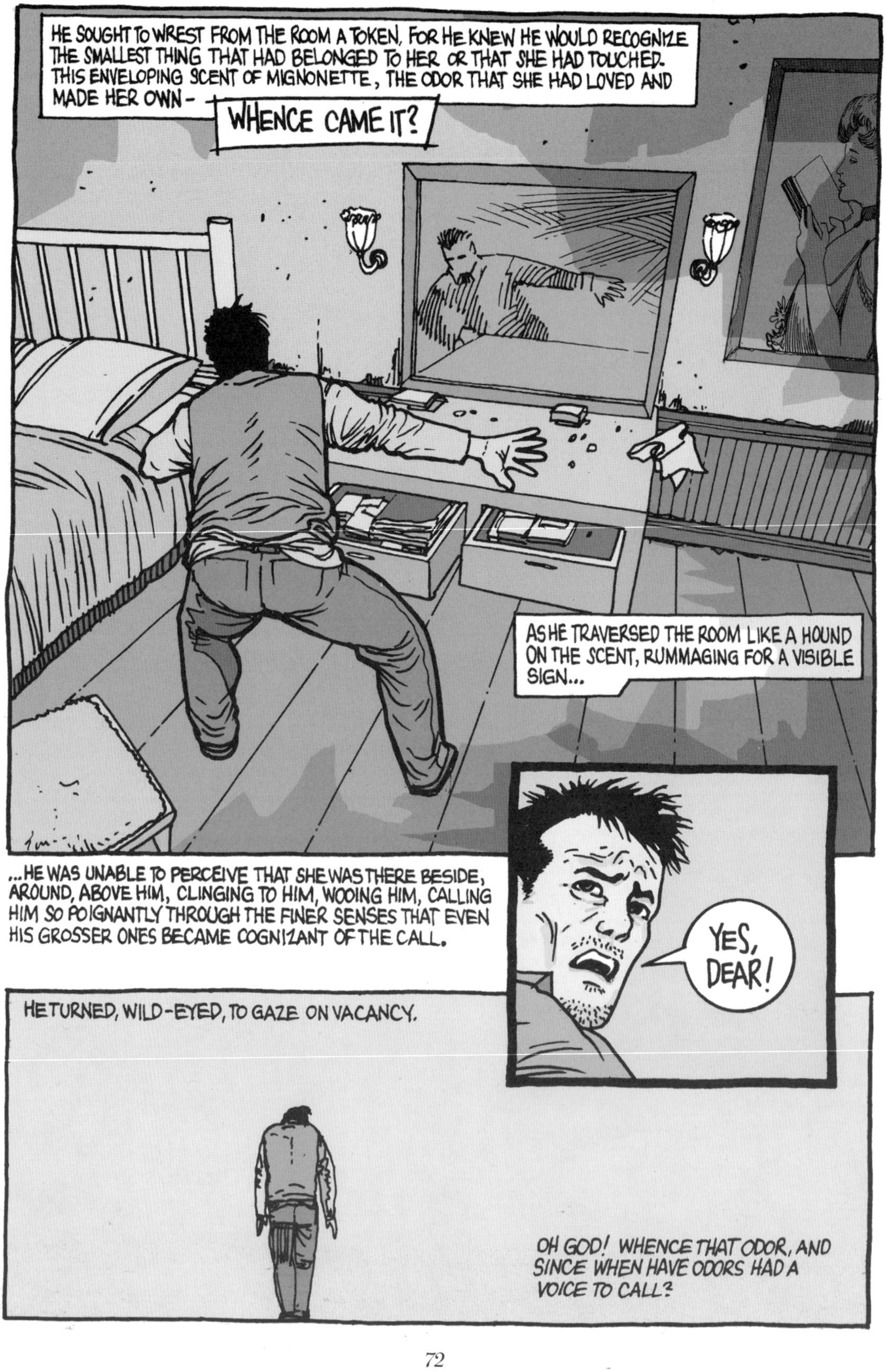
HE SOUGHT TO WREST FROM THE ROOM A TOKEN, FOR HE KNEW HE WOULD RECOGNIZE THE SMALLEST THING THAT HAD BELONGED TO HER OR THAT SHE HAD TOUCHED. THIS ENVELOPING SCENT OF MIGNONETTE, THE ODOR THAT SHE HAD LOVED AND MADE HER OWN -
WHENCE CAME IT?
AS HE TRAVERSED THE ROOM LIKE A HOUND ON THE SCENT, RUMMAGING FOR A VISIBLE SIGN...
...HE WAS UNABLE TO PERCEIVE THAT SHE WAS THERE BESIDE, AROUND, ABOVE HIM, CLINGING TO HIM, WOOING HIM, CALLING HIM SO POIGNANTLY THROUGH THE FINER SENSES THAT EVEN HIS GROSSER ONES BECAME COGNIZANT OF THE CALL.
YES, DEAR!
HE TURNED, WILD-EYED, TO GAZE ON VACANCY.
OH GOD! WHENCE THAT ODOR, AND SINCE WHEN HAVE ODORS HAD A VOICE TO CALL?

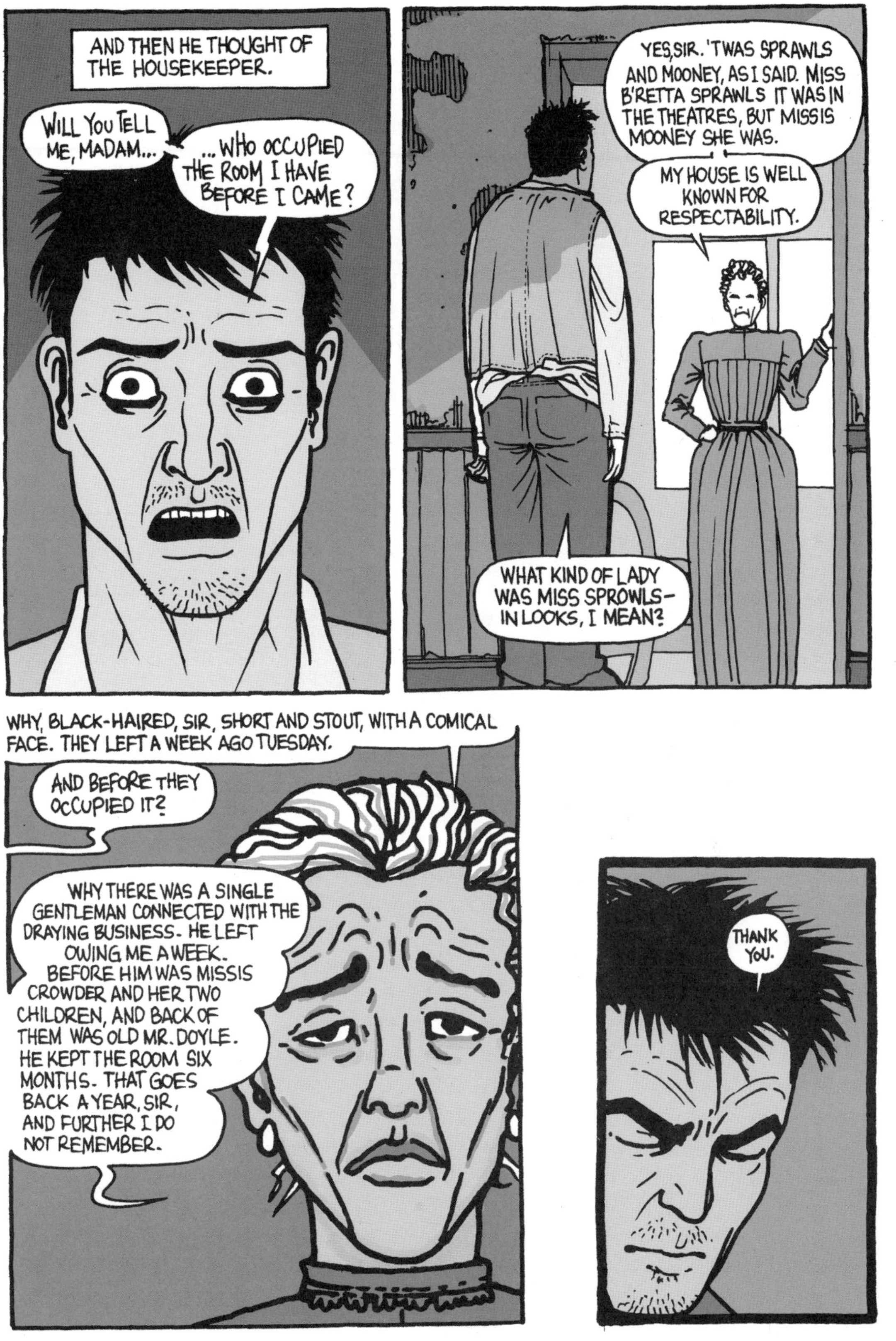
AND THEN HE THOUGHT OF THE HOUSEKEEPER.
WILL YOU TELL ME, MADAM...
...WHO OCCUPIED THE ROOM I HAVE BEFORE I CAME?
YES, SIR. 'TWAS SPRAWLS AND MOONEY, AS I SAID. MISS B'RETTA SPRAWLS IT WAS IN THE THEATRES, BUT MISSIS MOONEY SHE WAS.
MY HOUSE IS WELL KNOWN FOR RESPECTABILITY.
WHAT KIND OF LADY WAS MISS SPROWLS- IN LOOKS, I MEAN?
WHY, BLACK-HAIRED, SIR, SHORT AND STOUT, WITH A COMICAL FACE. THEY LEFT A WEEK AGO TUESDAY.
AND BEFORE THEY OCCUPIED IT?
WHY THERE WAS A SINGLE GENTLEMAN CONNECTED WITH THE DRAYING BUSINESS. HE LEFT OWING ME A WEEK. BEFORE HIM WAS MISSIS CROWDER AND HER TWO CHILDREN, AND BACK OF THEM WAS OLD MR. DOYLE. HE KEPT THE ROOM SIX MONTHS. THAT GOES BACK A YEAR, SIR, AND FURTHER I DO NOT REMEMBER.
THANK YOU.

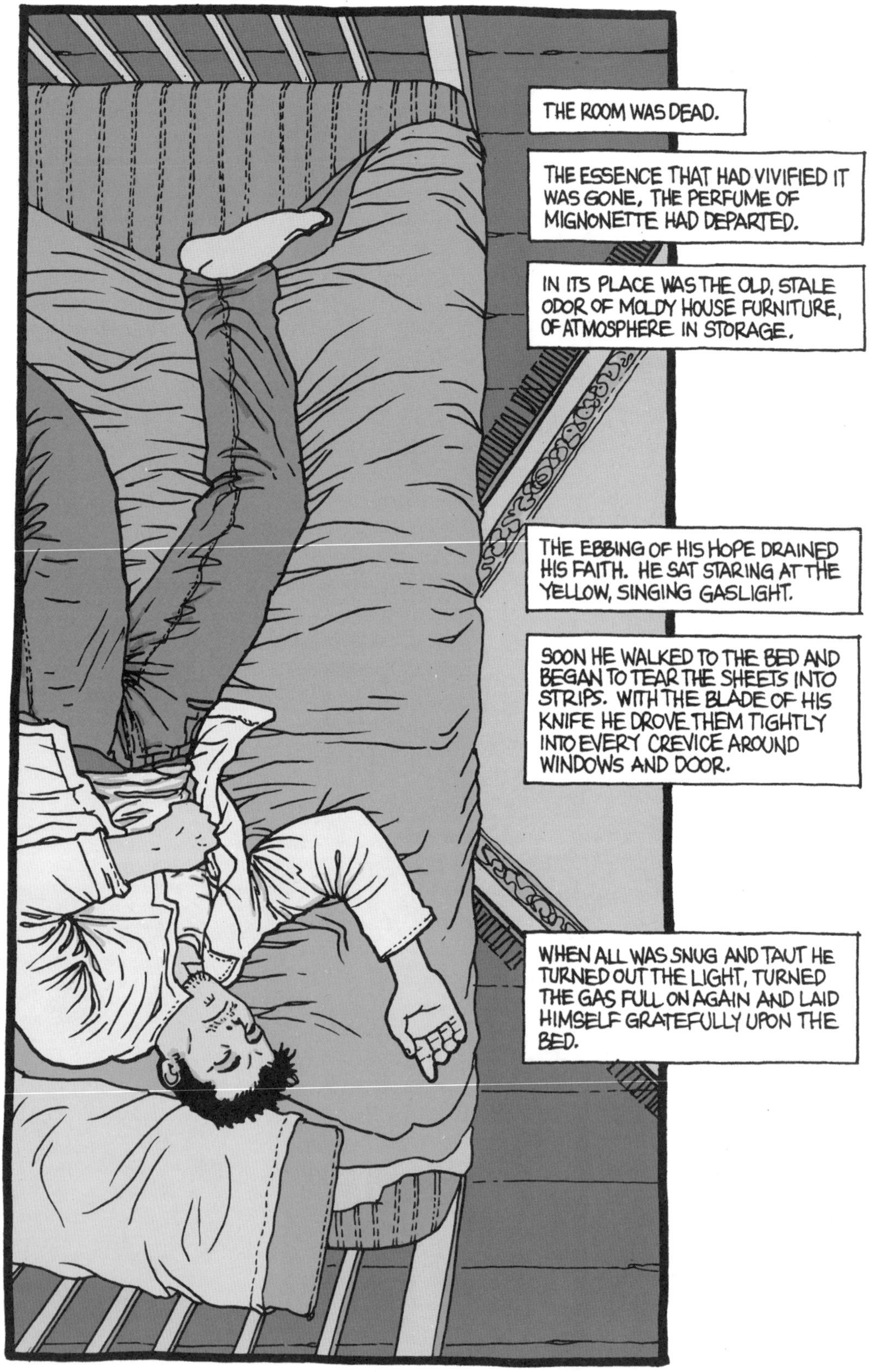
THE ROOM WAS DEAD.
THE ESSENCE THAT HAD VIVIFIED IT WAS GONE, THE PERFUME OF MIGNONETTE HAD DEPARTED.
IN ITS PLACE WAS THE OLD, STALE ODOR OF MOLDY HOUSE FURNITURE, OF ATMOSPHERE IN STORAGE.
THE EBBING OF HIS HOPE DRAINED HIS FAITH. HE SAT STARING AT THE YELLOW, SINGING GASLIGHT.
SOON HE WALKED TO THE BED AND BEGAN TO TEAR THE SHEETS INTO STRIPS. WITH THE BLADE OF HIS KNIFE HE DROVE THEM TIGHTLY INTO EVERY CREVICE AROUND WINDOWS AND DOOR.
WHEN ALL WAS SNUG AND TAUT HE TURNED OUT THE LIGHT, TURNED THE GAS FULL ON AGAIN AND LAID HIMSELF GRATEFULLY UPON THE BED.

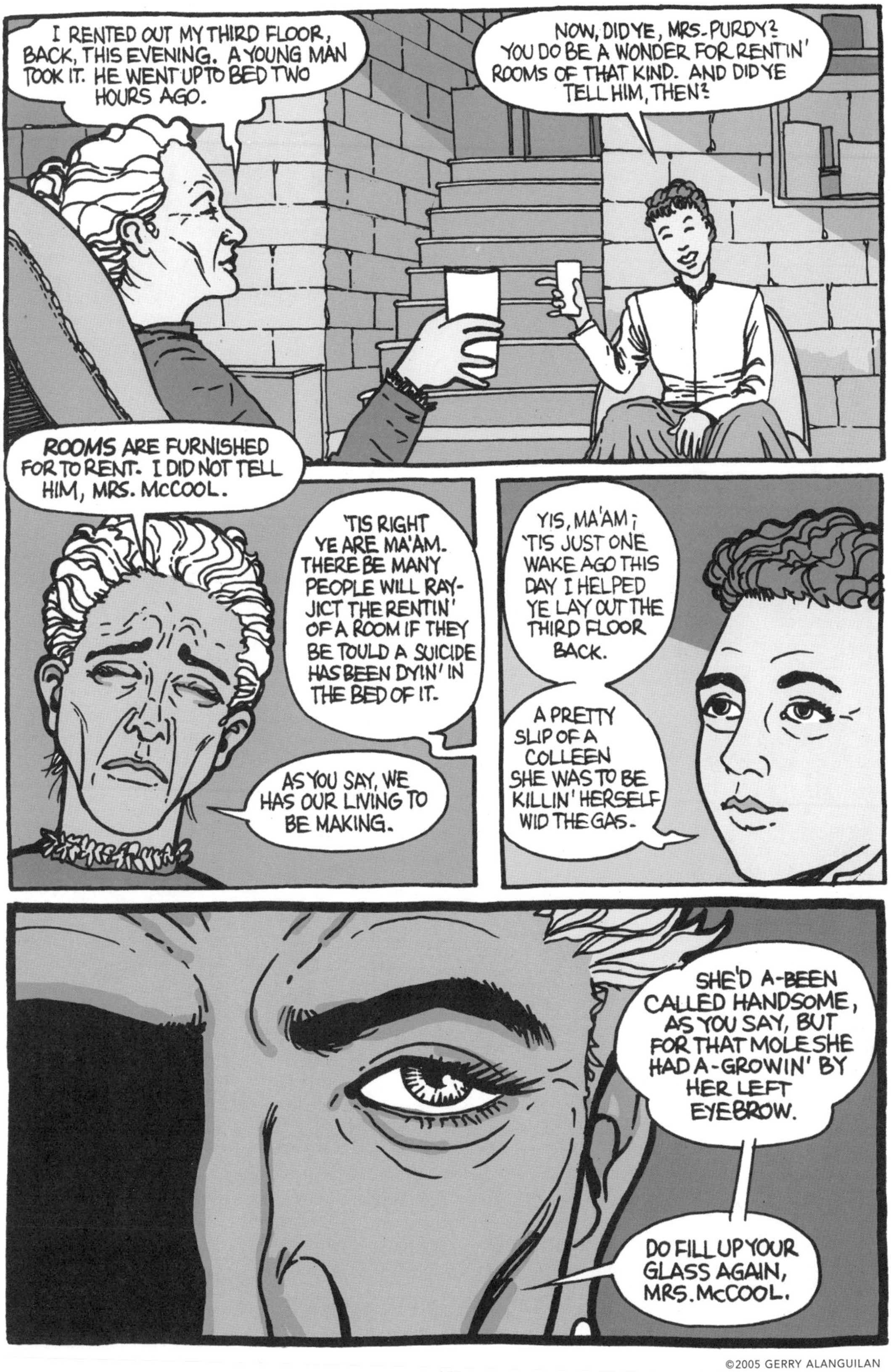
I RENTED OUT MY THIRD FLOOR, BACK, THIS EVENING. A YOUNG MAN TOOK IT. HE WENT UP TO BED TWO HOURS AGO.
NOW, DID YE, MRS. PURDY? YOU DO BE A WONDER FOR RENTIN' ROOMS OF THAT KIND. AND DID YE TELL HIM, THEN?
ROOMS ARE FURNISHED FOR TO RENT. I DID NOT TELL HIM, MRS. McCOOL.
'TIS RIGHT YE ARE MA'AM. THERE BE MANY PEOPLE WILL RAY-JICT THE RENTIN' OF A ROOM IF THEY BE TOULD A SUICIDE HAS BEEN DYIN' IN THE BED OF IT.
AS YOU SAY, WE HAS OUR LIVING TO BE MAKING.
YIS, MA'AM; 'TIS JUST ONE WAKE AGO THIS DAY I HELPED YE LAY OUT THE THIRD FLOOR BACK.
A PRETTY SLIP OF A COLLEEN SHE WAS TO BE KILLIN' HERSELF WID THE GAS.
SHE'D A-BEEN CALLED HANDSOME, AS YOU SAY, BUT FOR THAT MOLE SHE HAD A-GROWIN' BY HER LEFT EYEBROW.
DO FILL UP YOUR GLASS AGAIN, MRS. McCOOL.

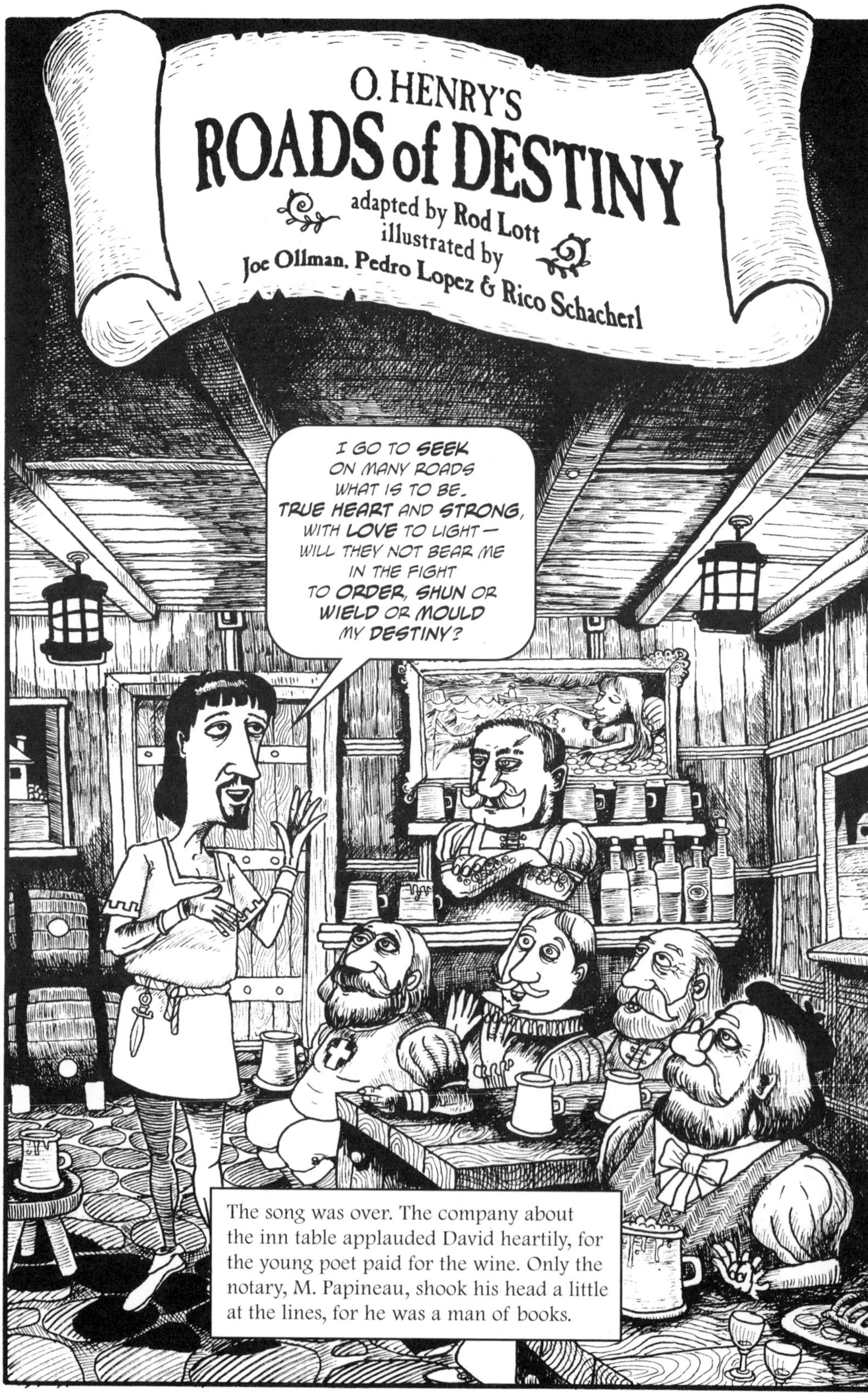
O. HENRY'S
ROADS of DESTINY
adapted by Rod Lott
illustrated by
Joe Ollman, Pedro Lopez & Rico Schacherl
I GO TO SEEK ON MANY ROADS WHAT IS TO BE. TRUE HEART AND STRONG, WITH LOVE TO LIGHT— WILL THEY NOT BEAR ME IN THE FIGHT TO ORDER, SHUN OR WIELD OR MOULD MY DESTINY?
The song was over. The company about the inn table applauded David heartily, for the young poet paid for the wine. Only the notary, M. Papineau, shook his head a little at the lines, for he was a man of books.

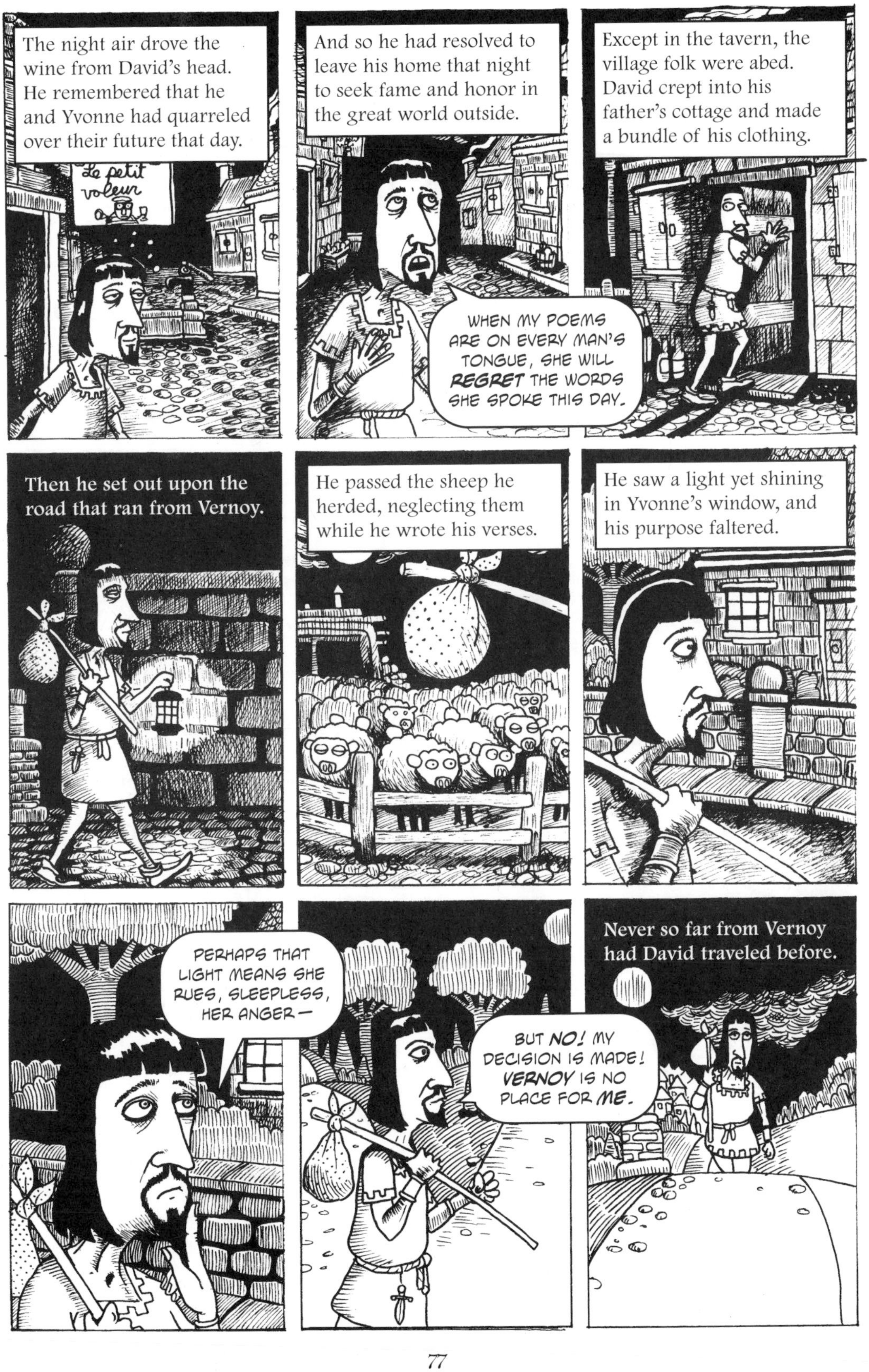
The night air drove the wine from David's head. He remembered that he and Yvonne had quarreled over their future that day.
Le petit voleur
And so he had resolved to leave his home that night to seek fame and honor in the great world outside.
WHEN MY POEMS ARE ON EVERY MAN'S TONGUE, SHE WILL REGRET THE WORDS SHE SPOKE THIS DAY.
Except in the tavern, the village folk were abed. David crept into his father's cottage and made a bundle of his clothing.
Then he set out upon the road that ran from Vernoy.
He passed the sheep he herded, neglecting them while he wrote his verses.
He saw a light yet shining in Yvonne's window, and his purpose faltered.
PERHAPS THAT LIGHT MEANS SHE RUES, SLEEPLESS, HER ANGER—
BUT NO! MY DECISION IS MADE! VERNOY IS NO PLACE FOR ME.
Never so far from Vernoy had David traveled before.

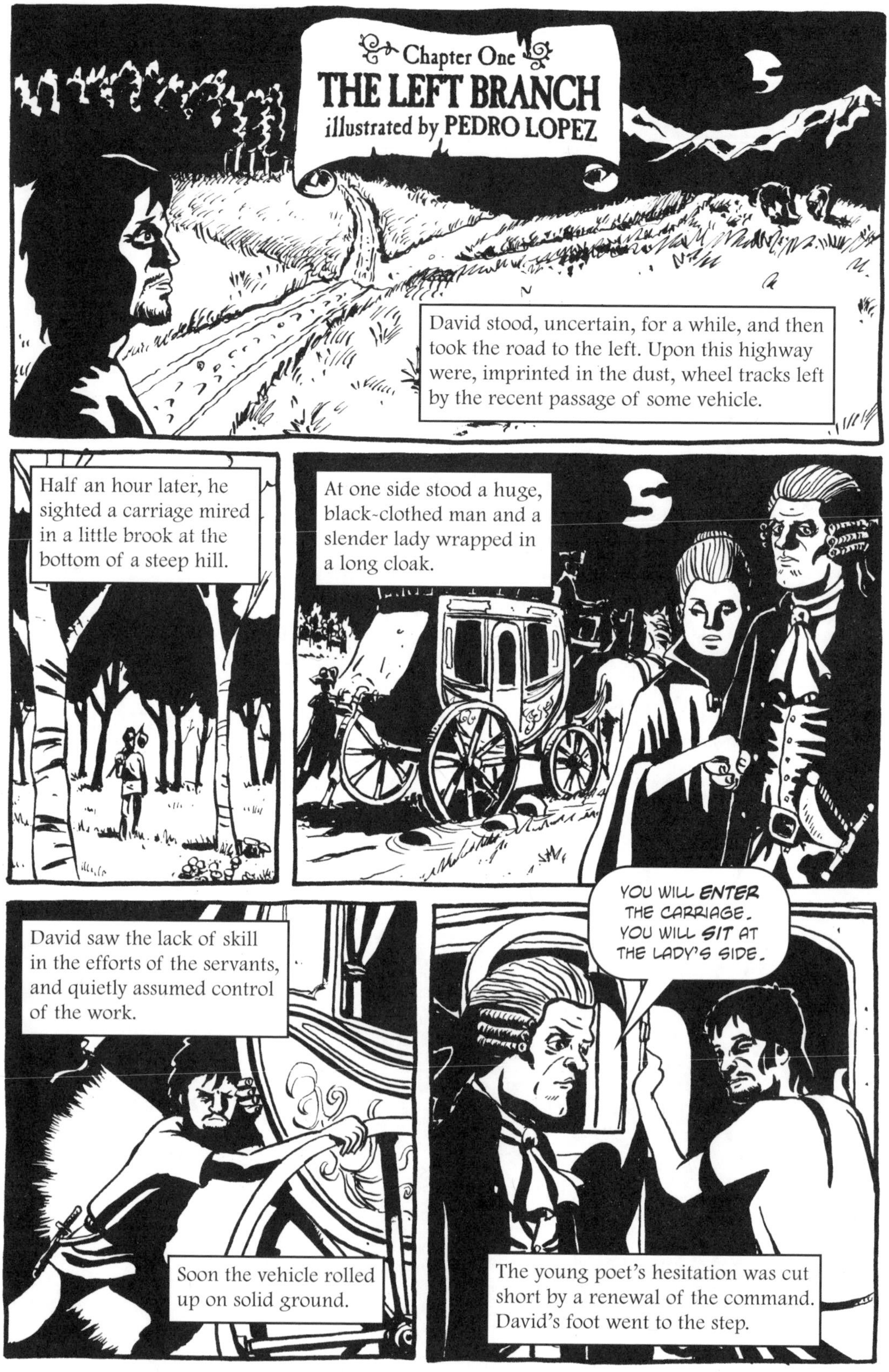
Chapter One
THE LEFT BRANCH
illustrated by PEDRO LOPEZ
David stood, uncertain, for a while, and then took the road to the left. Upon this highway were, imprinted in the dust, wheel tracks left by the recent passage of some vehicle.
Half an hour later, he sighted a carriage mired in a little brook at the bottom of a steep hill.
At one side stood a huge, black-clothed man and a slender lady wrapped in a long cloak.
David saw the lack of skill in the efforts of the servants, and quietly assumed control of the work.
Soon the vehicle rolled up on solid ground.
YOU WILL ENTER THE CARRIAGE. YOU WILL SIT AT THE LADY'S SIDE.
The young poet's hesitation was cut short by a renewal of the command. David's foot went to the step.

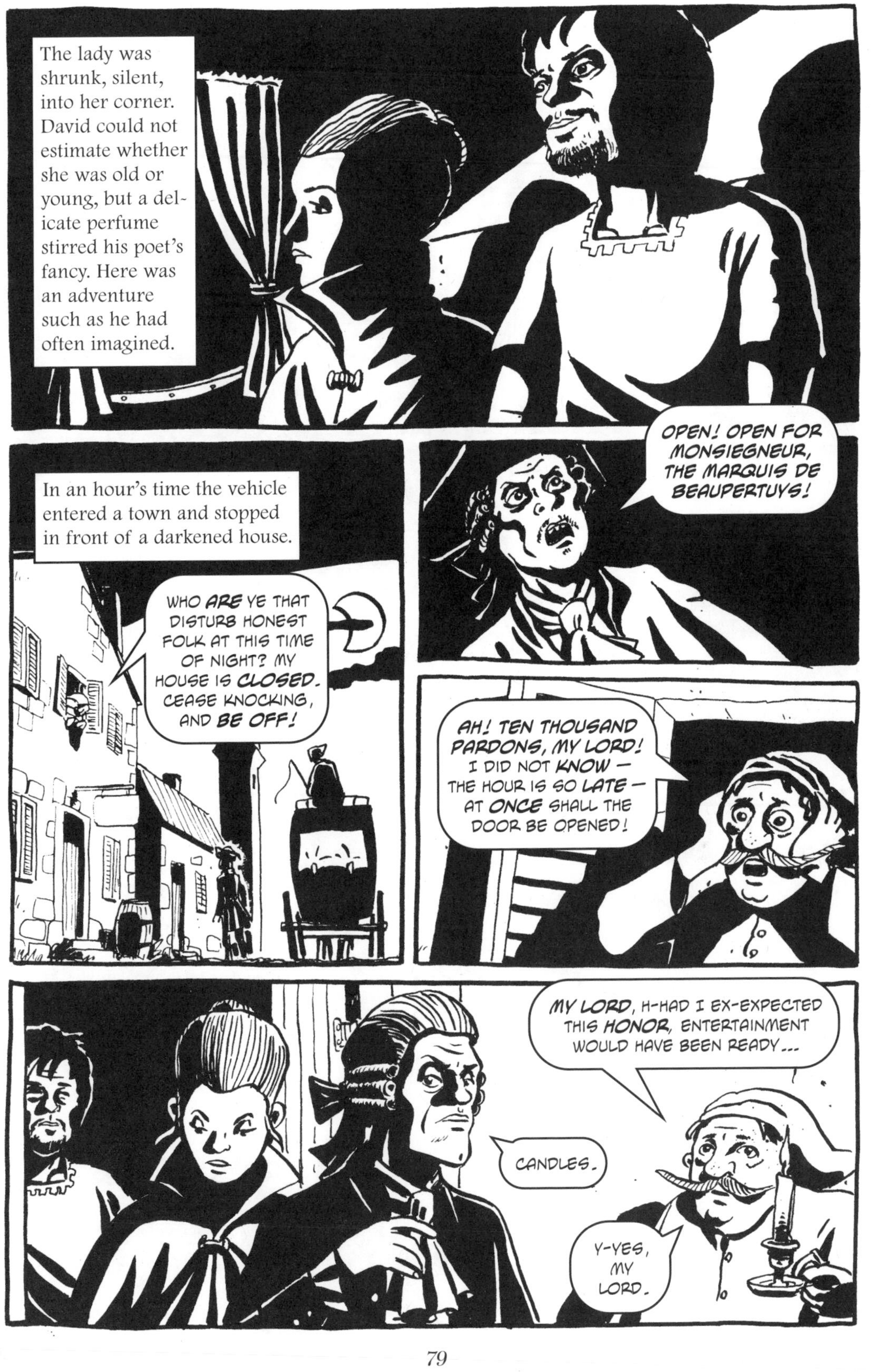
The lady was shrunk, silent, into her corner. David could not estimate whether she was old or young, but a delicate perfume stirred his poet's fancy. Here was an adventure such as he had often imagined.
In an hour's time the vehicle entered a town and stopped in front of a darkened house.
WHO ARE YE THAT DISTURB HONEST FOLK AT THIS TIME OF NIGHT? MY HOUSE IS CLOSED. CEASE KNOCKING, AND BE OFF!
OPEN! OPEN FOR MONSIEGNEUR, THE MARQUIS DE BEAUPERTUYS!
AH! TEN THOUSAND PARDONS, MY LORD! I DID NOT KNOW — THE HOUR IS SO LATE — AT ONCE SHALL THE DOOR BE OPENED!
MY LORD, H-HAD I EX-EXPECTED THIS HONOR, ENTERTAINMENT WOULD HAVE BEEN READY...
CANDLES.
Y-YES, MY LORD.

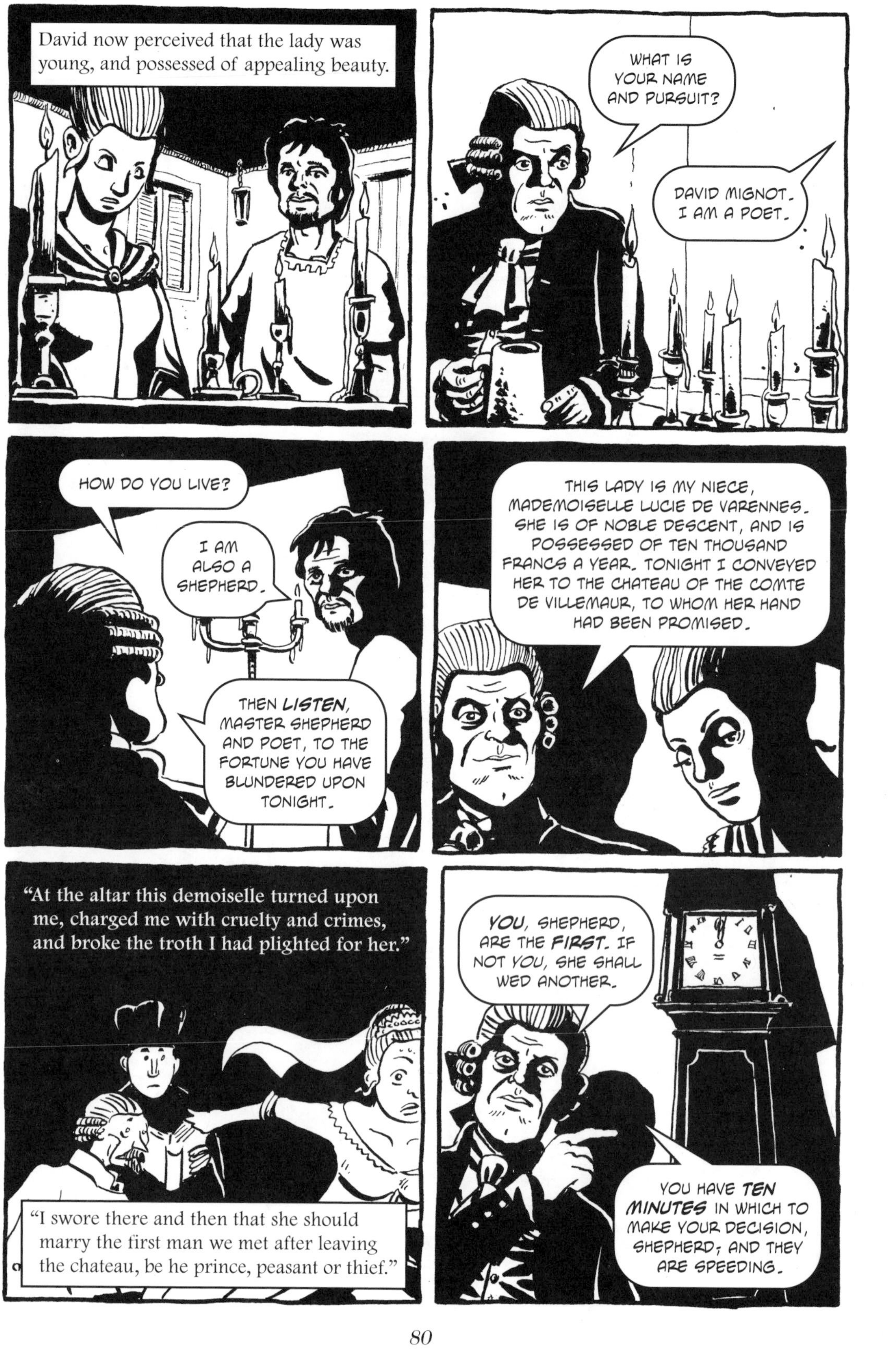
David now perceived that the lady was young, and possessed of appealing beauty.
WHAT IS YOUR NAME AND PURSUIT?
DAVID MIGNOT. I AM A POET.
HOW DO YOU LIVE?
I AM ALSO A SHEPHERD.
THEN LISTEN, MASTER SHEPHERD AND POET, TO THE FORTUNE YOU HAVE BLUNDERED UPON TONIGHT.
THIS LADY IS MY NIECE, MADEMOISELLE LUCIE DE VARENNES. SHE IS OF NOBLE DESCENT, AND IS POSSESSED OF TEN THOUSAND FRANCS A YEAR. TONIGHT I CONVEYED HER TO THE CHATEAU OF THE COMTE DE VILLEMAUR, TO WHOM HER HAND HAD BEEN PROMISED.
"At the altar this demoiselle turned upon me, charged me with cruelty and crimes, and broke the troth I had plighted for her."
"I swore there and then that she should marry the first man we met after leaving the chateau, be he prince, peasant or thief."
YOU, SHEPHERD, ARE THE FIRST. IF NOT YOU, SHE SHALL WED ANOTHER.
YOU HAVE TEN MINUTES IN WHICH TO MAKE YOUR DECISION, SHEPHERD; AND THEY ARE SPEEDING.

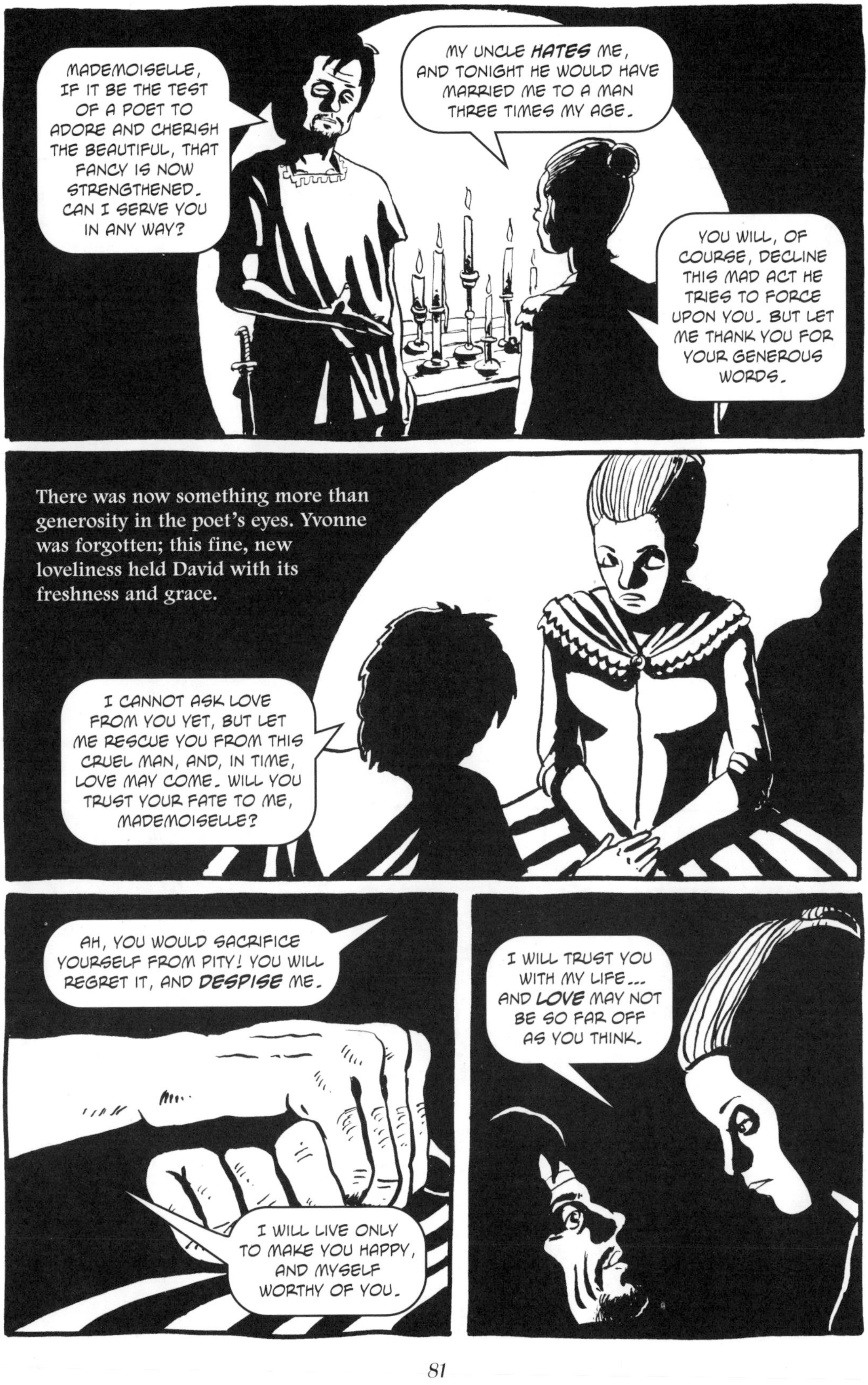
MADEMOISELLE, IF IT BE THE TEST OF A POET TO ADORE AND CHERISH THE BEAUTIFUL, THAT FANCY IS NOW STRENGTHENED. CAN I SERVE YOU IN ANY WAY?
MY UNCLE HATES ME, AND TONIGHT HE WOULD HAVE MARRIED ME TO A MAN THREE TIMES MY AGE.
YOU WILL, OF COURSE, DECLINE THIS MAD ACT HE TRIES TO FORCE UPON YOU. BUT LET ME THANK YOU FOR YOUR GENEROUS WORDS.
There was now something more than generosity in the poet's eyes. Yvonne was forgotten; this fine, new loveliness held David with its freshness and grace.
I CANNOT ASK LOVE FROM YOU YET, BUT LET ME RESCUE YOU FROM THIS CRUEL MAN, AND, IN TIME, LOVE MAY COME. WILL YOU TRUST YOUR FATE TO ME, MADEMOISELLE?
AH, YOU WOULD SACRIFICE YOURSELF FROM PITY! YOU WILL REGRET IT, AND DESPISE ME.
I WILL LIVE ONLY TO MAKE YOU HAPPY, AND MYSELF WORTHY OF YOU.
I WILL TRUST YOU WITH MY LIFE... AND LOVE MAY NOT BE SO FAR OFF AS YOU THINK.

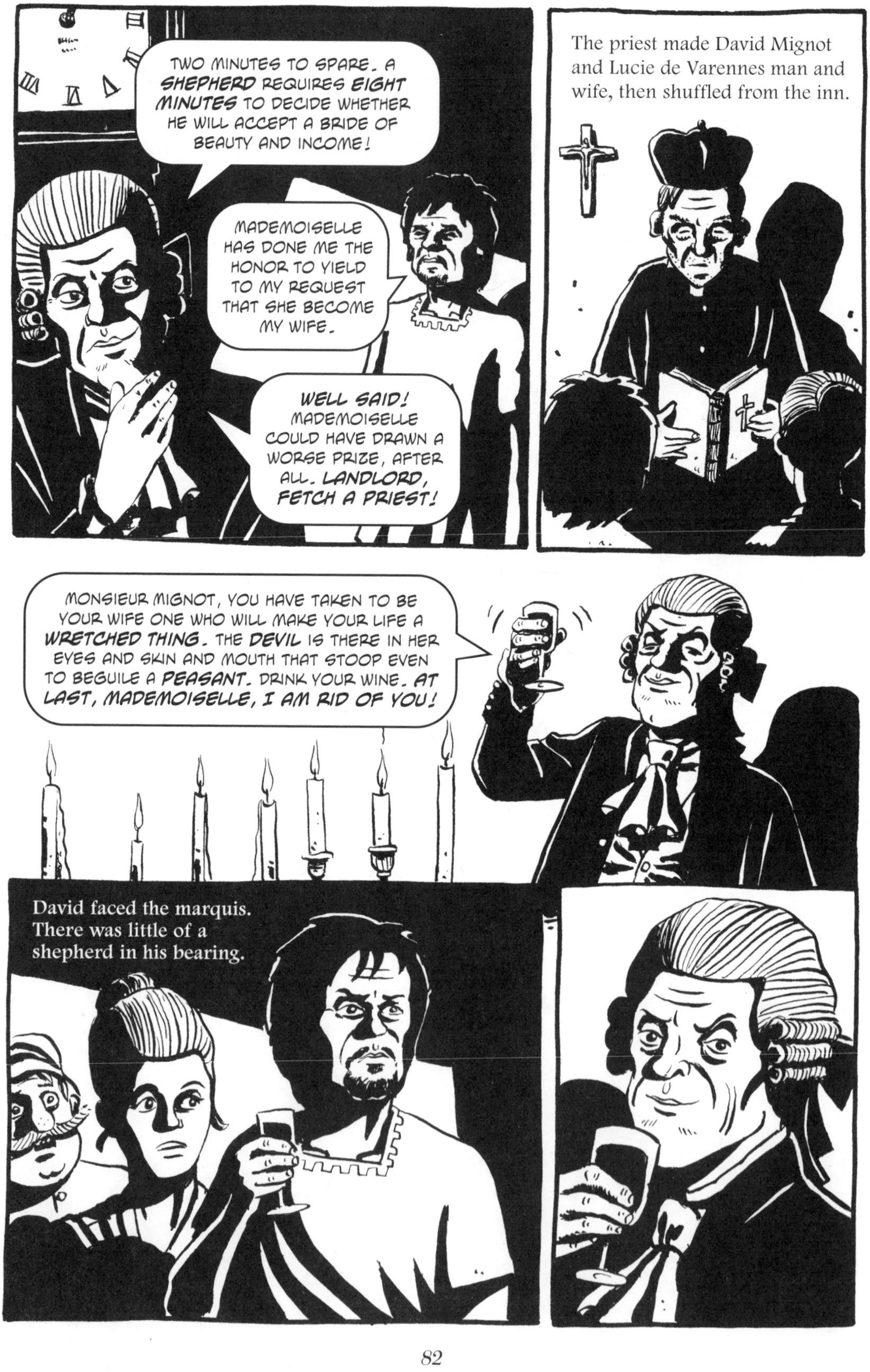
TWO MINUTES TO SPARE. A SHEPHERD REQUIRES EIGHT MINUTES TO DECIDE WHETHER HE WILL ACCEPT A BRIDE OF BEAUTY AND INCOME!
MADEMOISELLE HAS DONE ME THE HONOR TO YIELD TO MY REQUEST THAT SHE BECOME MY WIFE.
WELL SAID! MADEMOISELLE COULD HAVE DRAWN A WORSE PRIZE, AFTER ALL. LANDLORD, FETCH A PRIEST!
The priest made David Mignot and Lucie de Varennes man and wife, then shuffled from the inn.
MONSIEUR MIGNOT, YOU HAVE TAKEN TO BE YOUR WIFE ONE WHO WILL MAKE YOUR LIFE A WRETCHED THING. THE DEVIL IS THERE IN HER EYES AND SKIN AND MOUTH THAT STOOP EVEN TO BEGUILE A PEASANT. DRINK YOUR WINE. AT LAST, MADEMOISELLE, I AM RID OF YOU!
David faced the marquis. There was little of a shepherd in his bearing.

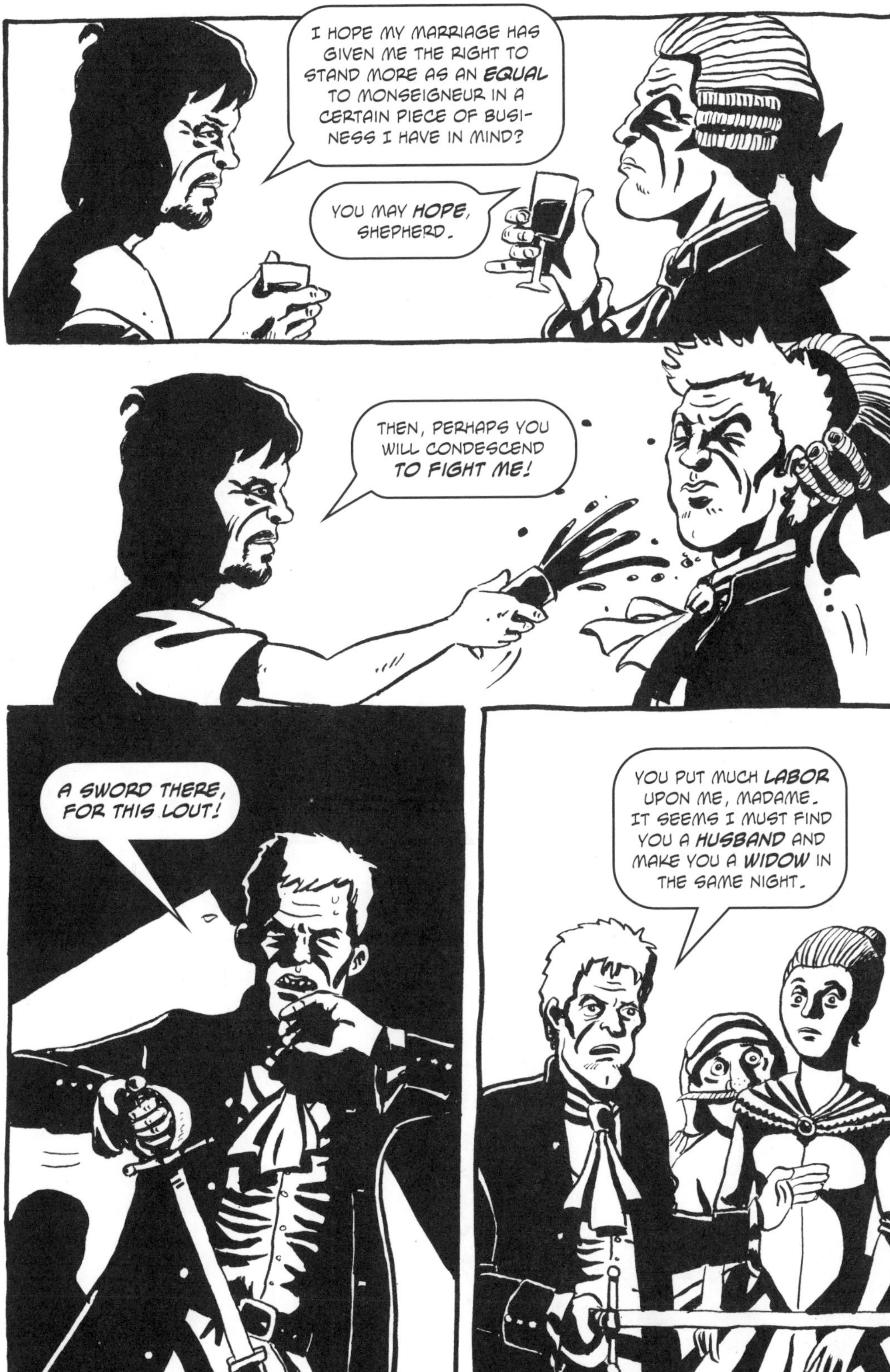
I HOPE MY MARRIAGE HAS GIVEN ME THE RIGHT TO STAND MORE AS AN EQUAL TO MONSEIGNEUR IN A CERTAIN PIECE OF BUSINESS I HAVE IN MIND?
YOU MAY HOPE, SHEPHERD.
THEN, PERHAPS YOU WILL CONDESCEND TO FIGHT ME!
A SWORD THERE, FOR THIS LOUT!
YOU PUT MUCH LABOR UPON ME, MADAME. IT SEEMS I MUST FIND YOU A HUSBAND AND MAKE YOU A WIDOW IN THE SAME NIGHT.

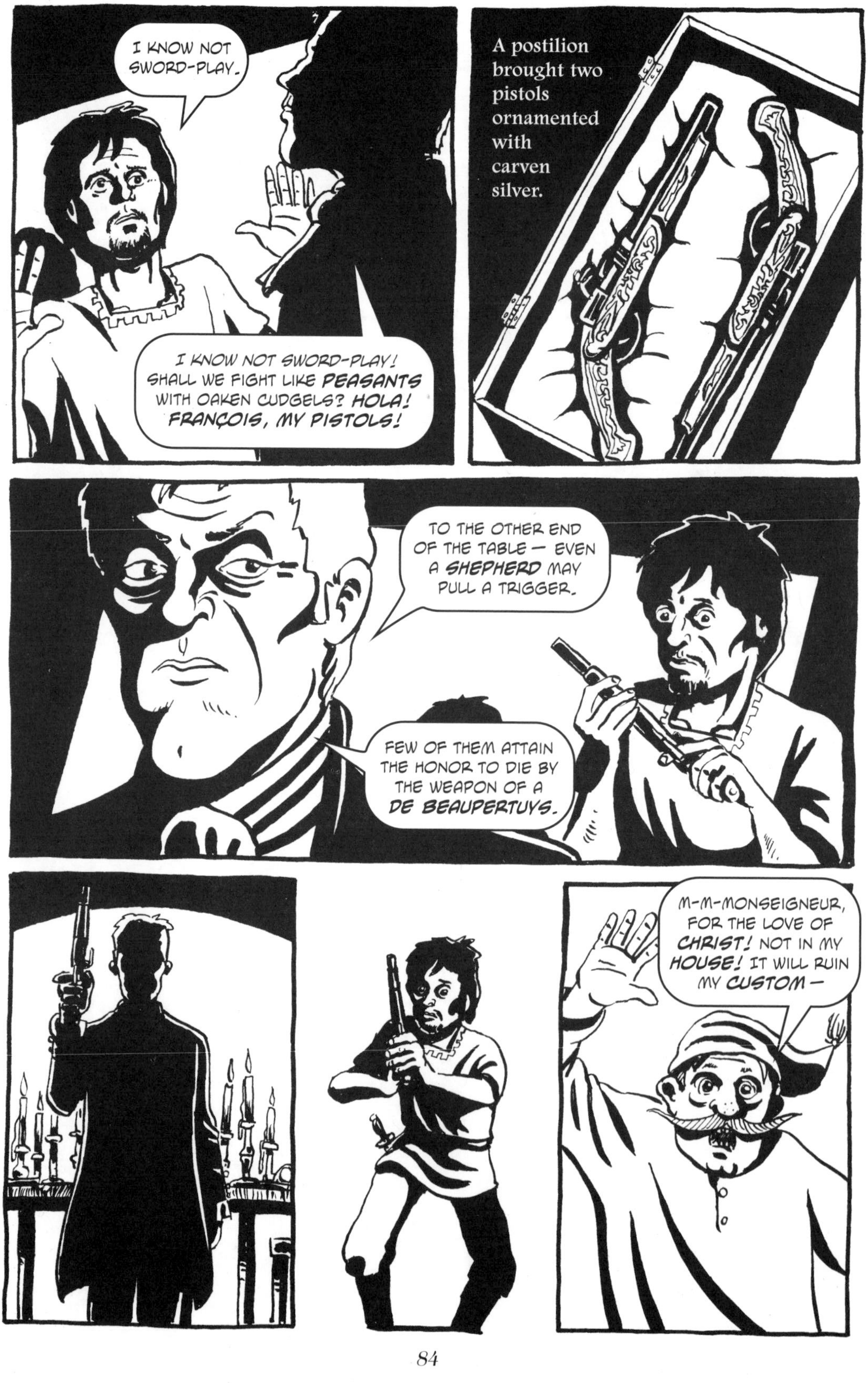
I KNOW NOT SWORD-PLAY.
I KNOW NOT SWORD-PLAY! SHALL WE FIGHT LIKE PEASANTS WITH OAKEN CUDGELS? HOLA! FRANÇOIS, MY PISTOLS!
A postilion brought two pistols ornamented with carven silver.
TO THE OTHER END OF THE TABLE — EVEN A SHEPHERD MAY PULL A TRIGGER.
FEW OF THEM ATTAIN THE HONOR TO DIE BY THE WEAPON OF A DE BEAUPERTUYS.
M-M-MONSEIGNEUR, FOR THE LOVE OF CHRIST! NOT IN MY HOUSE! IT WILL RUIN MY CUSTOM—

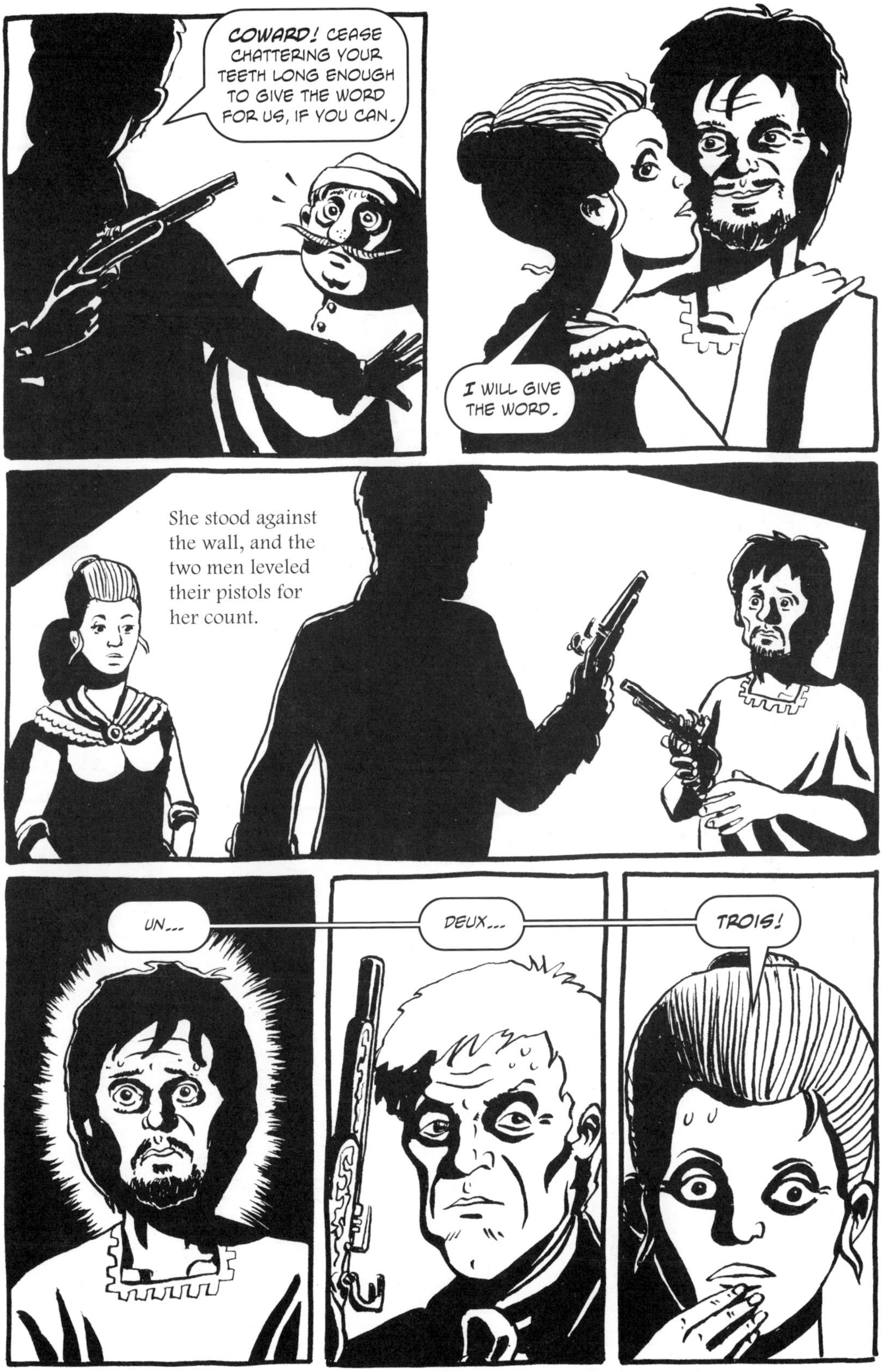
COWARD! CEASE CHATTERING YOUR TEETH LONG ENOUGH TO GIVE THE WORD FOR US, IF YOU CAN.
I WILL GIVE THE WORD.
She stood against the wall, and the two men leveled their pistols for her count.
UN...
DEUX...
TROIS!

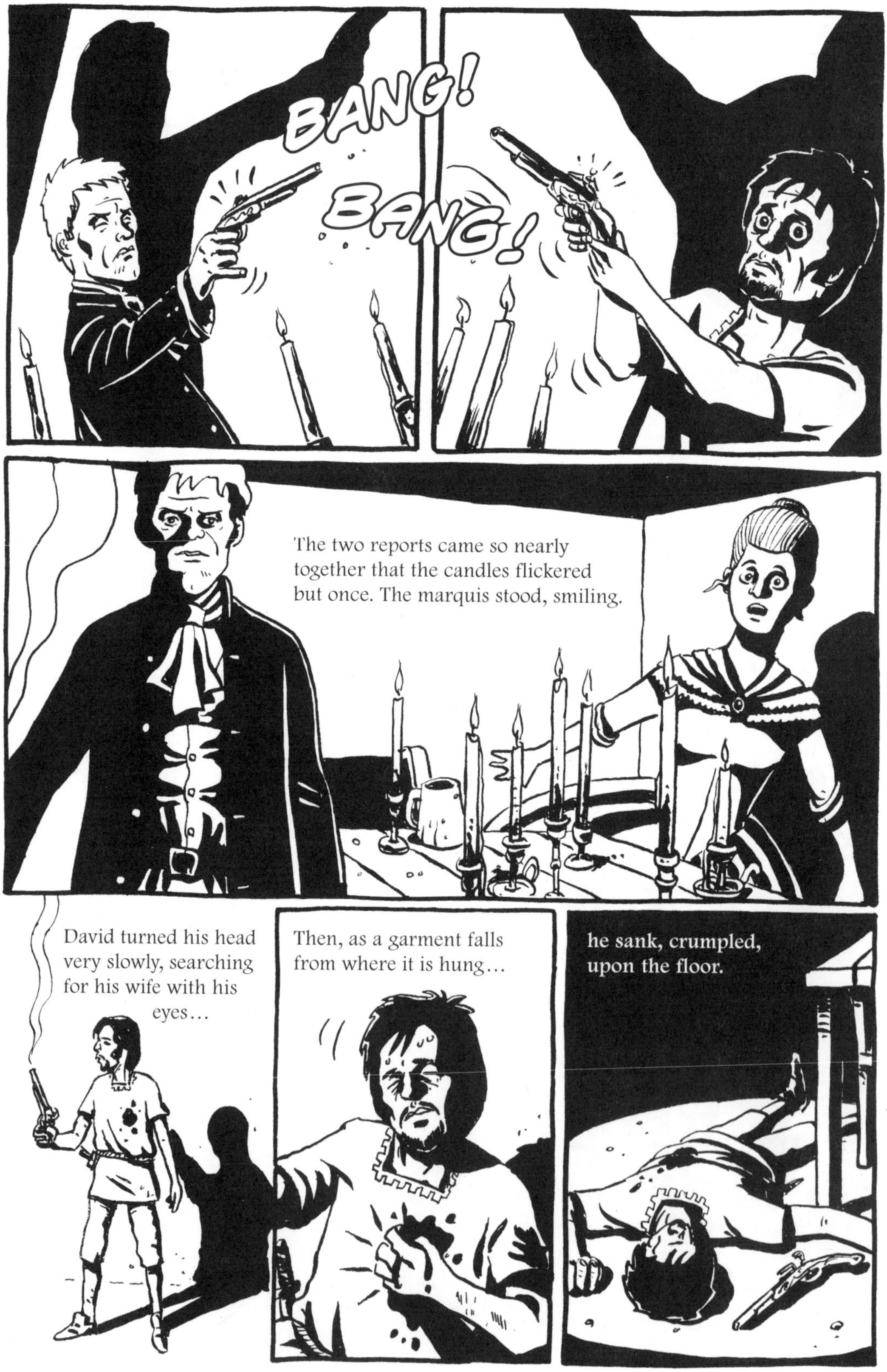
BANG!
BANG!
The two reports came so nearly together that the candles flickered but once. The marquis stood, smiling.
David turned his head very slowly, searching for his wife with his eyes…
Then, as a garment falls from where it is hung…
he sank, crumpled, upon the floor.

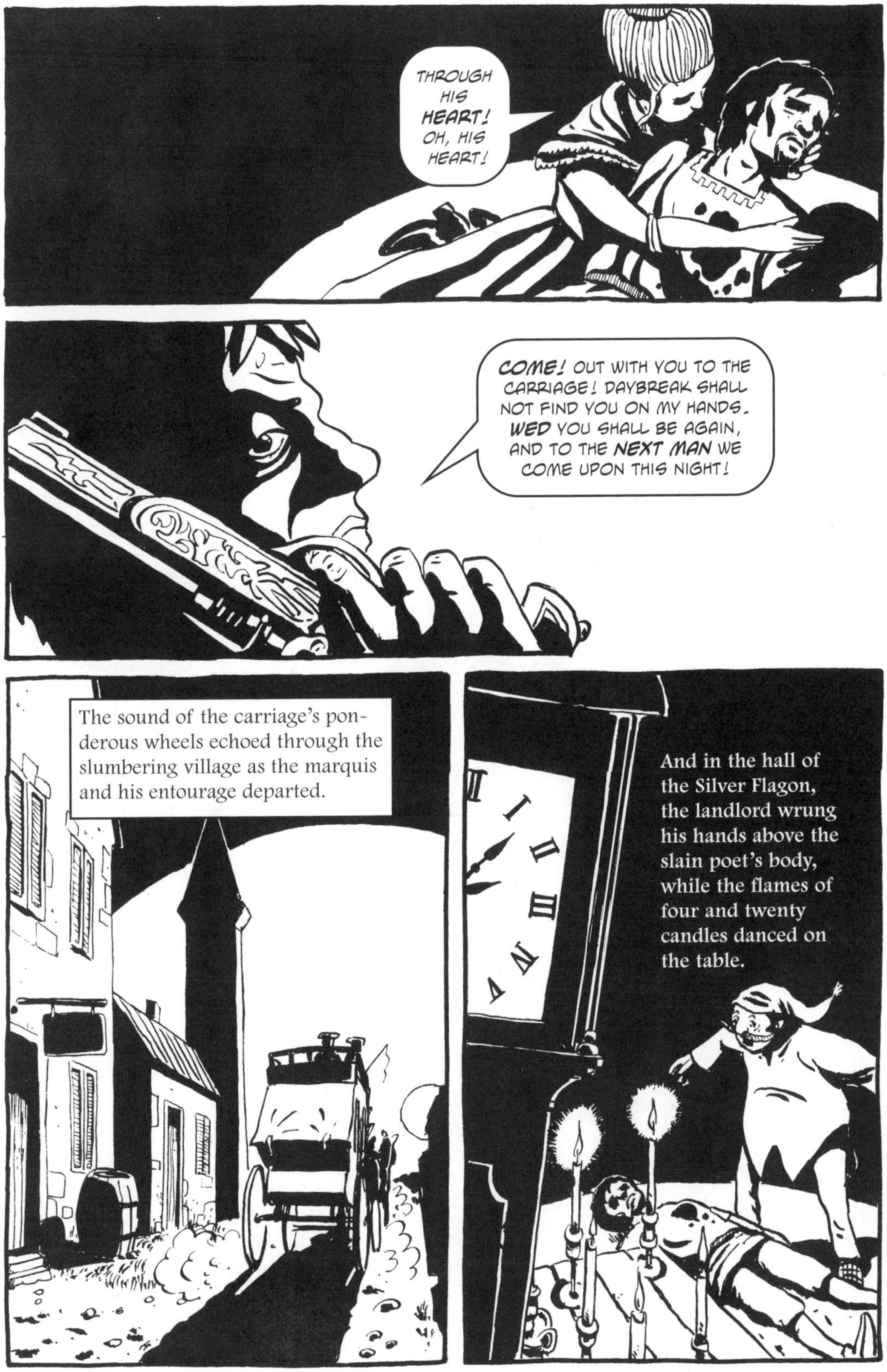
THROUGH HIS HEART! OH, HIS HEART!
COME! OUT WITH YOU TO THE CARRIAGE! DAYBREAK SHALL NOT FIND YOU ON MY HANDS. WED YOU SHALL BE AGAIN, AND TO THE NEXT MAN WE COME UPON THIS NIGHT!
The sound of the carriage's ponderous wheels echoed through the slumbering village as the marquis and his entourage departed.
And in the hall of the Silver Flagon, the landlord wrung his hands above the slain poet's body, while the flames of four and twenty candles danced on the table.

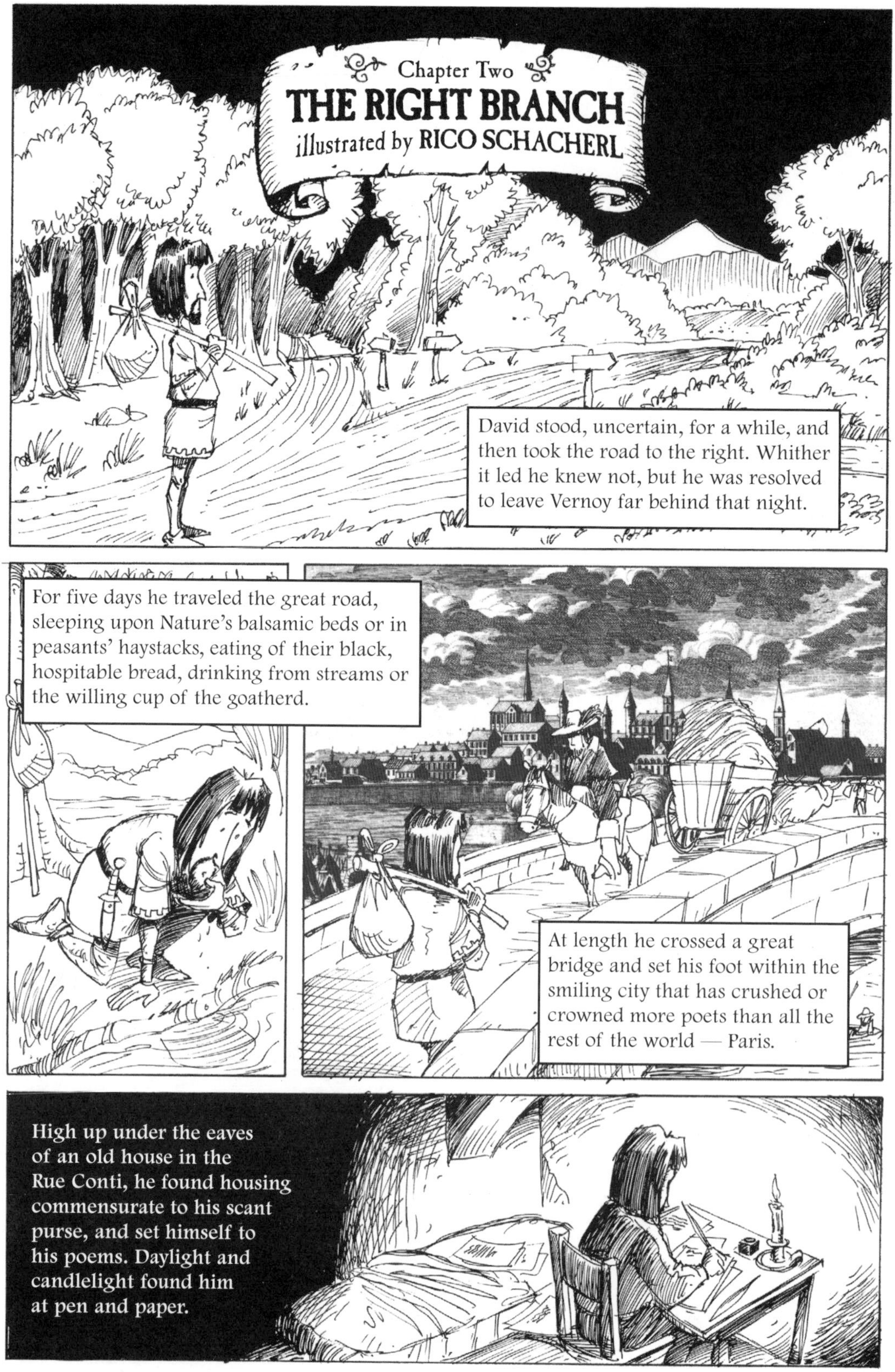
Chapter Two
THE RIGHT BRANCH
illustrated by RICO SCHACHERL
David stood, uncertain, for a while, and then took the road to the right. Whither it led he knew not, but he was resolved to leave Vernoy far behind that night.
For five days he traveled the great road, sleeping upon Nature's balsamic beds or in peasants' haystacks, eating of their black, hospitable bread, drinking from streams or the willing cup of the goatherd.
At length he crossed a great bridge and set his foot within the smiling city that has crushed or crowned more poets than all the rest of the world — Paris.
High up under the eaves of an old house in the Rue Conti, he found housing commensurate to his scant purse, and set himself to his poems. Daylight and candlelight found him at pen and paper.

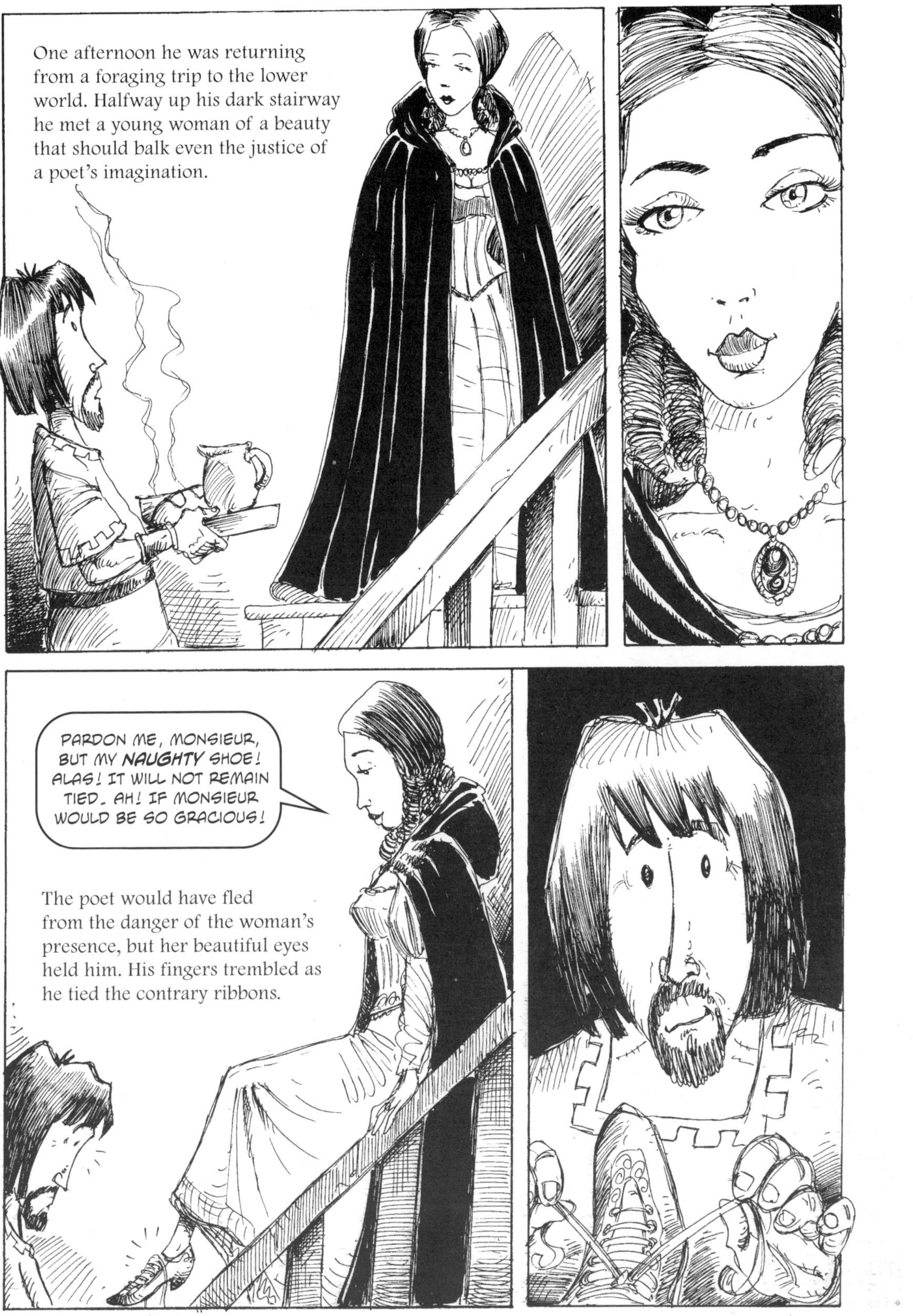
One afternoon he was returning from a foraging trip to the lower world. Halfway up his dark stairway he met a young woman of a beauty that should balk even the justice of a poet's imagination.
PARDON ME, MONSIEUR, BUT MY ***NAUGHTY*** SHOE! ALAS! IT WILL NOT REMAIN TIED. AH! IF MONSIEUR WOULD BE SO GRACIOUS!
The poet would have fled from the danger of the woman's presence, but her beautiful eyes held him. His fingers trembled as he tied the contrary ribbons.

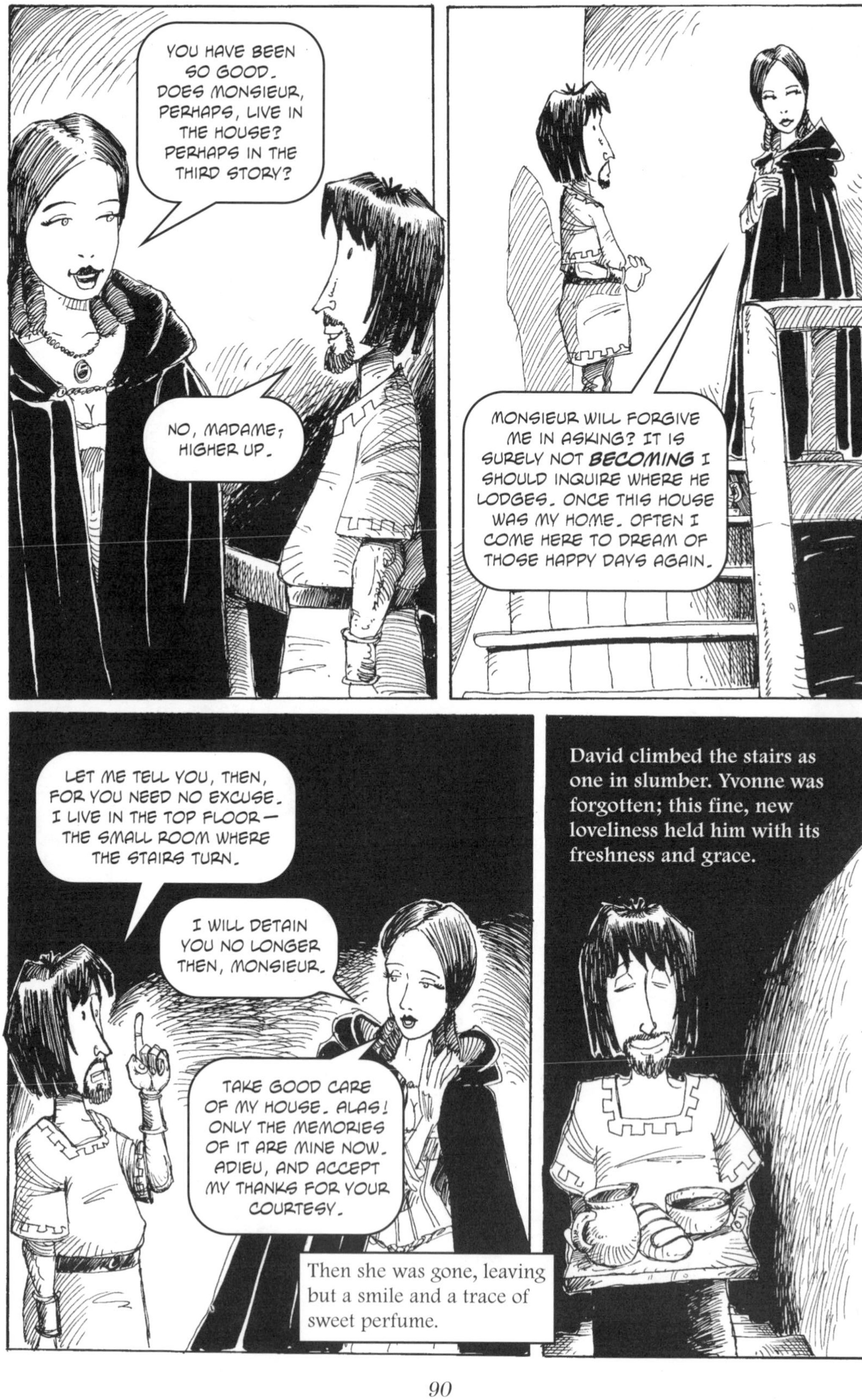
YOU HAVE BEEN SO GOOD. DOES MONSIEUR, PERHAPS, LIVE IN THE HOUSE? PERHAPS IN THE THIRD STORY?
NO, MADAME; HIGHER UP.
MONSIEUR WILL FORGIVE ME IN ASKING? IT IS SURELY NOT **BECOMING** I SHOULD INQUIRE WHERE HE LODGES. ONCE THIS HOUSE WAS MY HOME. OFTEN I COME HERE TO DREAM OF THOSE HAPPY DAYS AGAIN.
LET ME TELL YOU, THEN, FOR YOU NEED NO EXCUSE. I LIVE IN THE TOP FLOOR— THE SMALL ROOM WHERE THE STAIRS TURN.
I WILL DETAIN YOU NO LONGER THEN, MONSIEUR.
TAKE GOOD CARE OF MY HOUSE. ALAS! ONLY THE MEMORIES OF IT ARE MINE NOW. ADIEU, AND ACCEPT MY THANKS FOR YOUR COURTESY.
Then she was gone, leaving but a smile and a trace of sweet perfume.
David climbed the stairs as one in slumber. Yvonne was forgotten; this fine, new loveliness held him with its freshness and grace.

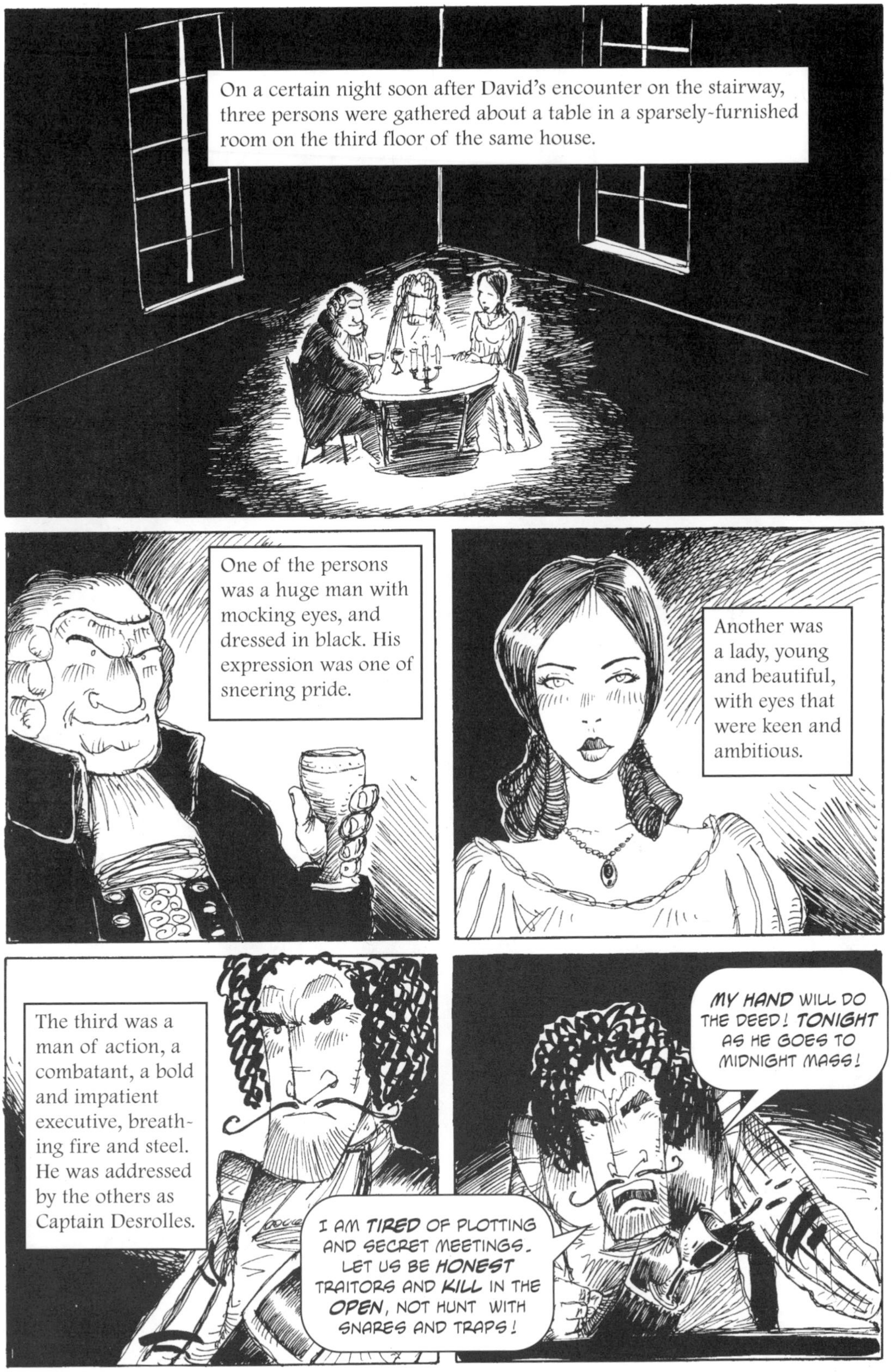
On a certain night soon after David's encounter on the stairway, three persons were gathered about a table in a sparsely-furnished room on the third floor of the same house.
One of the persons was a huge man with mocking eyes, and dressed in black. His expression was one of sneering pride.
Another was a lady, young and beautiful, with eyes that were keen and ambitious.
The third was a man of action, a combatant, a bold and impatient executive, breathing fire and steel. He was addressed by the others as Captain Desrolles.
I AM TIRED OF PLOTTING AND SECRET MEETINGS. LET US BE HONEST TRAITORS AND KILL IN THE OPEN, NOT HUNT WITH SNARES AND TRAPS!
MY HAND WILL DO THE DEED! TONIGHT AS HE GOES TO MIDNIGHT MASS!

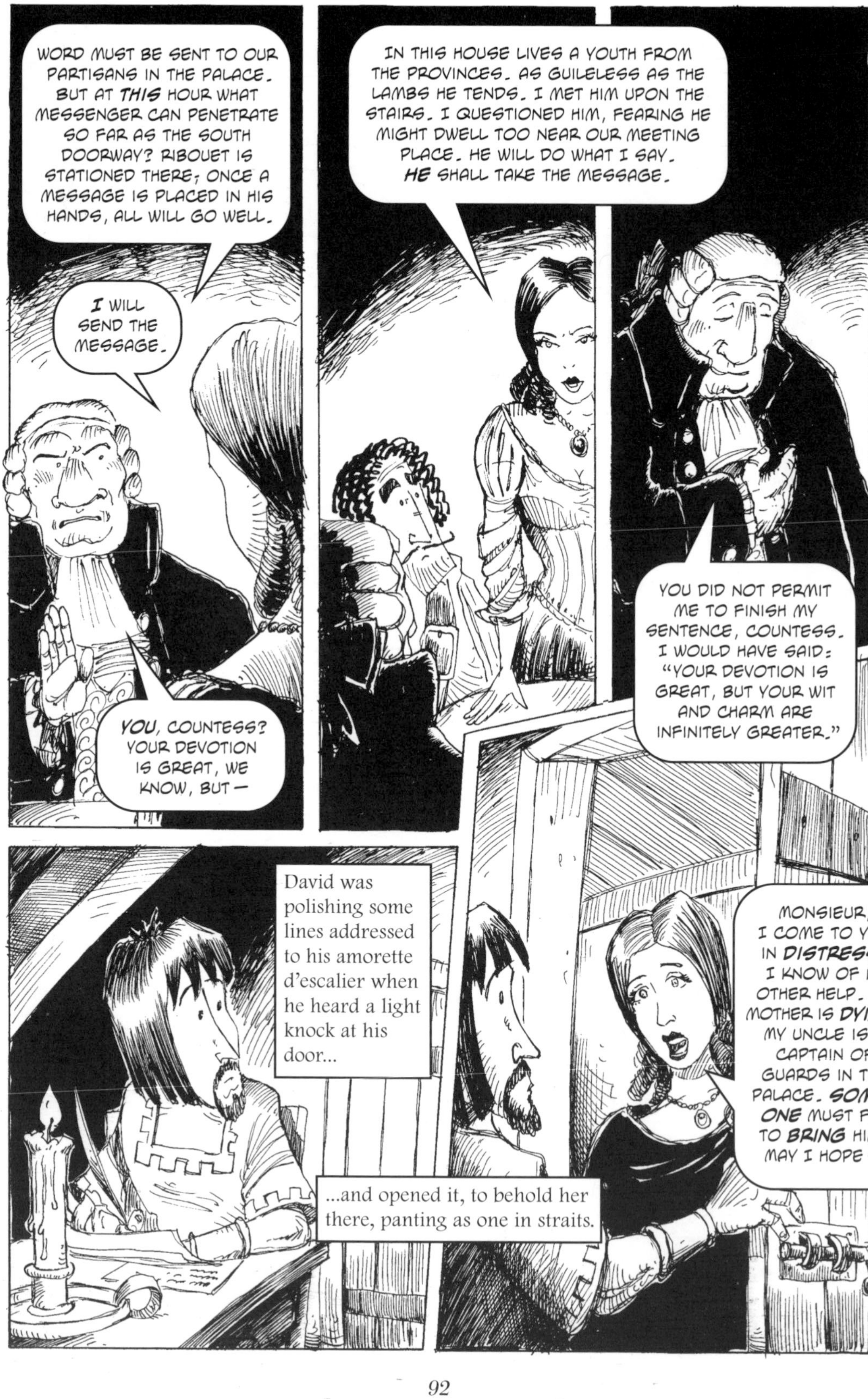
WORD MUST BE SENT TO OUR PARTISANS IN THE PALACE. BUT AT THIS HOUR WHAT MESSENGER CAN PENETRATE SO FAR AS THE SOUTH DOORWAY? RIBOUET IS STATIONED THERE; ONCE A MESSAGE IS PLACED IN HIS HANDS, ALL WILL GO WELL.
I WILL SEND THE MESSAGE.
YOU, COUNTESS? YOUR DEVOTION IS GREAT, WE KNOW, BUT—
IN THIS HOUSE LIVES A YOUTH FROM THE PROVINCES. AS GUILELESS AS THE LAMBS HE TENDS. I MET HIM UPON THE STAIRS. I QUESTIONED HIM, FEARING HE MIGHT DWELL TOO NEAR OUR MEETING PLACE. HE WILL DO WHAT I SAY. HE SHALL TAKE THE MESSAGE.
YOU DID NOT PERMIT ME TO FINISH MY SENTENCE, COUNTESS. I WOULD HAVE SAID: "YOUR DEVOTION IS GREAT, BUT YOUR WIT AND CHARM ARE INFINITELY GREATER."
David was polishing some lines addressed to his amorette d'escalier when he heard a light knock at his door...
...and opened it, to behold her there, panting as one in straits.
MONSIEUR, I COME TO YOU IN DISTRESS. I KNOW OF NO OTHER HELP. MY MOTHER IS DYING. MY UNCLE IS A CAPTAIN OF GUARDS IN THE PALACE. SOMEONE MUST FLY TO BRING HIM. MAY I HOPE—

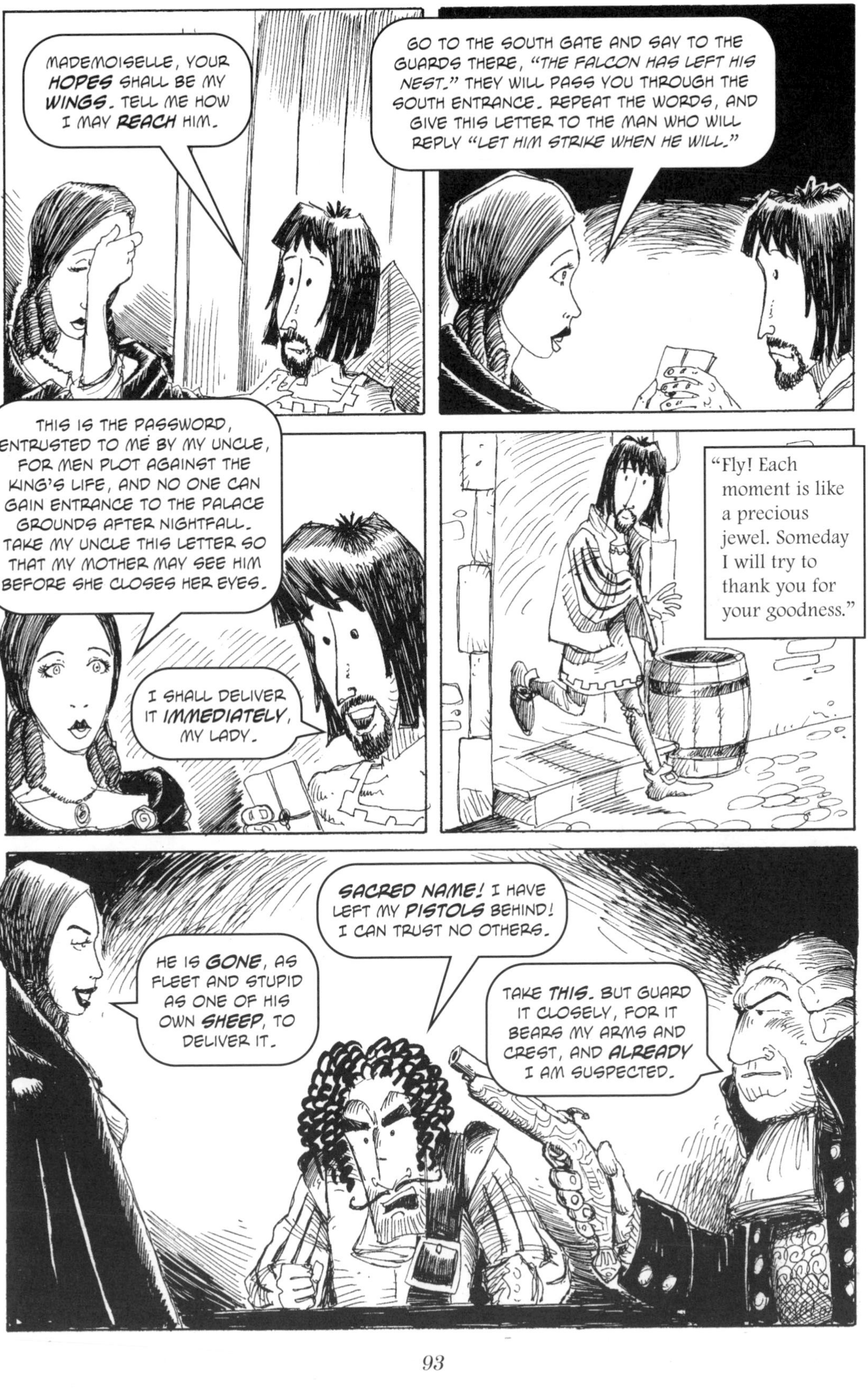
MADEMOISELLE, YOUR HOPES SHALL BE MY WINGS. TELL ME HOW I MAY REACH HIM.
GO TO THE SOUTH GATE AND SAY TO THE GUARDS THERE, "THE FALCON HAS LEFT HIS NEST." THEY WILL PASS YOU THROUGH THE SOUTH ENTRANCE. REPEAT THE WORDS, AND GIVE THIS LETTER TO THE MAN WHO WILL REPLY "LET HIM STRIKE WHEN HE WILL."
THIS IS THE PASSWORD, ENTRUSTED TO ME BY MY UNCLE, FOR MEN PLOT AGAINST THE KING'S LIFE, AND NO ONE CAN GAIN ENTRANCE TO THE PALACE GROUNDS AFTER NIGHTFALL. TAKE MY UNCLE THIS LETTER SO THAT MY MOTHER MAY SEE HIM BEFORE SHE CLOSES HER EYES.
I SHALL DELIVER IT IMMEDIATELY, MY LADY.
"Fly! Each moment is like a precious jewel. Someday I will try to thank you for your goodness."
HE IS GONE, AS FLEET AND STUPID AS ONE OF HIS OWN SHEEP, TO DELIVER IT.
SACRED NAME! I HAVE LEFT MY PISTOLS BEHIND! I CAN TRUST NO OTHERS.
TAKE THIS. BUT GUARD IT CLOSELY, FOR IT BEARS MY ARMS AND CREST, AND ALREADY I AM SUSPECTED.

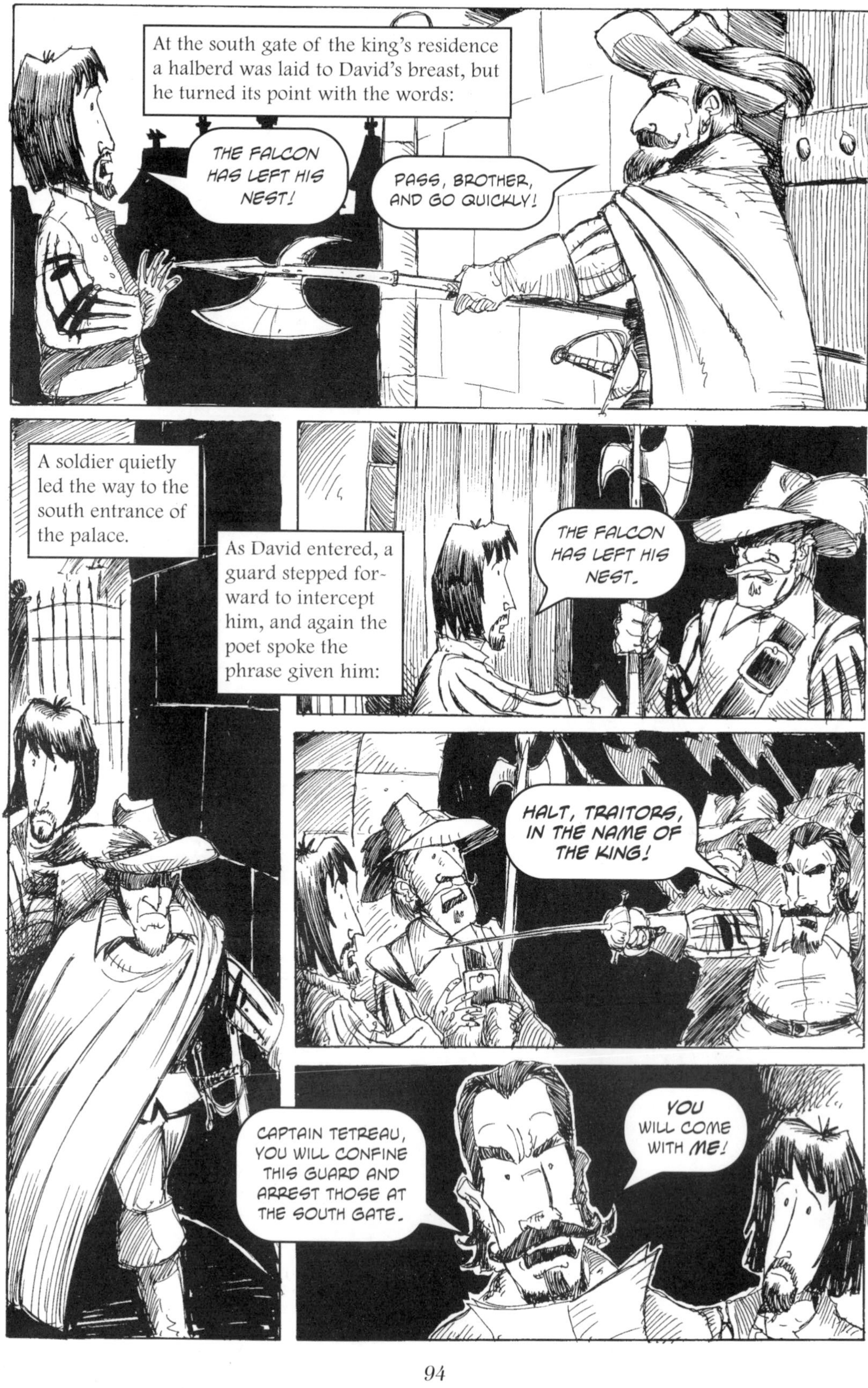
At the south gate of the king's residence a halberd was laid to David's breast, but he turned its point with the words:
THE FALCON HAS LEFT HIS NEST!
PASS, BROTHER, AND GO QUICKLY!
A soldier quietly led the way to the south entrance of the palace.
As David entered, a guard stepped forward to intercept him, and again the poet spoke the phrase given him:
THE FALCON HAS LEFT HIS NEST.
HALT, TRAITORS, IN THE NAME OF THE KING!
CAPTAIN TETREAU, YOU WILL CONFINE THIS GUARD AND ARREST THOSE AT THE SOUTH GATE.
YOU WILL COME WITH ME!

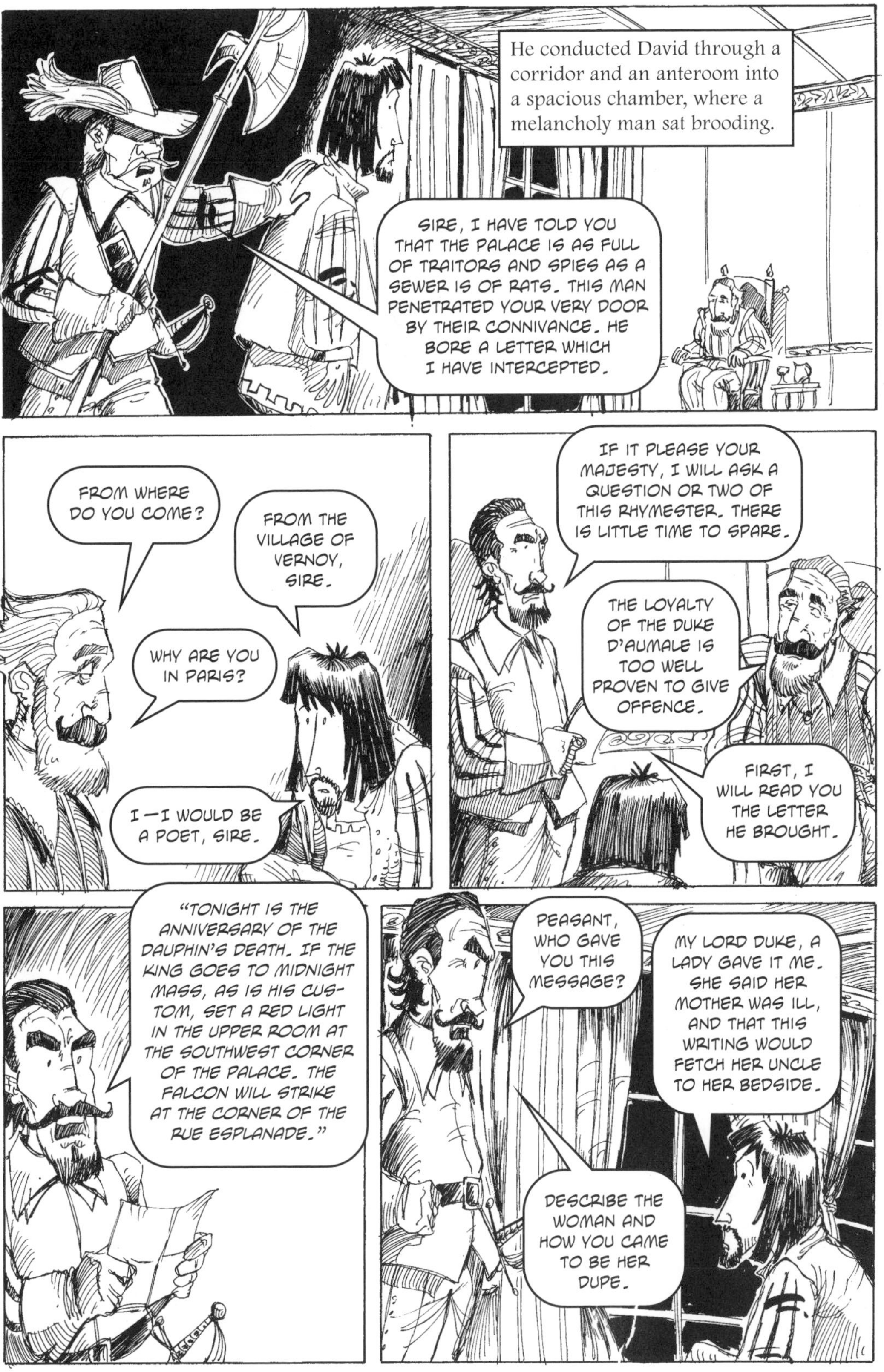
He conducted David through a corridor and an anteroom into a spacious chamber, where a melancholy man sat brooding.
SIRE, I HAVE TOLD YOU THAT THE PALACE IS AS FULL OF TRAITORS AND SPIES AS A SEWER IS OF RATS. THIS MAN PENETRATED YOUR VERY DOOR BY THEIR CONNIVANCE. HE BORE A LETTER WHICH I HAVE INTERCEPTED.
FROM WHERE DO YOU COME?
FROM THE VILLAGE OF VERNOY, SIRE.
WHY ARE YOU IN PARIS?
I—I WOULD BE A POET, SIRE.
IF IT PLEASE YOUR MAJESTY, I WILL ASK A QUESTION OR TWO OF THIS RHYMESTER. THERE IS LITTLE TIME TO SPARE.
THE LOYALTY OF THE DUKE D'AUMALE IS TOO WELL PROVEN TO GIVE OFFENCE.
FIRST, I WILL READ YOU THE LETTER HE BROUGHT.
"TONIGHT IS THE ANNIVERSARY OF THE DAUPHIN'S DEATH. IF THE KING GOES TO MIDNIGHT MASS, AS IS HIS CUSTOM, SET A RED LIGHT IN THE UPPER ROOM AT THE SOUTHWEST CORNER OF THE PALACE. THE FALCON WILL STRIKE AT THE CORNER OF THE RUE ESPLANADE."
PEASANT, WHO GAVE YOU THIS MESSAGE?
MY LORD DUKE, A LADY GAVE IT ME. SHE SAID HER MOTHER WAS ILL, AND THAT THIS WRITING WOULD FETCH HER UNCLE TO HER BEDSIDE.
DESCRIBE THE WOMAN AND HOW YOU CAME TO BE HER DUPE.

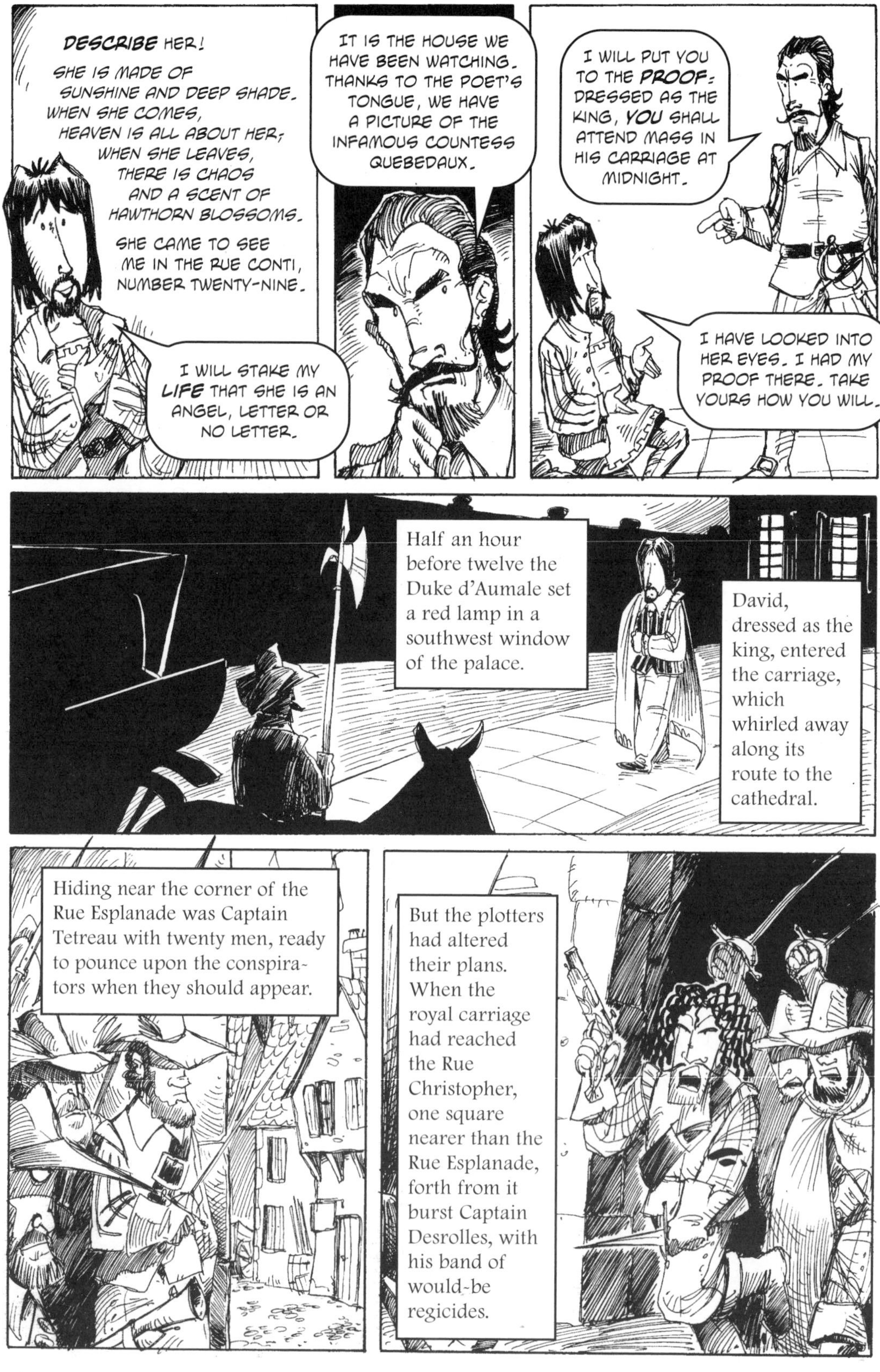
DESCRIBE HER!
SHE IS MADE OF SUNSHINE AND DEEP SHADE. WHEN SHE COMES, HEAVEN IS ALL ABOUT HER; WHEN SHE LEAVES, THERE IS CHAOS AND A SCENT OF HAWTHORN BLOSSOMS.
SHE CAME TO SEE ME IN THE RUE CONTI, NUMBER TWENTY-NINE.
I WILL STAKE MY LIFE THAT SHE IS AN ANGEL, LETTER OR NO LETTER.
IT IS THE HOUSE WE HAVE BEEN WATCHING. THANKS TO THE POET'S TONGUE, WE HAVE A PICTURE OF THE INFAMOUS COUNTESS QUEBEDAUX.
I WILL PUT YOU TO THE PROOF: DRESSED AS THE KING, YOU SHALL ATTEND MASS IN HIS CARRIAGE AT MIDNIGHT.
I HAVE LOOKED INTO HER EYES. I HAD MY PROOF THERE. TAKE YOURS HOW YOU WILL.
Half an hour before twelve the Duke d'Aumale set a red lamp in a southwest window of the palace.
David, dressed as the king, entered the carriage, which whirled away along its route to the cathedral.
Hiding near the corner of the Rue Esplanade was Captain Tetreau with twenty men, ready to pounce upon the conspirators when they should appear.
But the plotters had altered their plans. When the royal carriage had reached the Rue Christopher, one square nearer than the Rue Esplanade, forth from it burst Captain Desrolles, with his band of would-be regicides.

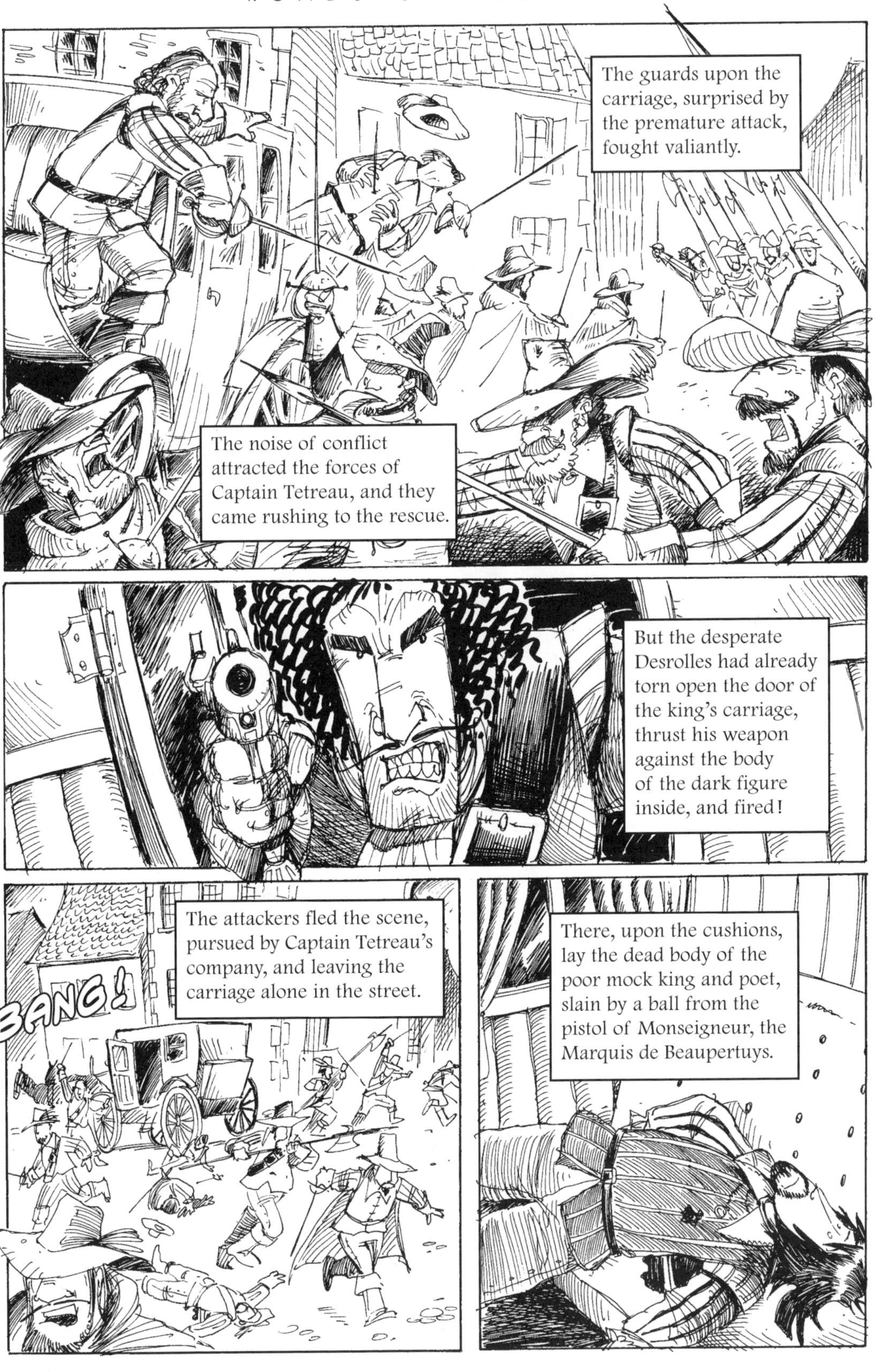
The guards upon the carriage, surprised by the premature attack, fought valiantly.
The noise of conflict attracted the forces of Captain Tetreau, and they came rushing to the rescue.
But the desperate Desrolles had already torn open the door of the king's carriage, thrust his weapon against the body of the dark figure inside, and fired!
The attackers fled the scene, pursued by Captain Tetreau's company, and leaving the carriage alone in the street.
BANG!
There, upon the cushions, lay the dead body of the poor mock king and poet, slain by a ball from the pistol of Monseigneur, the Marquis de Beaupertuys.

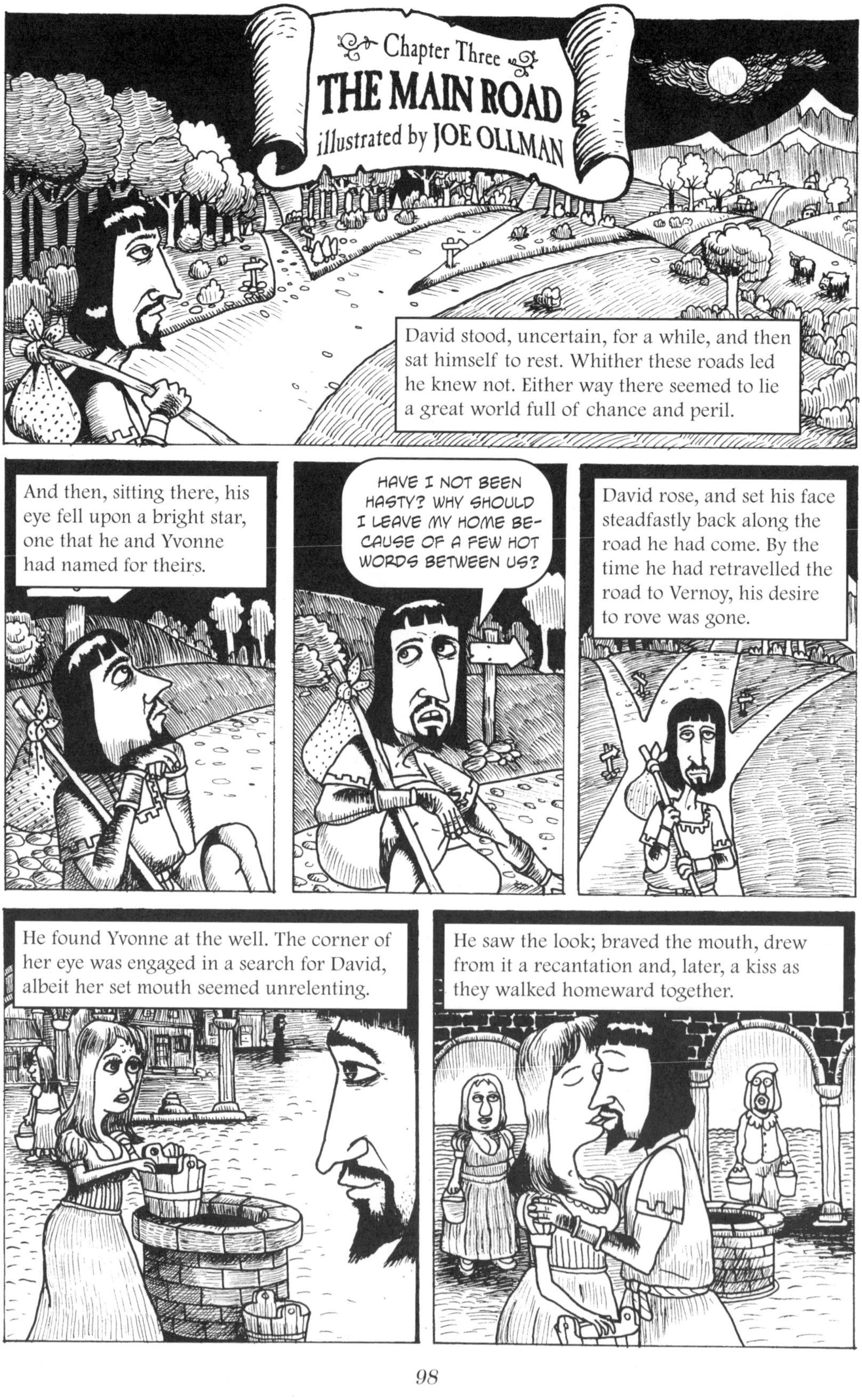
Chapter Three
THE MAIN ROAD
illustrated by JOE OLLMAN
David stood, uncertain, for a while, and then sat himself to rest. Whither these roads led he knew not. Either way there seemed to lie a great world full of chance and peril.
And then, sitting there, his eye fell upon a bright star, one that he and Yvonne had named for theirs.
HAVE I NOT BEEN HASTY? WHY SHOULD I LEAVE MY HOME BECAUSE OF A FEW HOT WORDS BETWEEN US?
David rose, and set his face steadfastly back along the road he had come. By the time he had retravelled the road to Vernoy, his desire to rove was gone.
He found Yvonne at the well. The corner of her eye was engaged in a search for David, albeit her set mouth seemed unrelenting.
He saw the look; braved the mouth, drew from it a recantation and, later, a kiss as they walked homeward together.

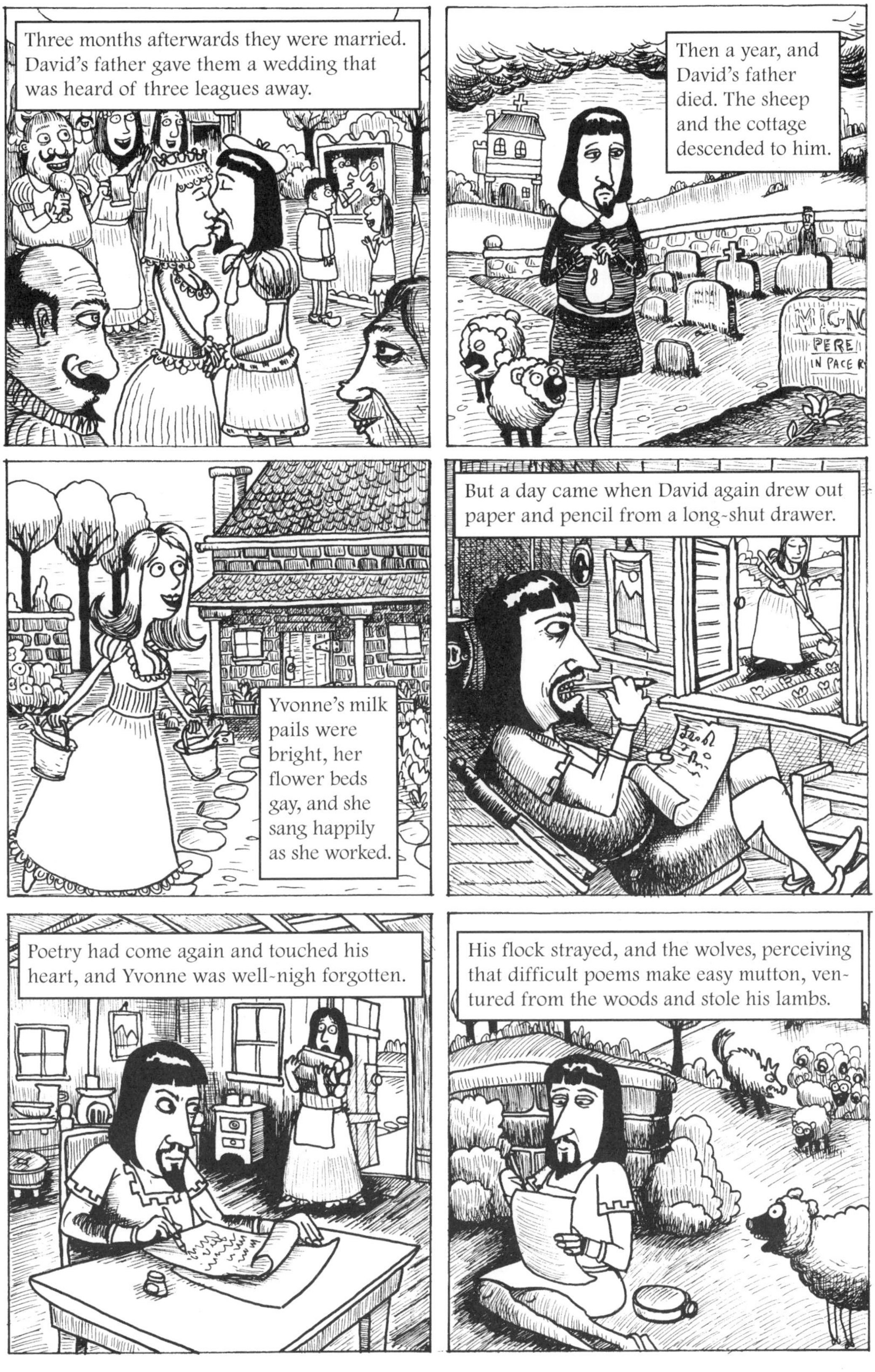
Three months afterwards they were married. David's father gave them a wedding that was heard of three leagues away.
Then a year, and David's father died. The sheep and the cottage descended to him.
Yvonne's milk pails were bright, her flower beds gay, and she sang happily as she worked.
But a day came when David again drew out paper and pencil from a long-shut drawer.
Poetry had come again and touched his heart, and Yvonne was well-nigh forgotten.
His flock strayed, and the wolves, perceiving that difficult poems make easy mutton, ventured from the woods and stole his lambs.

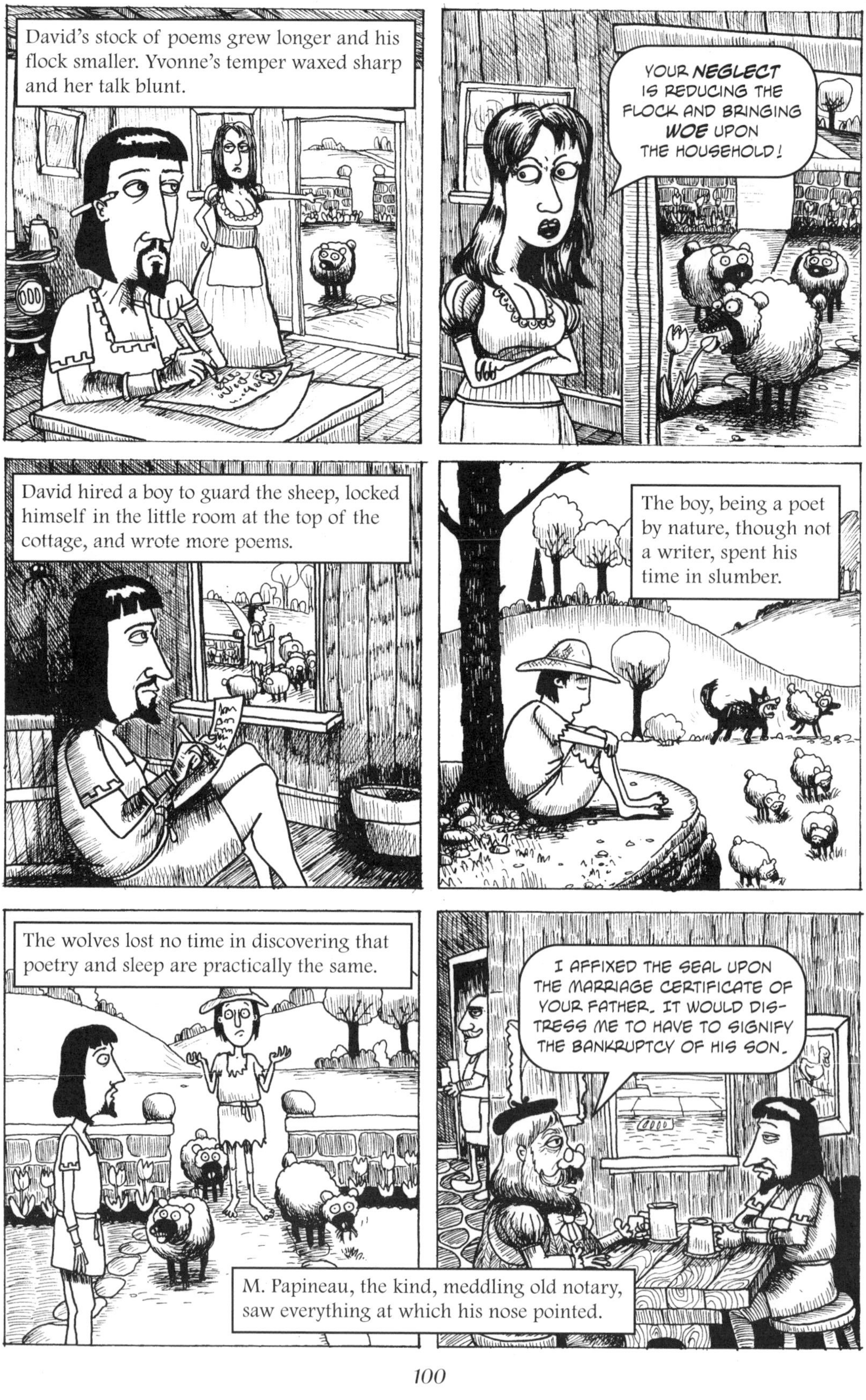
David's stock of poems grew longer and his flock smaller. Yvonne's temper waxed sharp and her talk blunt.
YOUR NEGLECT IS REDUCING THE FLOCK AND BRINGING WOE UPON THE HOUSEHOLD!
David hired a boy to guard the sheep, locked himself in the little room at the top of the cottage, and wrote more poems.
The boy, being a poet by nature, though not a writer, spent his time in slumber.
The wolves lost no time in discovering that poetry and sleep are practically the same.
M. Papineau, the kind, meddling old notary, saw everything at which his nose pointed.
I AFFIXED THE SEAL UPON THE MARRIAGE CERTIFICATE OF YOUR FATHER. IT WOULD DISTRESS ME TO HAVE TO SIGNIFY THE BANKRUPTCY OF HIS SON.

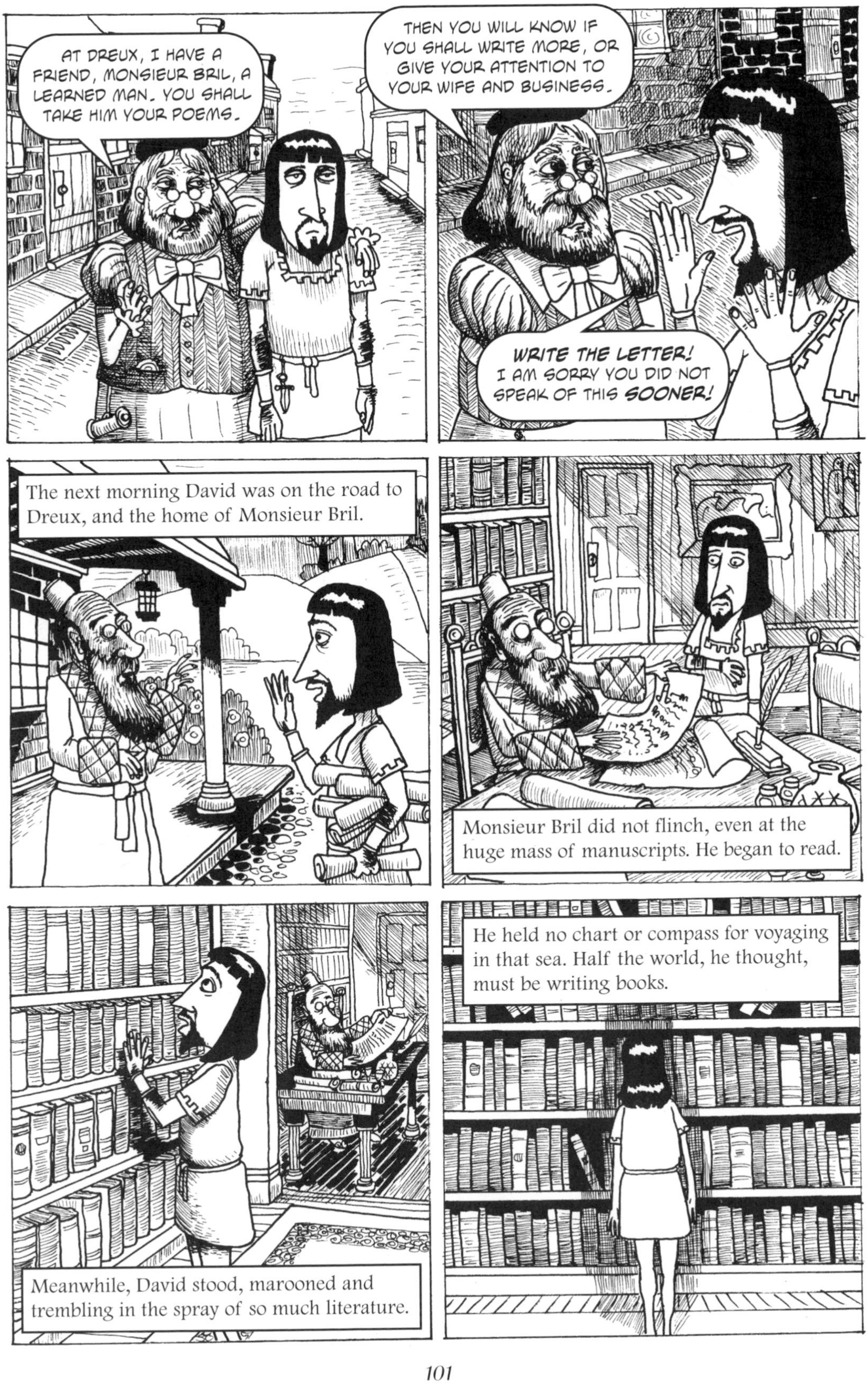
AT DREUX, I HAVE A FRIEND, MONSIEUR BRIL, A LEARNED MAN. YOU SHALL TAKE HIM YOUR POEMS.
THEN YOU WILL KNOW IF YOU SHALL WRITE MORE, OR GIVE YOUR ATTENTION TO YOUR WIFE AND BUSINESS.
WRITE THE LETTER! I AM SORRY YOU DID NOT SPEAK OF THIS SOONER!
The next morning David was on the road to Dreux, and the home of Monsieur Bril.
Monsieur Bril did not flinch, even at the huge mass of manuscripts. He began to read.
Meanwhile, David stood, marooned and trembling in the spray of so much literature.
He held no chart or compass for voyaging in that sea. Half the world, he thought, must be writing books.

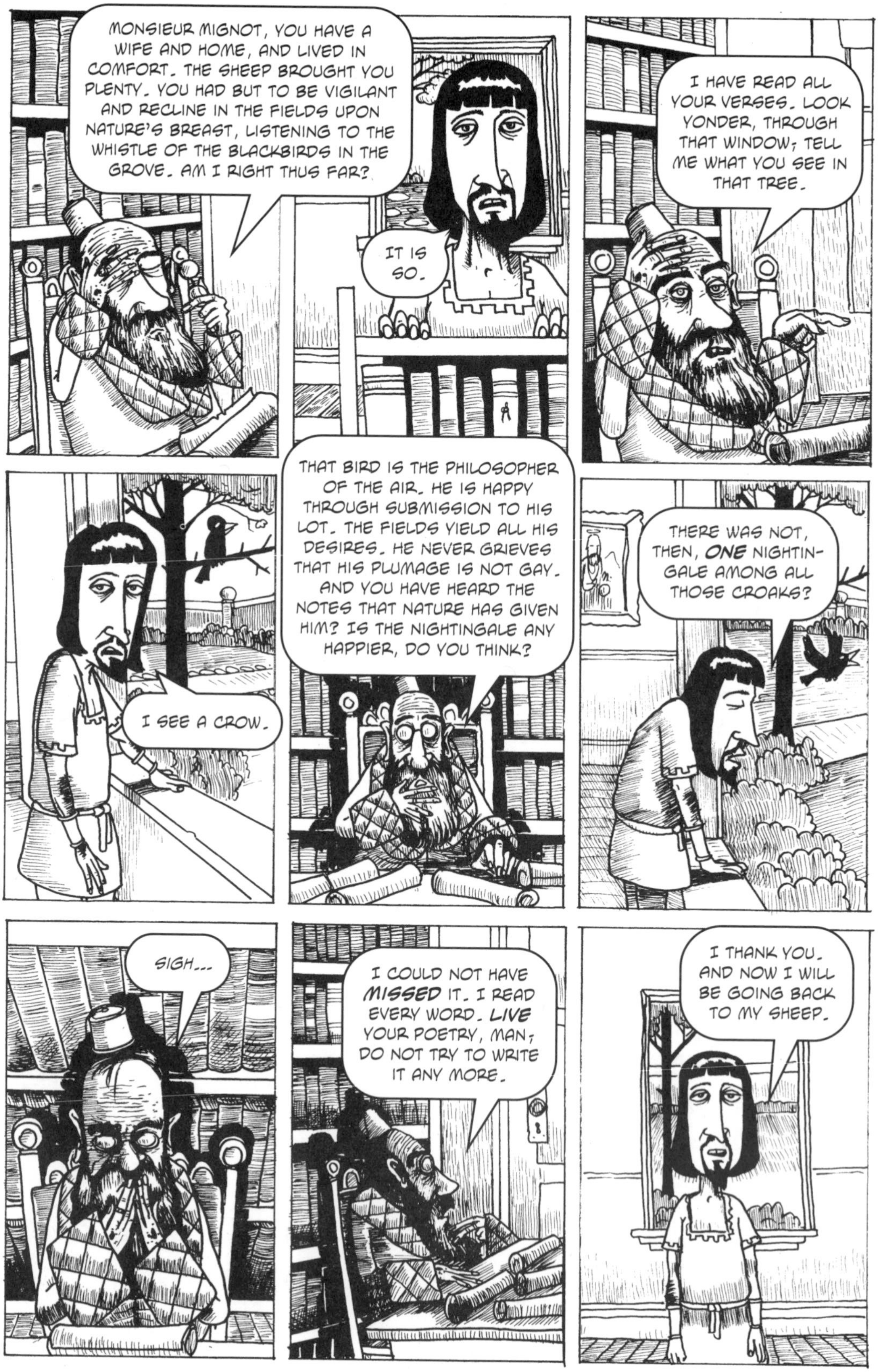
MONSIEUR MIGNOT, YOU HAVE A WIFE AND HOME, AND LIVED IN COMFORT. THE SHEEP BROUGHT YOU PLENTY. YOU HAD BUT TO BE VIGILANT AND RECLINE IN THE FIELDS UPON NATURE'S BREAST, LISTENING TO THE WHISTLE OF THE BLACKBIRDS IN THE GROVE. AM I RIGHT THUS FAR?
IT IS SO.
I HAVE READ ALL YOUR VERSES. LOOK YONDER, THROUGH THAT WINDOW; TELL ME WHAT YOU SEE IN THAT TREE.
I SEE A CROW.
THAT BIRD IS THE PHILOSOPHER OF THE AIR. HE IS HAPPY THROUGH SUBMISSION TO HIS LOT. THE FIELDS YIELD ALL HIS DESIRES. HE NEVER GRIEVES THAT HIS PLUMAGE IS NOT GAY. AND YOU HAVE HEARD THE NOTES THAT NATURE HAS GIVEN HIM? IS THE NIGHTINGALE ANY HAPPIER, DO YOU THINK?
THERE WAS NOT, THEN, ONE NIGHTINGALE AMONG ALL THOSE CROAKS?
SIGH...
I COULD NOT HAVE MISSED IT. I READ EVERY WORD. LIVE YOUR POETRY, MAN; DO NOT TRY TO WRITE IT ANY MORE.
I THANK YOU. AND NOW I WILL BE GOING BACK TO MY SHEEP.

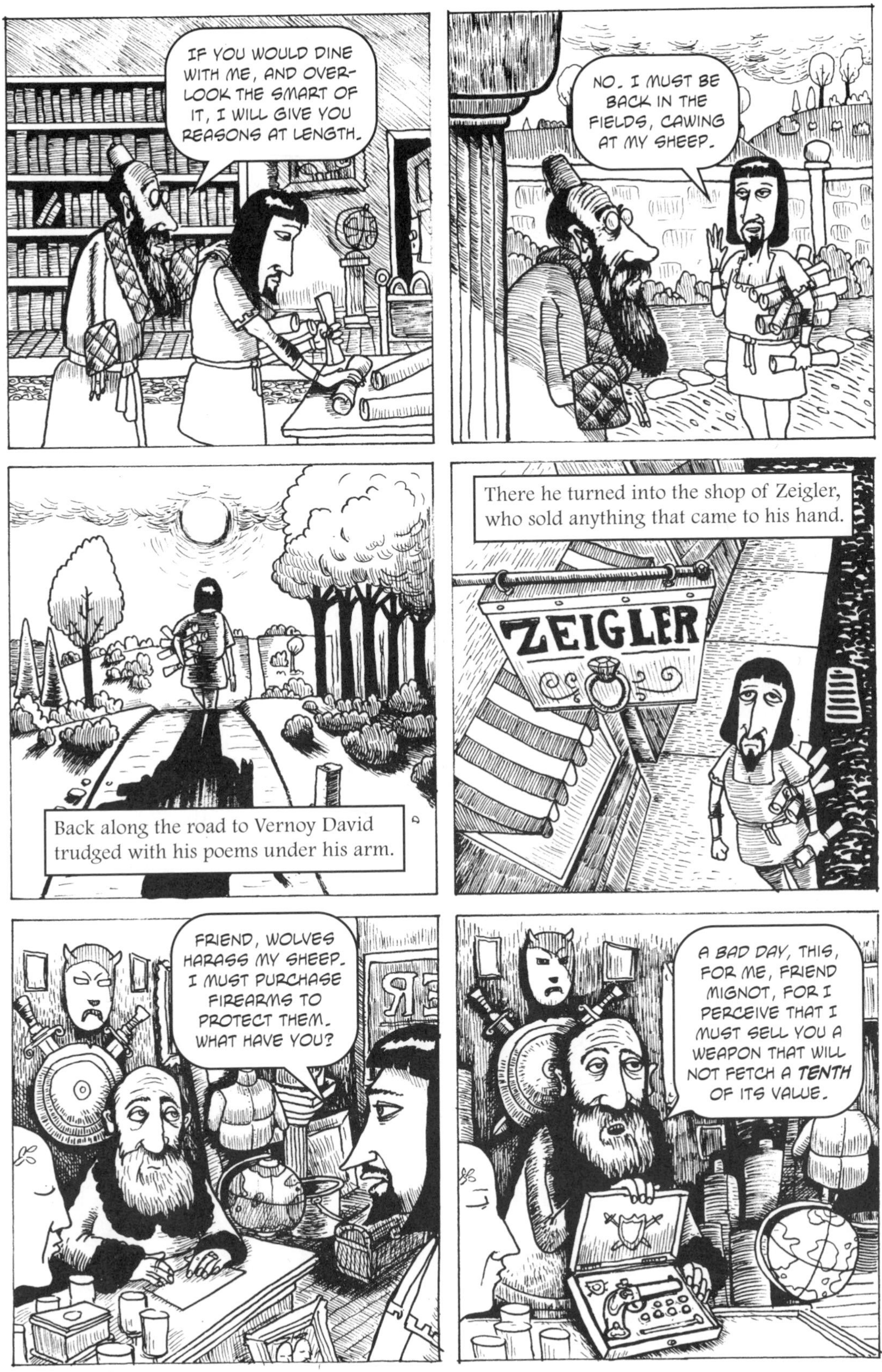
IF YOU WOULD DINE WITH ME, AND OVERLOOK THE SMART OF IT, I WILL GIVE YOU REASONS AT LENGTH.
NO. I MUST BE BACK IN THE FIELDS, CAWING AT MY SHEEP.
Back along the road to Vernoy David trudged with his poems under his arm.
There he turned into the shop of Zeigler, who sold anything that came to his hand.
ZEIGLER
FRIEND, WOLVES HARASS MY SHEEP. I MUST PURCHASE FIREARMS TO PROTECT THEM. WHAT HAVE YOU?
A BAD DAY, THIS, FOR ME, FRIEND MIGNOT, FOR I PERCEIVE THAT I MUST SELL YOU A WEAPON THAT WILL NOT FETCH A ***TENTH*** OF ITS VALUE.

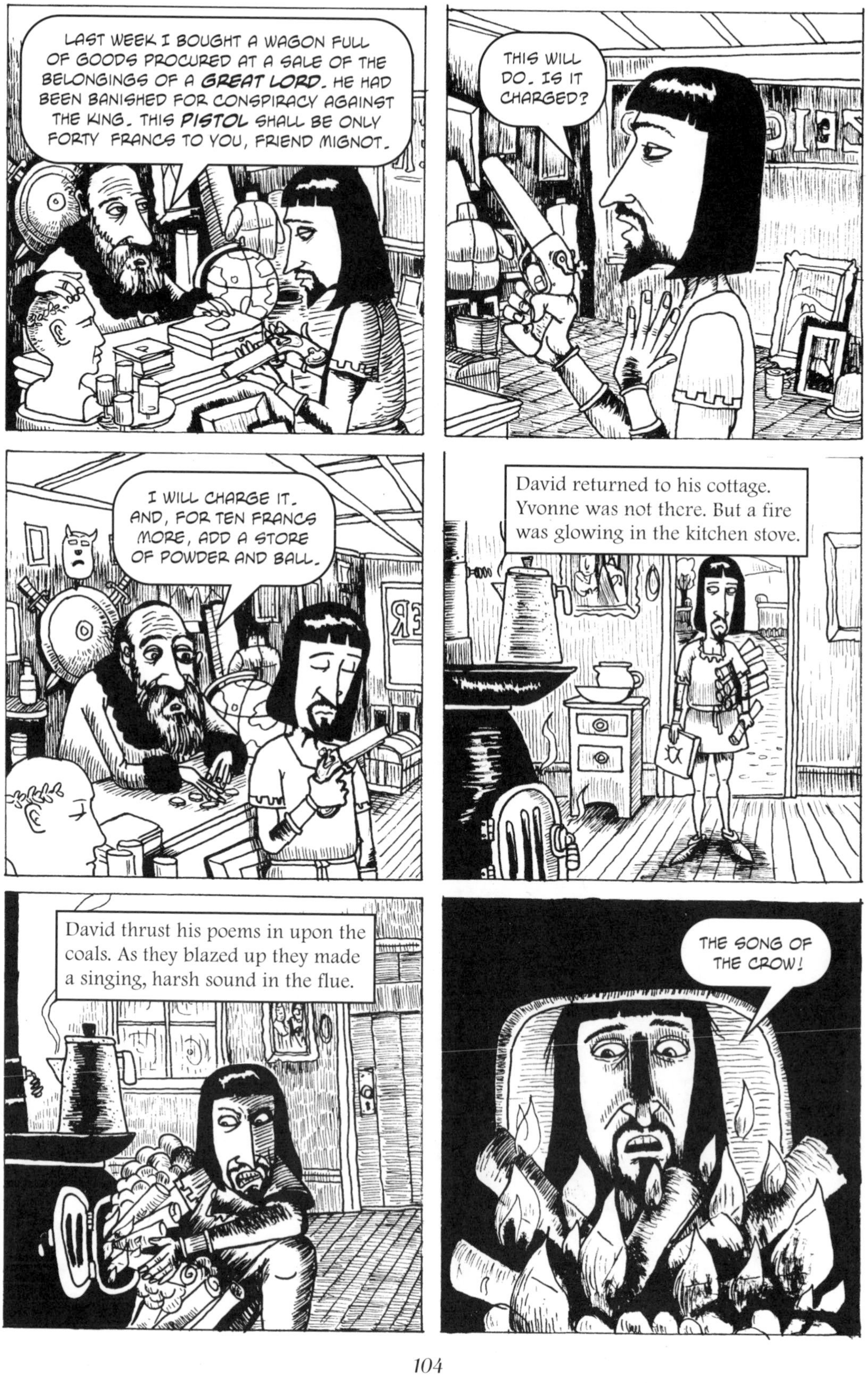
LAST WEEK I BOUGHT A WAGON FULL OF GOODS PROCURED AT A SALE OF THE BELONGINGS OF A GREAT LORD. HE HAD BEEN BANISHED FOR CONSPIRACY AGAINST THE KING. THIS PISTOL SHALL BE ONLY FORTY FRANCS TO YOU, FRIEND MIGNOT.
THIS WILL DO. IS IT CHARGED?
I WILL CHARGE IT. AND, FOR TEN FRANCS MORE, ADD A STORE OF POWDER AND BALL.
David returned to his cottage. Yvonne was not there. But a fire was glowing in the kitchen stove.
David thrust his poems in upon the coals. As they blazed up they made a singing, harsh sound in the flue.
THE SONG OF THE CROW!

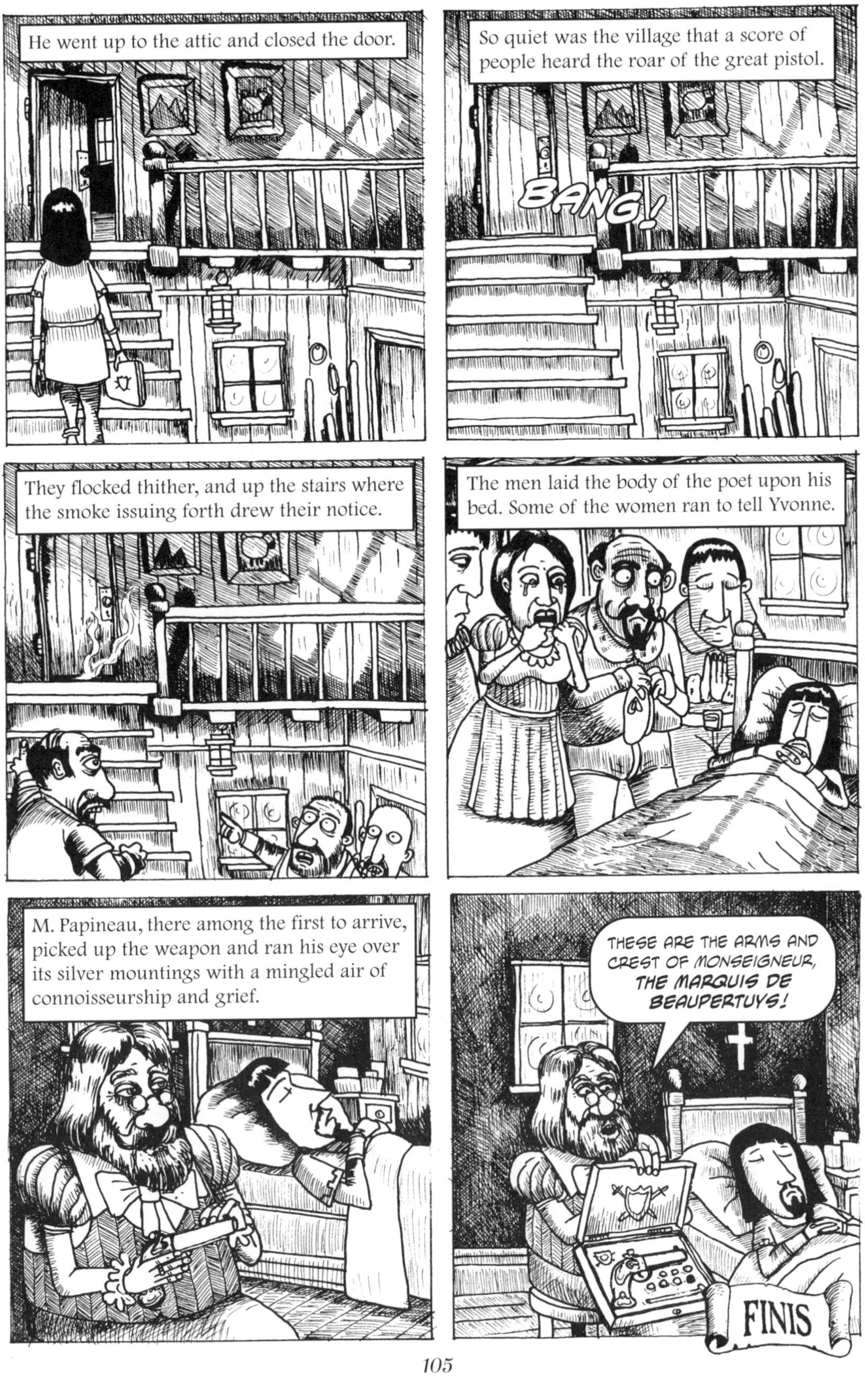
He went up to the attic and closed the door.
So quiet was the village that a score of people heard the roar of the great pistol.
BANG!
They flocked thither, and up the stairs where the smoke issuing forth drew their notice.
The men laid the body of the poet upon his bed. Some of the women ran to tell Yvonne.
M. Papineau, there among the first to arrive, picked up the weapon and ran his eye over its silver mountings with a mingled air of connoisseurship and grief.
THESE ARE THE ARMS AND CREST OF MONSEIGNEUR, THE MARQUIS DE BEAUPERTUYS!
FINIS

THE FRIENDLY CALL

by O. Henry

(Adapted +) Illustrated by Peter Gullerud ... 2004

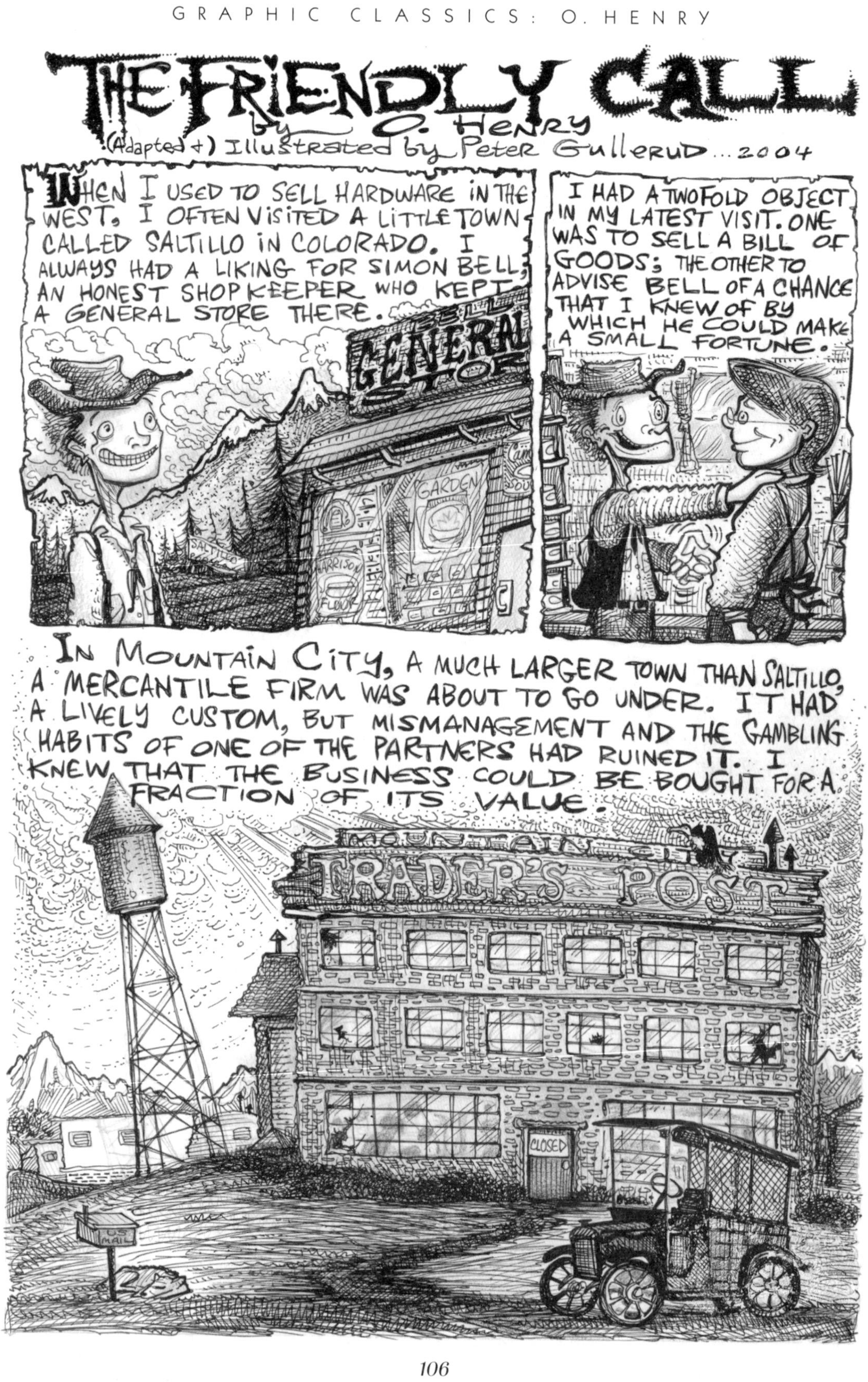
WHEN I USED TO SELL HARDWARE IN THE WEST, I OFTEN VISITED A LITTLE TOWN CALLED SALTILLO IN COLORADO. I ALWAYS HAD A LIKING FOR SIMON BELL, AN HONEST SHOPKEEPER WHO KEPT A GENERAL STORE THERE.
GENERAL
GARDEN
HARRISON
FLOUR
I HAD A TWOFOLD OBJECT IN MY LATEST VISIT. ONE WAS TO SELL A BILL OF GOODS; THE OTHER TO ADVISE BELL OF A CHANCE THAT I KNEW OF BY WHICH HE COULD MAKE A SMALL FORTUNE.
IN MOUNTAIN CITY, A MUCH LARGER TOWN THAN SALTILLO, A MERCANTILE FIRM WAS ABOUT TO GO UNDER. IT HAD A LIVELY CUSTOM, BUT MISMANAGEMENT AND THE GAMBLING HABITS OF ONE OF THE PARTNERS HAD RUINED IT. I KNEW THAT THE BUSINESS COULD BE BOUGHT FOR A FRACTION OF ITS VALUE.
TRADER'S POST
CLOSED
US MAIL

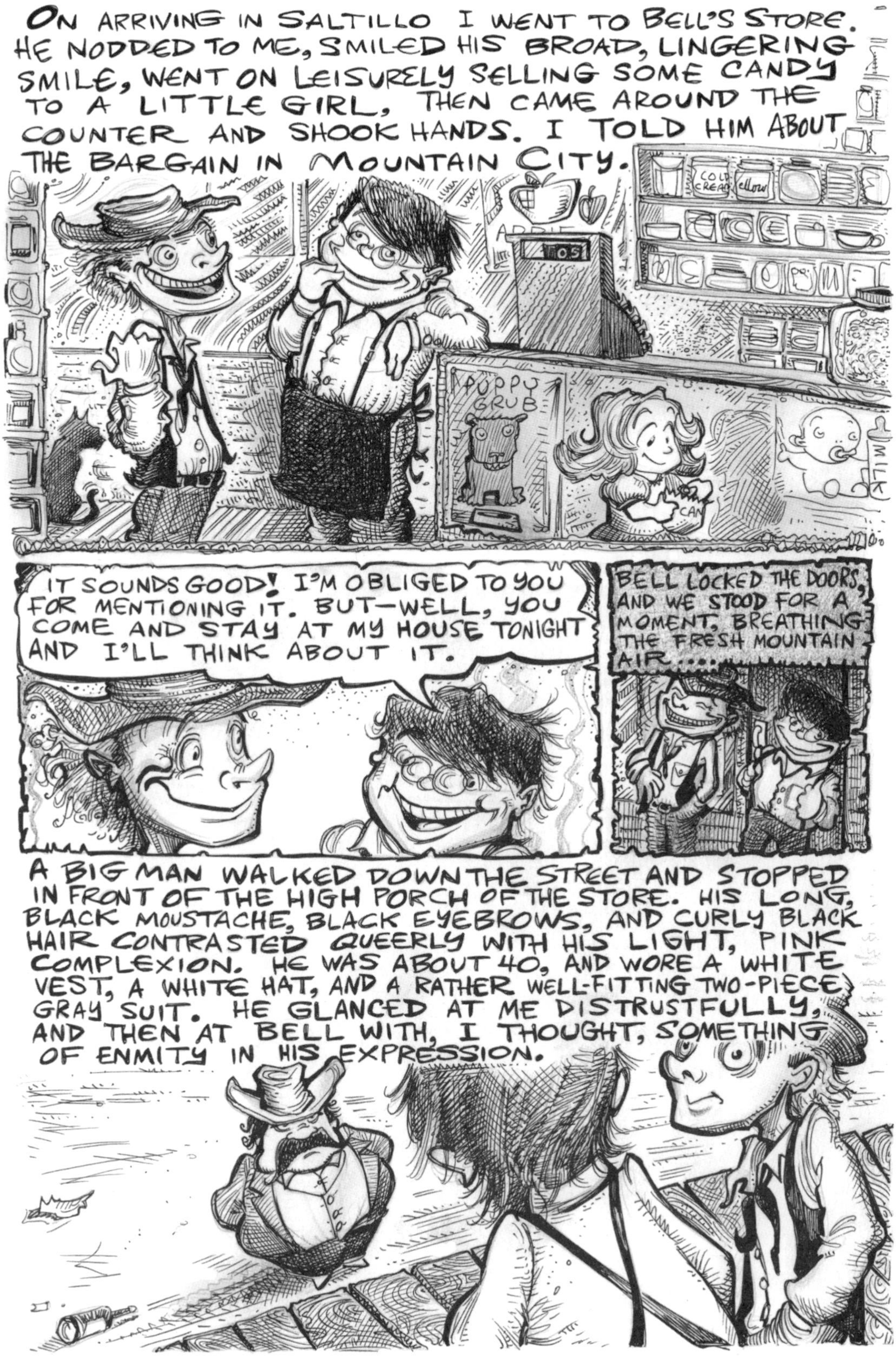
ON ARRIVING IN SALTILLO I WENT TO BELL'S STORE. HE NODDED TO ME, SMILED HIS BROAD, LINGERING SMILE, WENT ON LEISURELY SELLING SOME CANDY TO A LITTLE GIRL, THEN CAME AROUND THE COUNTER AND SHOOK HANDS. I TOLD HIM ABOUT THE BARGAIN IN MOUNTAIN CITY.
PUPPY GRUB
MILK
IT SOUNDS GOOD! I'M OBLIGED TO YOU FOR MENTIONING IT. BUT—WELL, YOU COME AND STAY AT MY HOUSE TONIGHT AND I'LL THINK ABOUT IT.
BELL LOCKED THE DOORS, AND WE STOOD FOR A MOMENT, BREATHING THE FRESH MOUNTAIN AIR....
A BIG MAN WALKED DOWN THE STREET AND STOPPED IN FRONT OF THE HIGH PORCH OF THE STORE. HIS LONG, BLACK MOUSTACHE, BLACK EYEBROWS, AND CURLY BLACK HAIR CONTRASTED QUEERLY WITH HIS LIGHT, PINK COMPLEXION. HE WAS ABOUT 40, AND WORE A WHITE VEST, A WHITE HAT, AND A RATHER WELL-FITTING TWO-PIECE GRAY SUIT. HE GLANCED AT ME DISTRUSTFULLY, AND THEN AT BELL WITH, I THOUGHT, SOMETHING OF ENMITY IN HIS EXPRESSION.

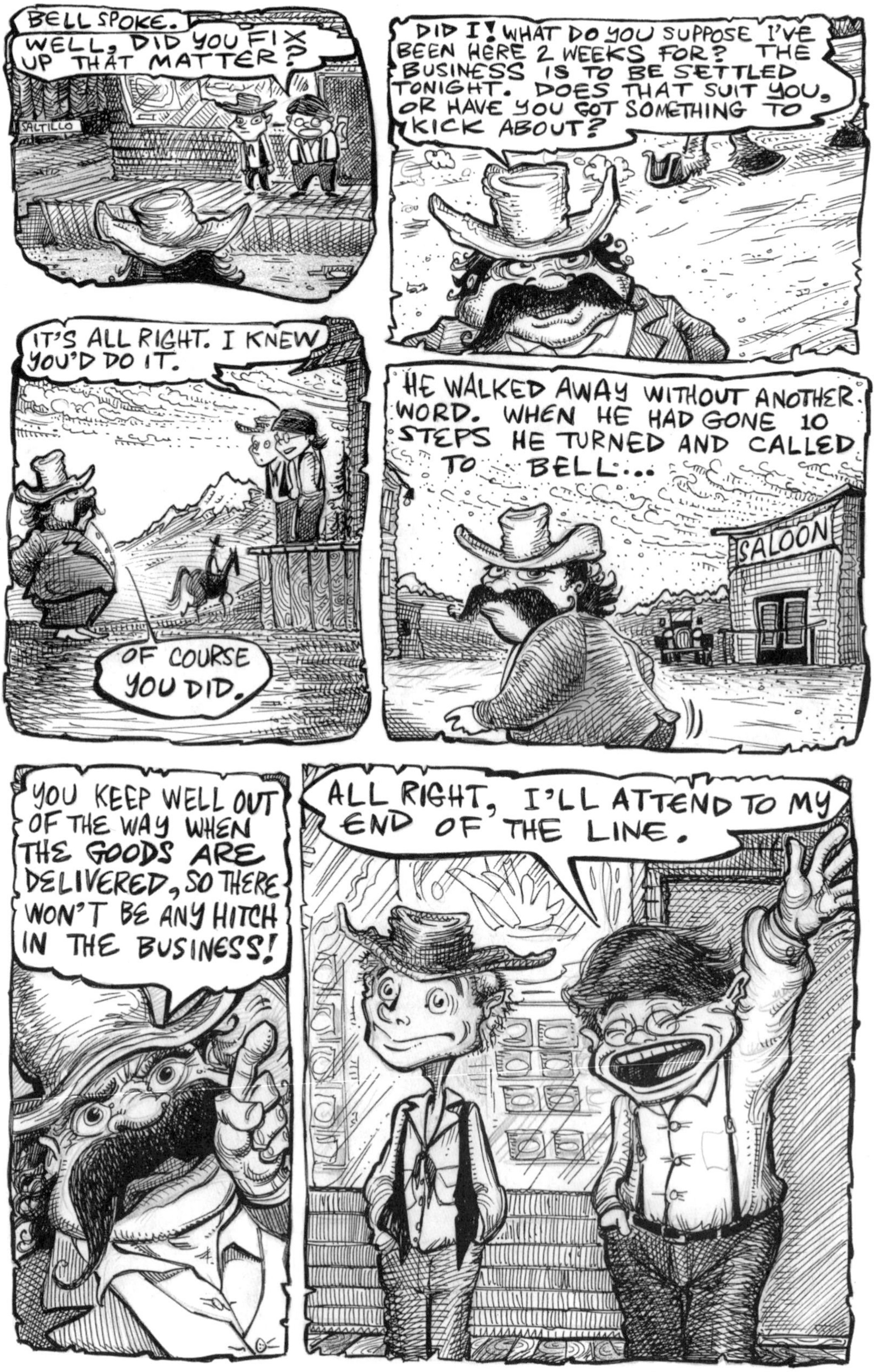
BELL SPOKE.
WELL, DID YOU FIX UP THAT MATTER?
SALTILLO
DID I! WHAT DO YOU SUPPOSE I'VE BEEN HERE 2 WEEKS FOR? THE BUSINESS IS TO BE SETTLED TONIGHT. DOES THAT SUIT YOU, OR HAVE YOU GOT SOMETHING TO KICK ABOUT?
IT'S ALL RIGHT. I KNEW YOU'D DO IT.
OF COURSE YOU DID.
HE WALKED AWAY WITHOUT ANOTHER WORD. WHEN HE HAD GONE 10 STEPS HE TURNED AND CALLED TO BELL...
SALOON
YOU KEEP WELL OUT OF THE WAY WHEN THE GOODS ARE DELIVERED, SO THERE WON'T BE ANY HITCH IN THE BUSINESS!
ALL RIGHT, I'LL ATTEND TO MY END OF THE LINE.

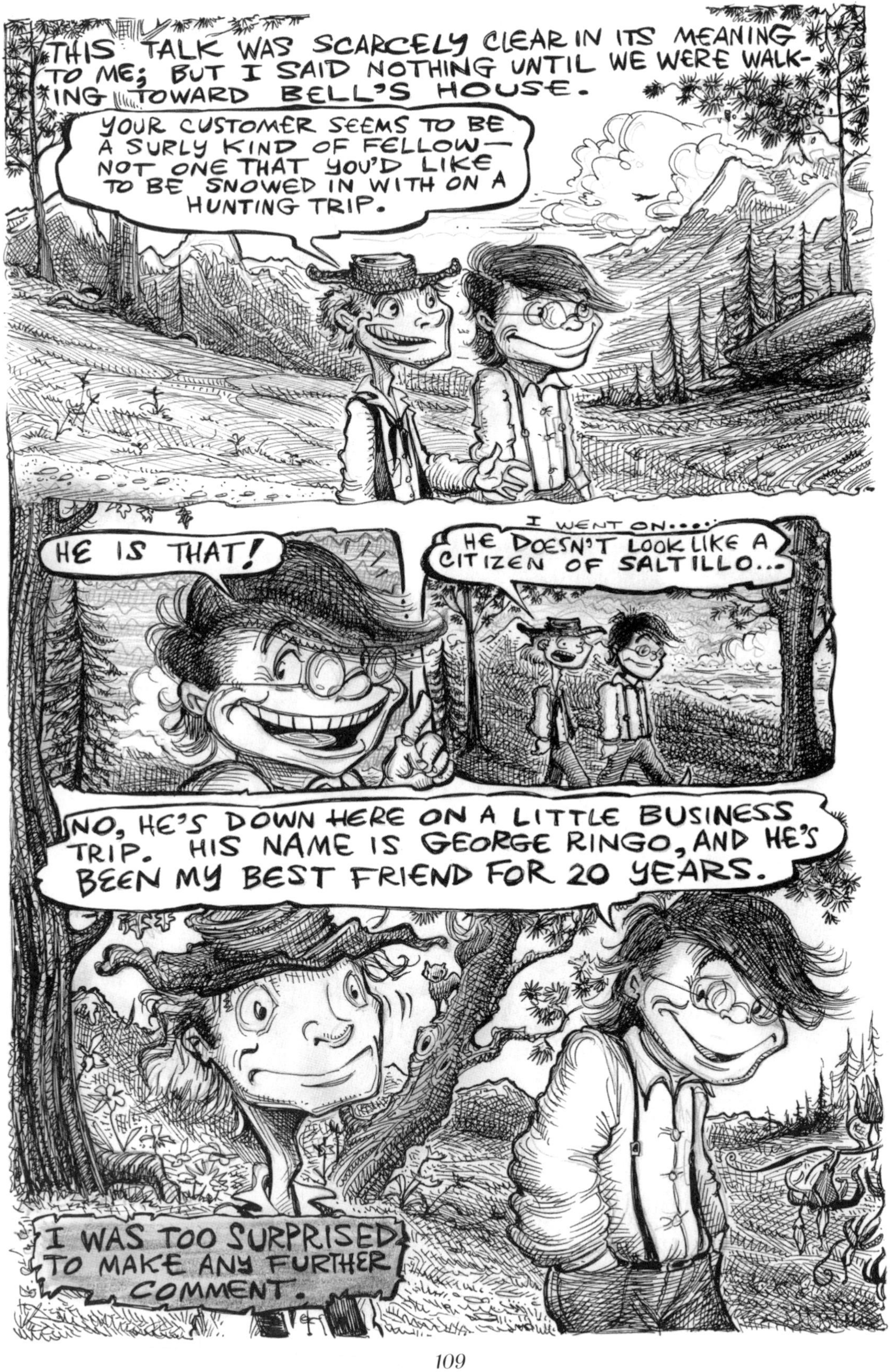
THIS TALK WAS SCARCELY CLEAR IN ITS MEANING TO ME; BUT I SAID NOTHING UNTIL WE WERE WALKING TOWARD BELL'S HOUSE.
YOUR CUSTOMER SEEMS TO BE A SURLY KIND OF FELLOW— NOT ONE THAT YOU'D LIKE TO BE SNOWED IN WITH ON A HUNTING TRIP.
HE IS THAT!
I WENT ON...
HE DOESN'T LOOK LIKE A CITIZEN OF SALTILLO...
NO, HE'S DOWN HERE ON A LITTLE BUSINESS TRIP. HIS NAME IS GEORGE RINGO, AND HE'S BEEN MY BEST FRIEND FOR 20 YEARS.
I WAS TOO SURPRISED TO MAKE ANY FURTHER COMMENT.

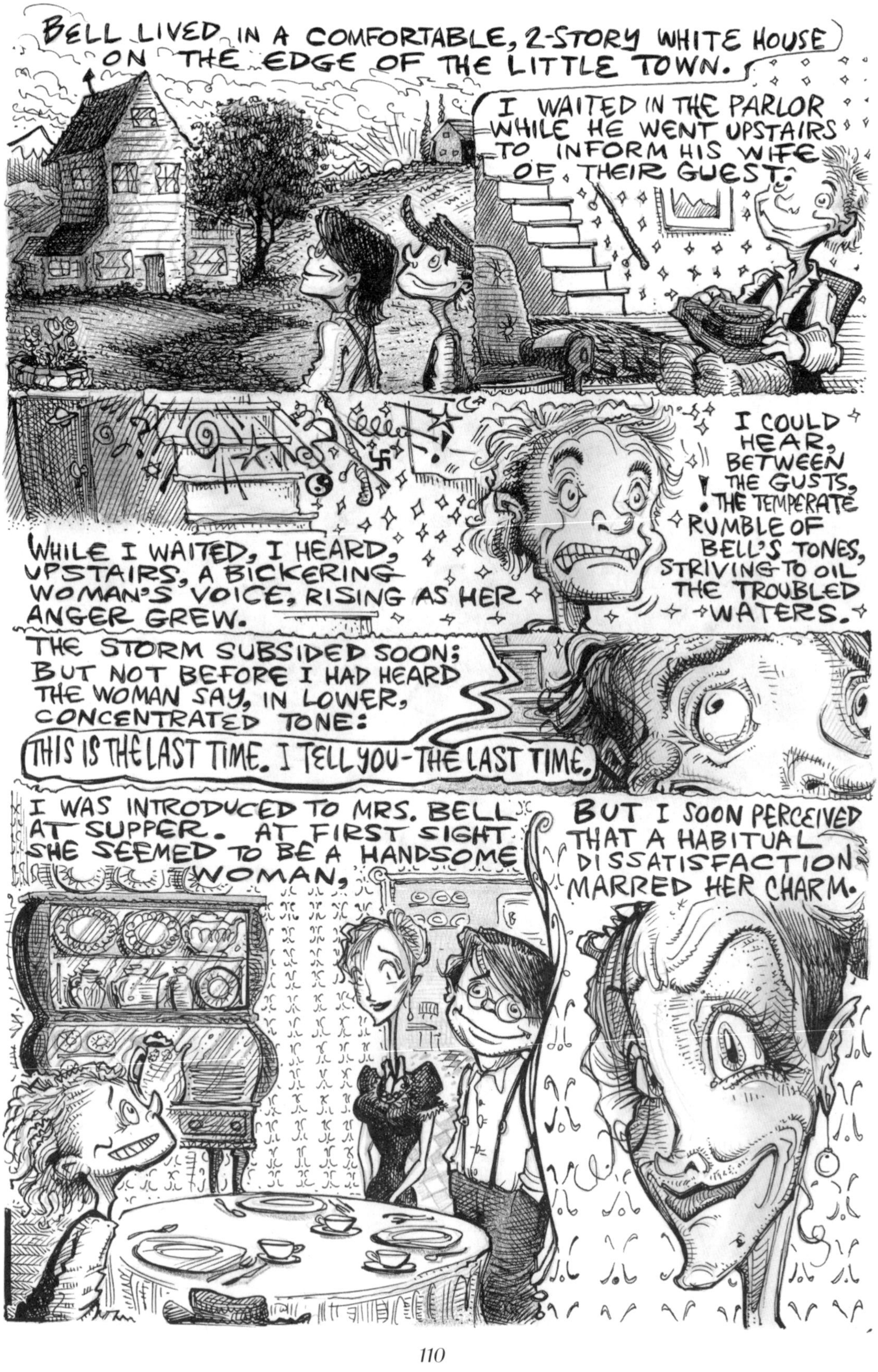
BELL LIVED IN A COMFORTABLE, 2-STORY WHITE HOUSE ON THE EDGE OF THE LITTLE TOWN.
I WAITED IN THE PARLOR WHILE HE WENT UPSTAIRS TO INFORM HIS WIFE OF THEIR GUEST.
WHILE I WAITED, I HEARD, UPSTAIRS, A BICKERING WOMAN'S VOICE, RISING AS HER ANGER GREW.
I COULD HEAR, BETWEEN THE GUSTS, THE TEMPERATE RUMBLE OF BELL'S TONES, STRIVING TO OIL THE TROUBLED WATERS.
THE STORM SUBSIDED SOON; BUT NOT BEFORE I HAD HEARD THE WOMAN SAY, IN LOWER, CONCENTRATED TONE:
THIS IS THE LAST TIME. I TELL YOU-THE LAST TIME.
I WAS INTRODUCED TO MRS. BELL AT SUPPER. AT FIRST SIGHT SHE SEEMED TO BE A HANDSOME WOMAN,
BUT I SOON PERCEIVED THAT A HABITUAL DISSATISFACTION MARRED HER CHARM.

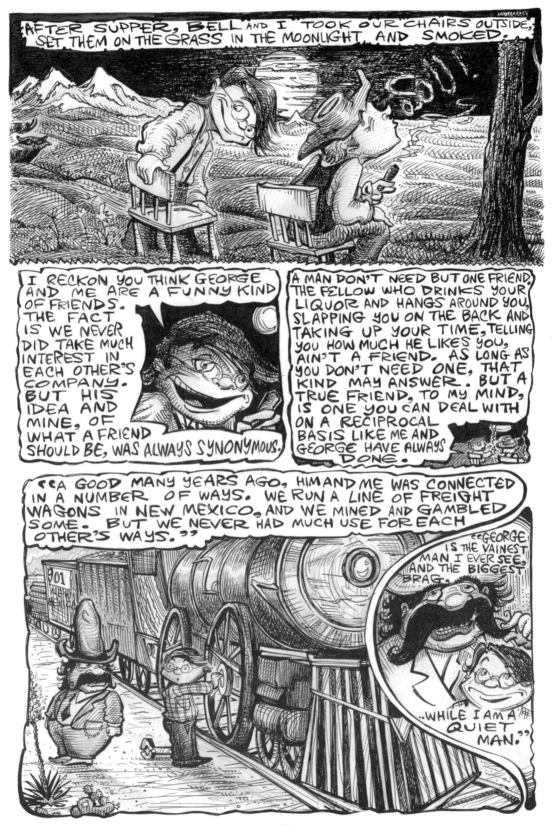

AFTER SUPPER, BELL AND I TOOK OUR CHAIRS OUTSIDE, SET THEM ON THE GRASS IN THE MOONLIGHT, AND SMOKED.

I RECKON YOU THINK GEORGE AND ME ARE A FUNNY KIND OF FRIENDS. THE FACT IS WE NEVER DID TAKE MUCH INTEREST IN EACH OTHER'S COMPANY. BUT HIS IDEA AND MINE, OF WHAT A FRIEND SHOULD BE, WAS ALWAYS SYNONYMOUS.

A MAN DON'T NEED BUT ONE FRIEND. THE FELLOW WHO DRINKS YOUR LIQUOR AND HANGS AROUND YOU, SLAPPING YOU ON THE BACK AND TAKING UP YOUR TIME, TELLING YOU HOW MUCH HE LIKES YOU, AIN'T A FRIEND. AS LONG AS YOU DON'T NEED ONE, THAT KIND MAY ANSWER. BUT A TRUE FRIEND, TO MY MIND, IS ONE YOU CAN DEAL WITH ON A RECIPROCAL BASIS LIKE ME AND GEORGE HAVE ALWAYS DONE.

"A GOOD MANY YEARS AGO, HIM AND ME WAS CONNECTED IN A NUMBER OF WAYS. WE RUN A LINE OF FREIGHT WAGONS IN NEW MEXICO, AND WE MINED AND GAMBLED SOME. BUT WE NEVER HAD MUCH USE FOR EACH OTHER'S WAYS."

"GEORGE IS THE VAINEST MAN I EVER SEE, AND THE BIGGEST BRAG... ...WHILE I AM A QUIET MAN."

901

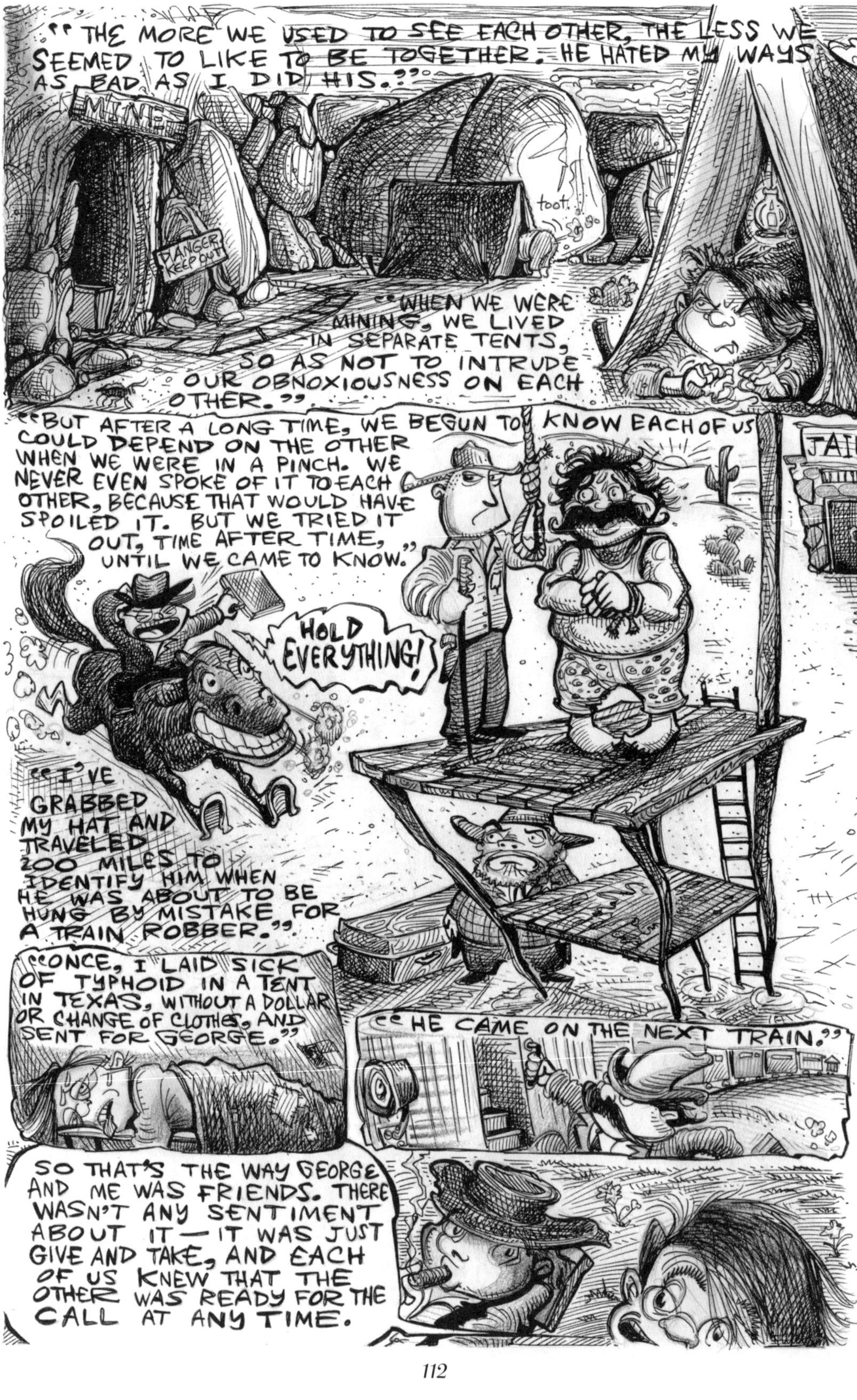
"THE MORE WE USED TO SEE EACH OTHER, THE LESS WE SEEMED TO LIKE TO BE TOGETHER. HE HATED MY WAYS AS BAD AS I DID HIS."
MINE
DANGER KEEP OUT
toot
"WHEN WE WERE MINING, WE LIVED IN SEPARATE TENTS, SO AS NOT TO INTRUDE OUR OBNOXIOUSNESS ON EACH OTHER."
"BUT AFTER A LONG TIME, WE BEGUN TO KNOW EACH OF US COULD DEPEND ON THE OTHER WHEN WE WERE IN A PINCH. WE NEVER EVEN SPOKE OF IT TO EACH OTHER, BECAUSE THAT WOULD HAVE SPOILED IT. BUT WE TRIED IT OUT, TIME AFTER TIME, UNTIL WE CAME TO KNOW."
JAIL
HOLD EVERYTHING!
"I'VE GRABBED MY HAT AND TRAVELED 200 MILES TO IDENTIFY HIM WHEN HE WAS ABOUT TO BE HUNG BY MISTAKE FOR A TRAIN ROBBER."
"ONCE, I LAID SICK OF TYPHOID IN A TENT IN TEXAS, WITHOUT A DOLLAR OR CHANGE OF CLOTHES, AND SENT FOR GEORGE."
"HE CAME ON THE NEXT TRAIN."
SO THAT'S THE WAY GEORGE AND ME WAS FRIENDS. THERE WASN'T ANY SENTIMENT ABOUT IT — IT WAS JUST GIVE AND TAKE, AND EACH OF US KNEW THAT THE OTHER WAS READY FOR THE CALL AT ANY TIME.

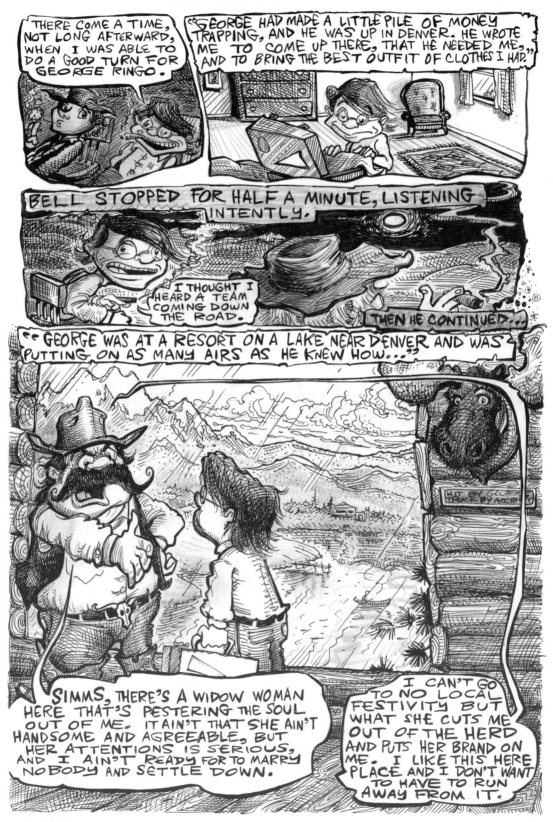

THERE COME A TIME, NOT LONG AFTERWARD, WHEN I WAS ABLE TO DO A GOOD TURN FOR GEORGE RINGO.

"GEORGE HAD MADE A LITTLE PILE OF MONEY TRAPPING, AND HE WAS UP IN DENVER. HE WROTE ME TO COME UP THERE, THAT HE NEEDED ME, AND TO BRING THE BEST OUTFIT OF CLOTHES I HAD."

BELL STOPPED FOR HALF A MINUTE, LISTENING INTENTLY.

I THOUGHT I HEARD A TEAM COMING DOWN THE ROAD.

THEN HE CONTINUED...

"GEORGE WAS AT A RESORT ON A LAKE NEAR DENVER AND WAS PUTTING ON AS MANY AIRS AS HE KNEW HOW..."

HIT BY GEORGE TRUCK BY ACCIDENT

SIMMS, THERE'S A WIDOW WOMAN HERE THAT'S PESTERING THE SOUL OUT OF ME. IT AIN'T THAT SHE AIN'T HANDSOME AND AGREEABLE, BUT HER ATTENTIONS IS SERIOUS, AND I AIN'T READY FOR TO MARRY NOBODY AND SETTLE DOWN.

I CAN'T GO TO NO LOCAL FESTIVITY BUT WHAT SHE CUTS ME OUT OF THE HERD AND PUTS HER BRAND ON ME. I LIKE THIS HERE PLACE AND I DON'T WANT TO HAVE TO RUN AWAY FROM IT.

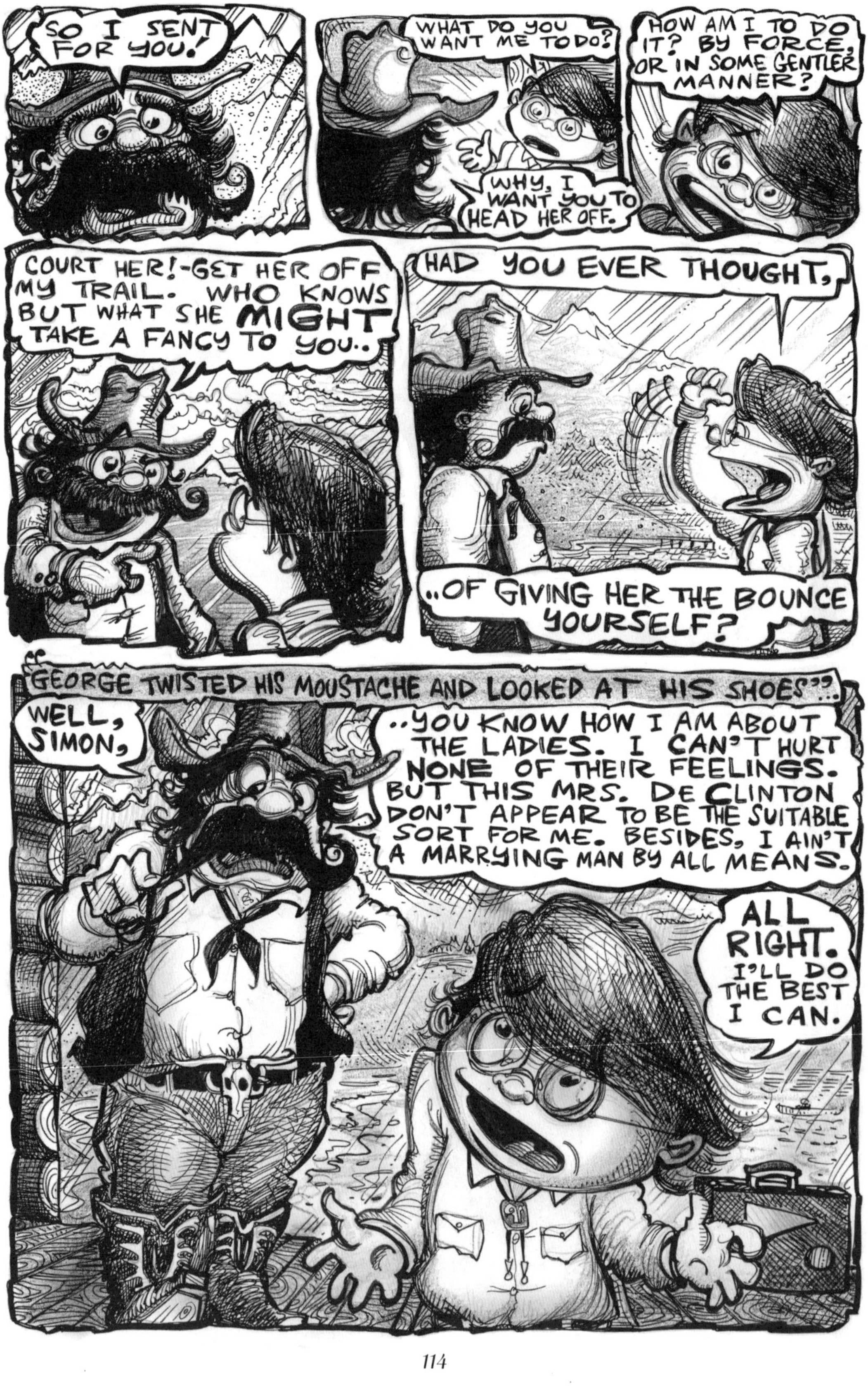
SO I SENT FOR YOU!
WHAT DO YOU WANT ME TO DO?
WHY, I WANT YOU TO HEAD HER OFF.
HOW AM I TO DO IT? BY FORCE, OR IN SOME GENTLER MANNER?
COURT HER!-GET HER OFF MY TRAIL. WHO KNOWS BUT WHAT SHE MIGHT TAKE A FANCY TO YOU..
HAD YOU EVER THOUGHT,
..OF GIVING HER THE BOUNCE YOURSELF?
"GEORGE TWISTED HIS MOUSTACHE AND LOOKED AT HIS SHOES"..
WELL, SIMON,
..YOU KNOW HOW I AM ABOUT THE LADIES. I CAN'T HURT NONE OF THEIR FEELINGS. BUT THIS MRS. DE CLINTON DON'T APPEAR TO BE THE SUITABLE SORT FOR ME. BESIDES, I AIN'T A MARRYING MAN BY ALL MEANS.
ALL RIGHT. I'LL DO THE BEST I CAN.

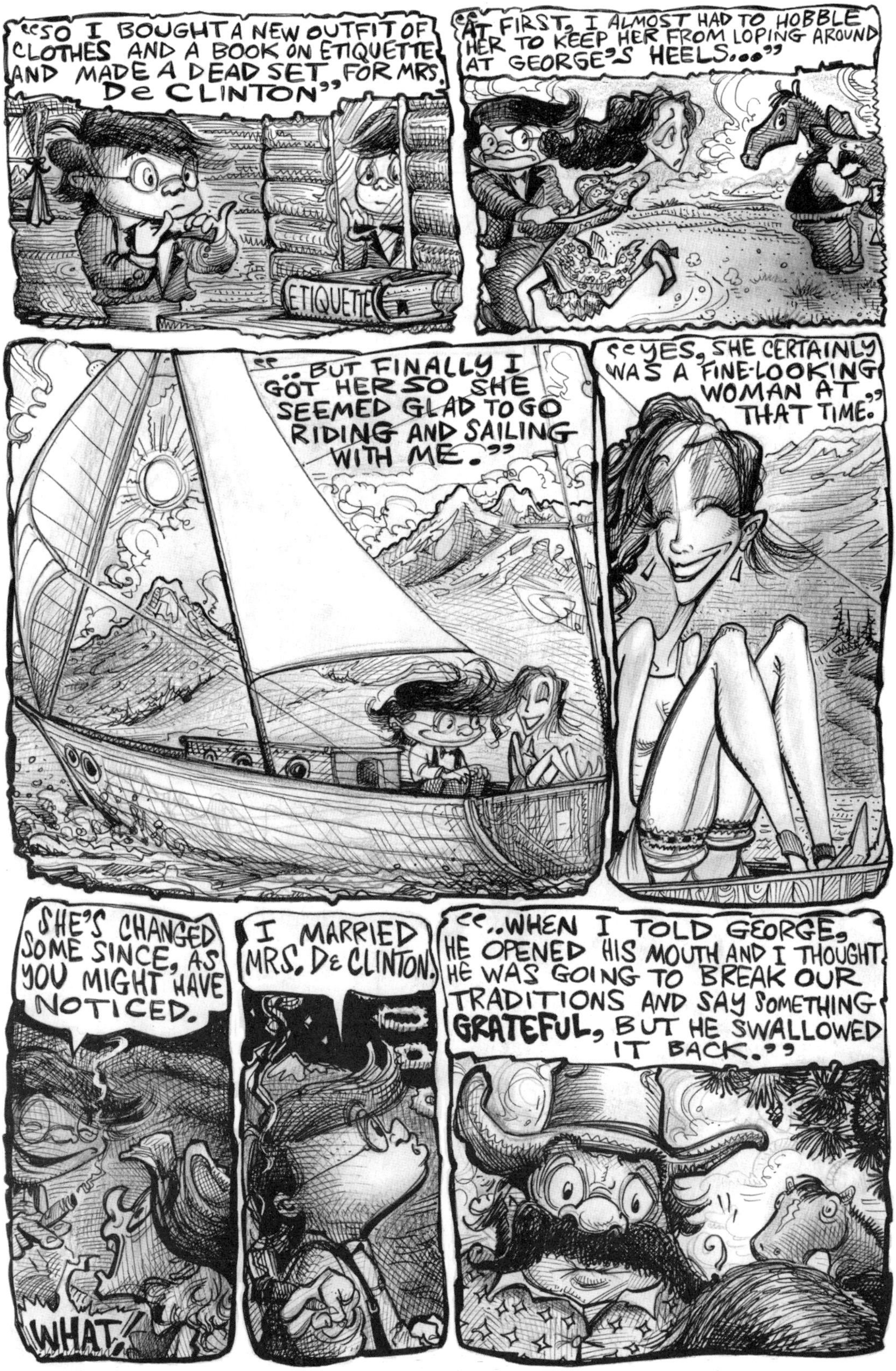
"SO I BOUGHT A NEW OUTFIT OF CLOTHES AND A BOOK ON ETIQUETTE AND MADE A DEAD SET FOR MRS. De CLINTON"
ETIQUETTE
"AT FIRST, I ALMOST HAD TO HOBBLE HER TO KEEP HER FROM LOPING AROUND AT GEORGE'S HEELS..."
".. BUT FINALLY I GOT HER SO SHE SEEMED GLAD TO GO RIDING AND SAILING WITH ME."
"YES, SHE CERTAINLY WAS A FINE-LOOKING WOMAN AT THAT TIME."
SHE'S CHANGED SOME SINCE, AS YOU MIGHT HAVE NOTICED.
WHAT!
I MARRIED MRS. De CLINTON.
"..WHEN I TOLD GEORGE, HE OPENED HIS MOUTH AND I THOUGHT HE WAS GOING TO BREAK OUR TRADITIONS AND SAY SOMETHING GRATEFUL, BUT HE SWALLOWED IT BACK."

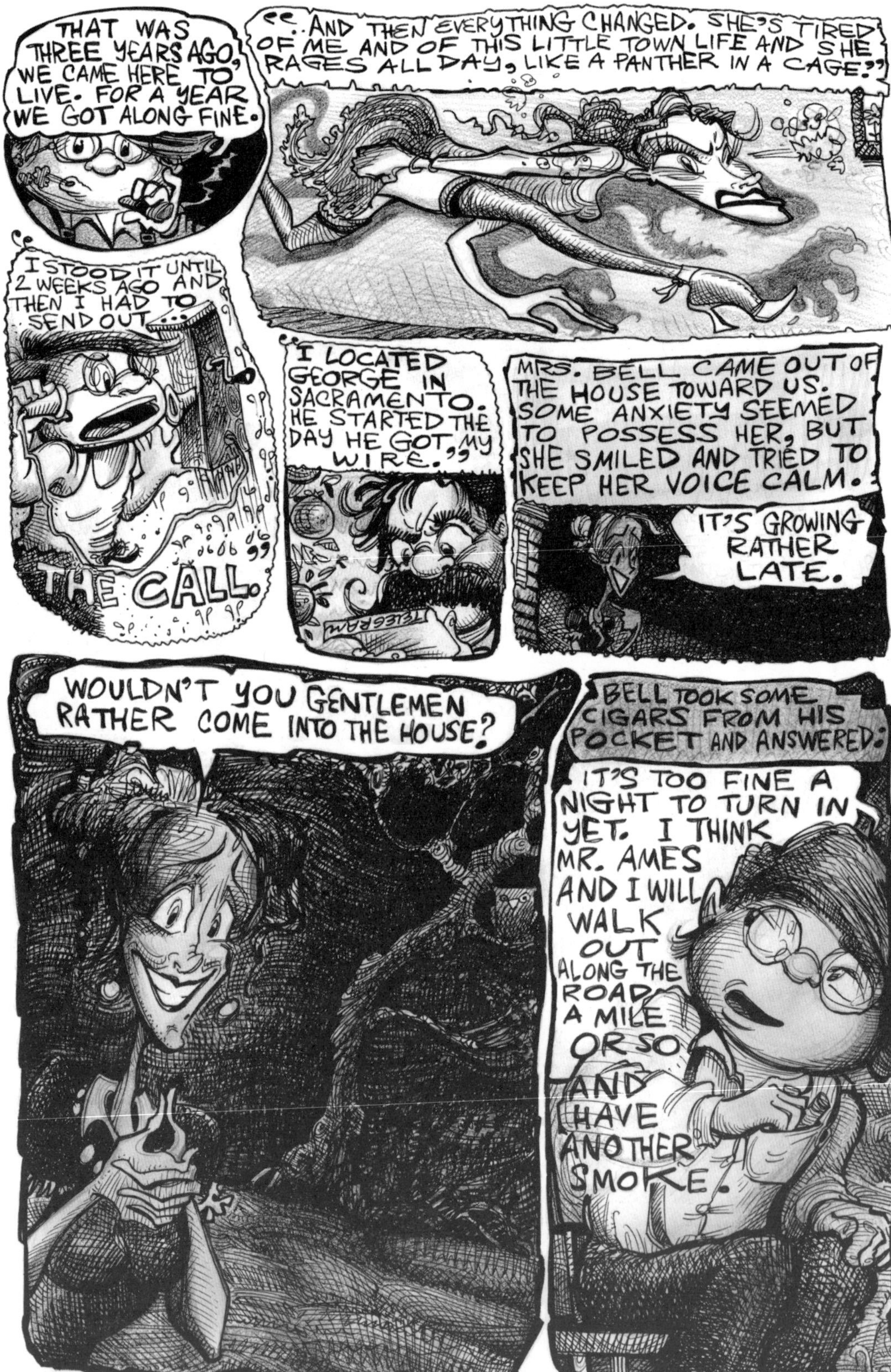
THAT WAS THREE YEARS AGO, WE CAME HERE TO LIVE. FOR A YEAR WE GOT ALONG FINE.
"...AND THEN EVERYTHING CHANGED. SHE'S TIRED OF ME AND OF THIS LITTLE TOWN LIFE AND SHE RAGES ALL DAY, LIKE A PANTHER IN A CAGE."
"I STOOD IT UNTIL 2 WEEKS AGO AND THEN I HAD TO SEND OUT...
THE CALL.
"I LOCATED GEORGE IN SACRAMENTO. HE STARTED THE DAY HE GOT MY WIRE."
TELEGRAM
MRS. BELL CAME OUT OF THE HOUSE TOWARD US. SOME ANXIETY SEEMED TO POSSESS HER, BUT SHE SMILED AND TRIED TO KEEP HER VOICE CALM.
IT'S GROWING RATHER LATE.
WOULDN'T YOU GENTLEMEN RATHER COME INTO THE HOUSE?
BELL TOOK SOME CIGARS FROM HIS POCKET AND ANSWERED:
IT'S TOO FINE A NIGHT TO TURN IN YET. I THINK MR. AMES AND I WILL WALK OUT ALONG THE ROAD A MILE OR SO AND HAVE ANOTHER SMOKE.

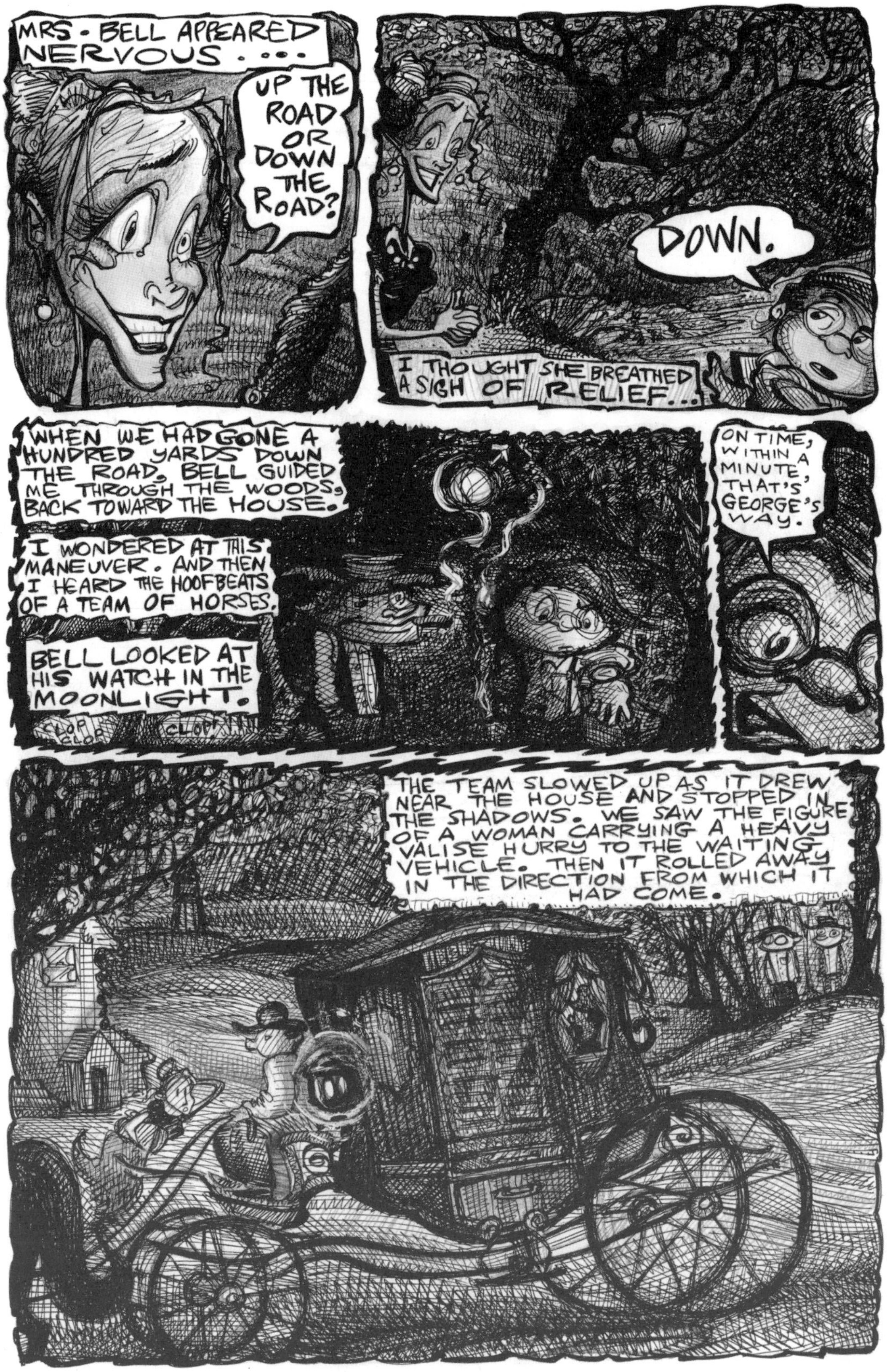
MRS. BELL APPEARED NERVOUS....
UP THE ROAD OR DOWN THE ROAD?
DOWN.
I THOUGHT SHE BREATHED A SIGH OF RELIEF...
WHEN WE HAD GONE A HUNDRED YARDS DOWN THE ROAD, BELL GUIDED ME THROUGH THE WOODS, BACK TOWARD THE HOUSE.
I WONDERED AT THIS MANEUVER. AND THEN I HEARD THE HOOFBEATS OF A TEAM OF HORSES.
BELL LOOKED AT HIS WATCH IN THE MOONLIGHT.
CLOP CLOP
CLOP
ON TIME, WITHIN A MINUTE, THAT'S GEORGE'S WAY.
THE TEAM SLOWED UP AS IT DREW NEAR THE HOUSE AND STOPPED IN THE SHADOWS. WE SAW THE FIGURE OF A WOMAN CARRYING A HEAVY VALISE HURRY TO THE WAITING VEHICLE. THEN IT ROLLED AWAY IN THE DIRECTION FROM WHICH IT HAD COME.

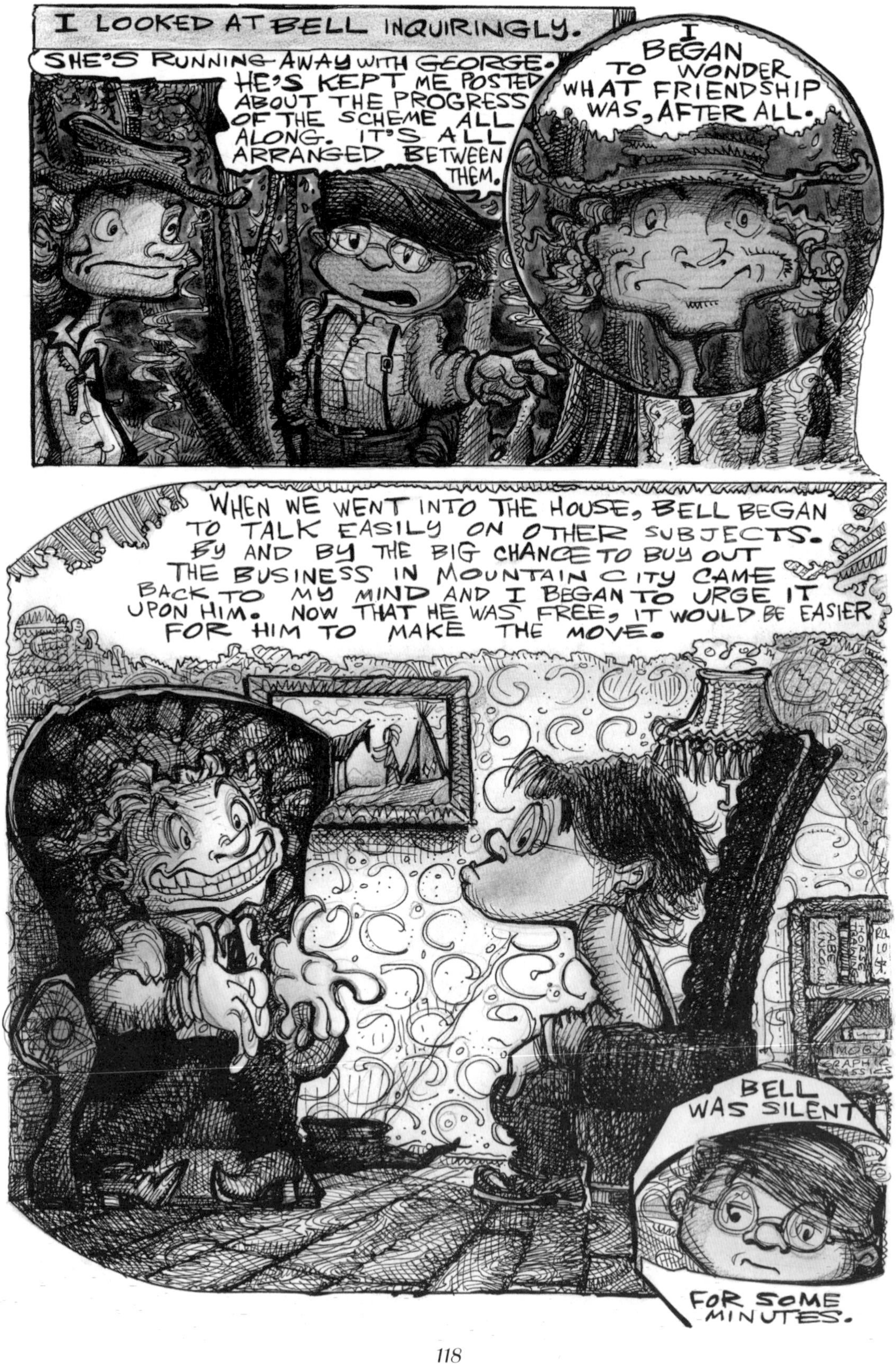
I LOOKED AT BELL INQUIRINGLY.
SHE'S RUNNING AWAY WITH GEORGE. HE'S KEPT ME POSTED ABOUT THE PROGRESS OF THE SCHEME ALL ALONG. IT'S ALL ARRANGED BETWEEN THEM.
I BEGAN TO WONDER WHAT FRIENDSHIP WAS, AFTER ALL.
WHEN WE WENT INTO THE HOUSE, BELL BEGAN TO TALK EASILY ON OTHER SUBJECTS. BY AND BY THE BIG CHANCE TO BUY OUT THE BUSINESS IN MOUNTAIN CITY CAME BACK TO MY MIND AND I BEGAN TO URGE IT UPON HIM. NOW THAT HE WAS FREE, IT WOULD BE EASIER FOR HIM TO MAKE THE MOVE.
BELL WAS SILENT
FOR SOME MINUTES.

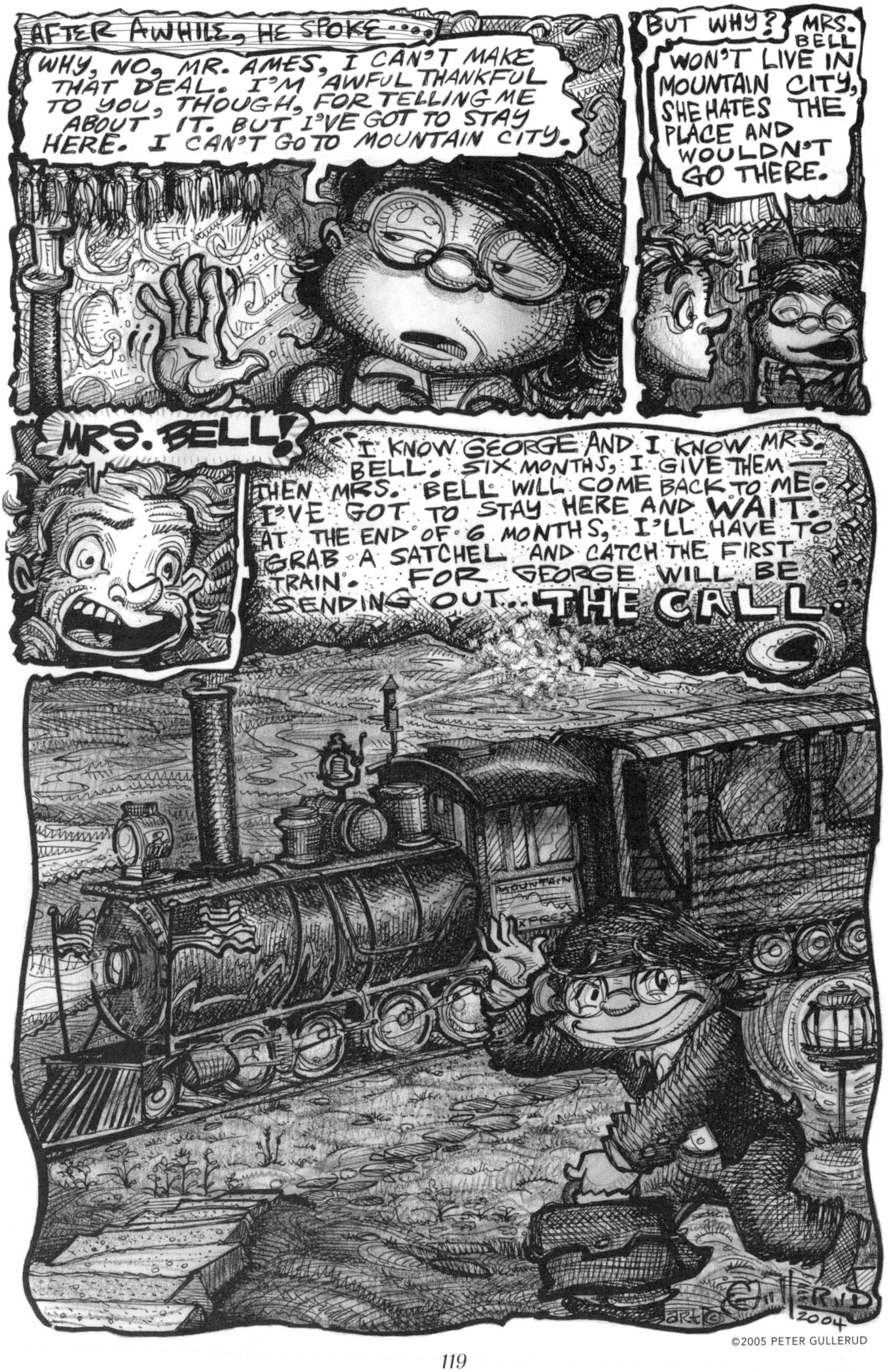
AFTER AWHILE, HE SPOKE...
WHY, NO, MR. AMES, I CAN'T MAKE THAT DEAL. I'M AWFUL THANKFUL TO YOU, THOUGH, FOR TELLING ME ABOUT IT. BUT I'VE GOT TO STAY HERE. I CAN'T GO TO MOUNTAIN CITY.
BUT WHY?
MRS. BELL WON'T LIVE IN MOUNTAIN CITY, SHE HATES THE PLACE AND WOULDN'T GO THERE.
MRS. BELL!
"I KNOW GEORGE AND I KNOW MRS. BELL. SIX MONTHS, I GIVE THEM — THEN MRS. BELL WILL COME BACK TO ME. I'VE GOT TO STAY HERE AND WAIT. AT THE END OF 6 MONTHS, I'LL HAVE TO GRAB A SATCHEL AND CATCH THE FIRST TRAIN. FOR GEORGE WILL BE SENDING OUT... THE CALL.
MOUNTAIN
XPRESS
GULLERUD 2004

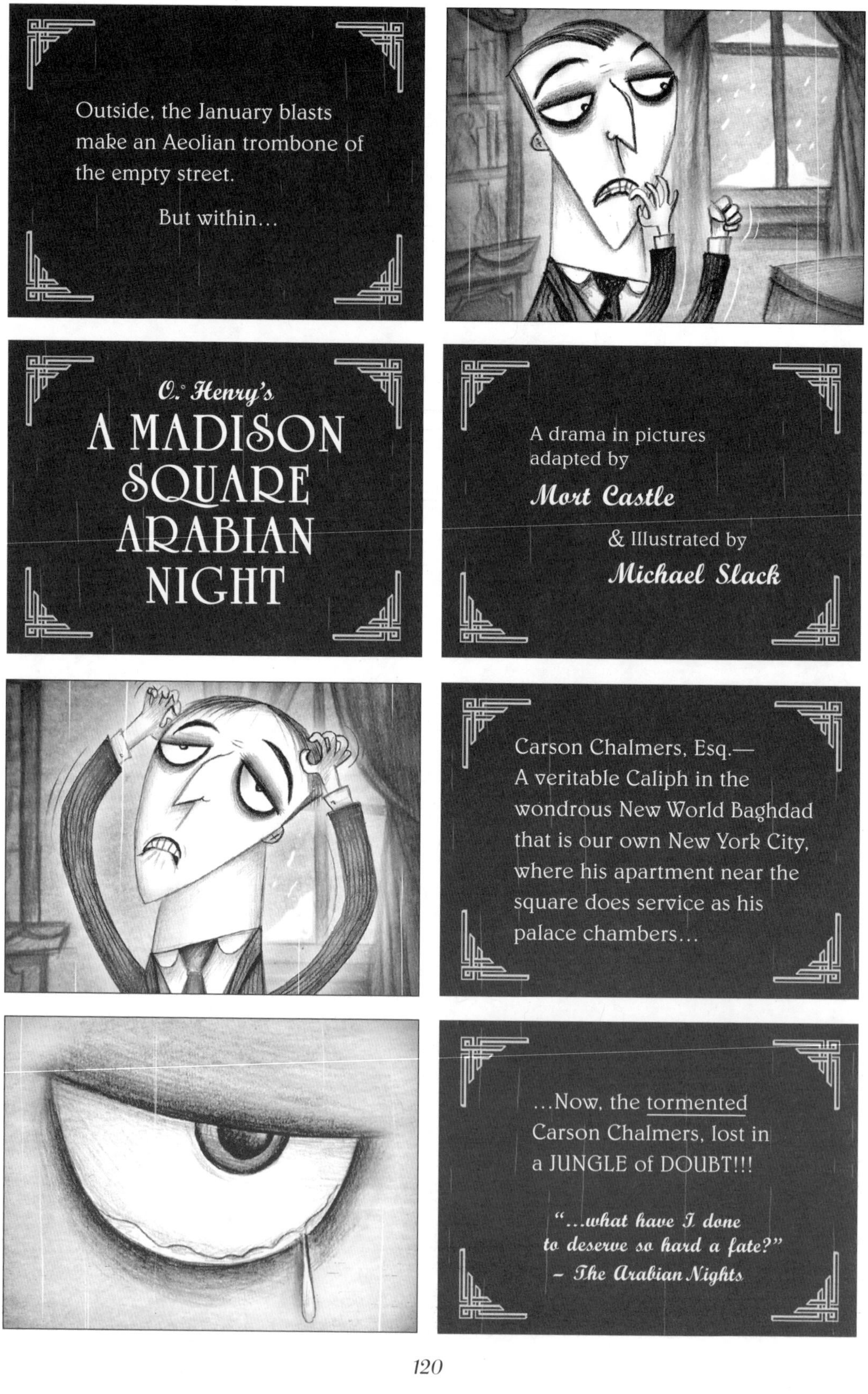
Outside, the January blasts make an Aeolian trombone of the empty street.
But within...
O. Henry's
A MADISON SQUARE ARABIAN NIGHT
A drama in pictures adapted by
Mort Castle
& Illustrated by
Michael Slack
Carson Chalmers, Esq.— A veritable Caliph in the wondrous New World Baghdad that is our own New York City, where his apartment near the square does service as his palace chambers...
...Now, the tormented Carson Chalmers, lost in a JUNGLE of DOUBT!!!
"...what have I done to deserve so hard a fate?"
– The Arabian Nights

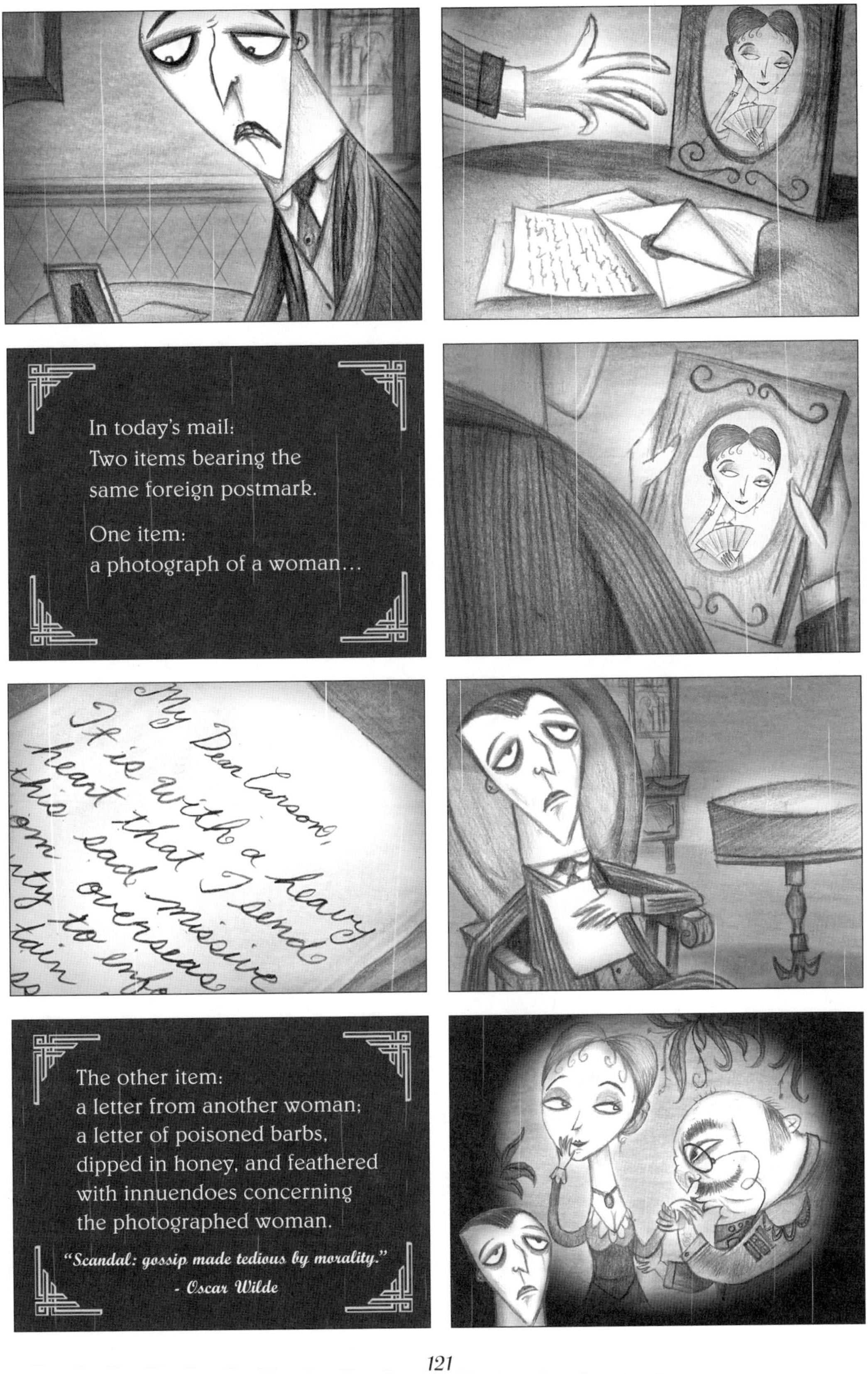
In today's mail:
Two items bearing the
same foreign postmark.
One item:
a photograph of a woman...
My Dear Carson,
It is with a heavy
heart that I send
this sad missive
The other item:
a letter from another woman;
a letter of poisoned barbs,
dipped in honey, and feathered
with innuendoes concerning
the photographed woman.
"Scandal: gossip made tedious by morality."
- Oscar Wilde

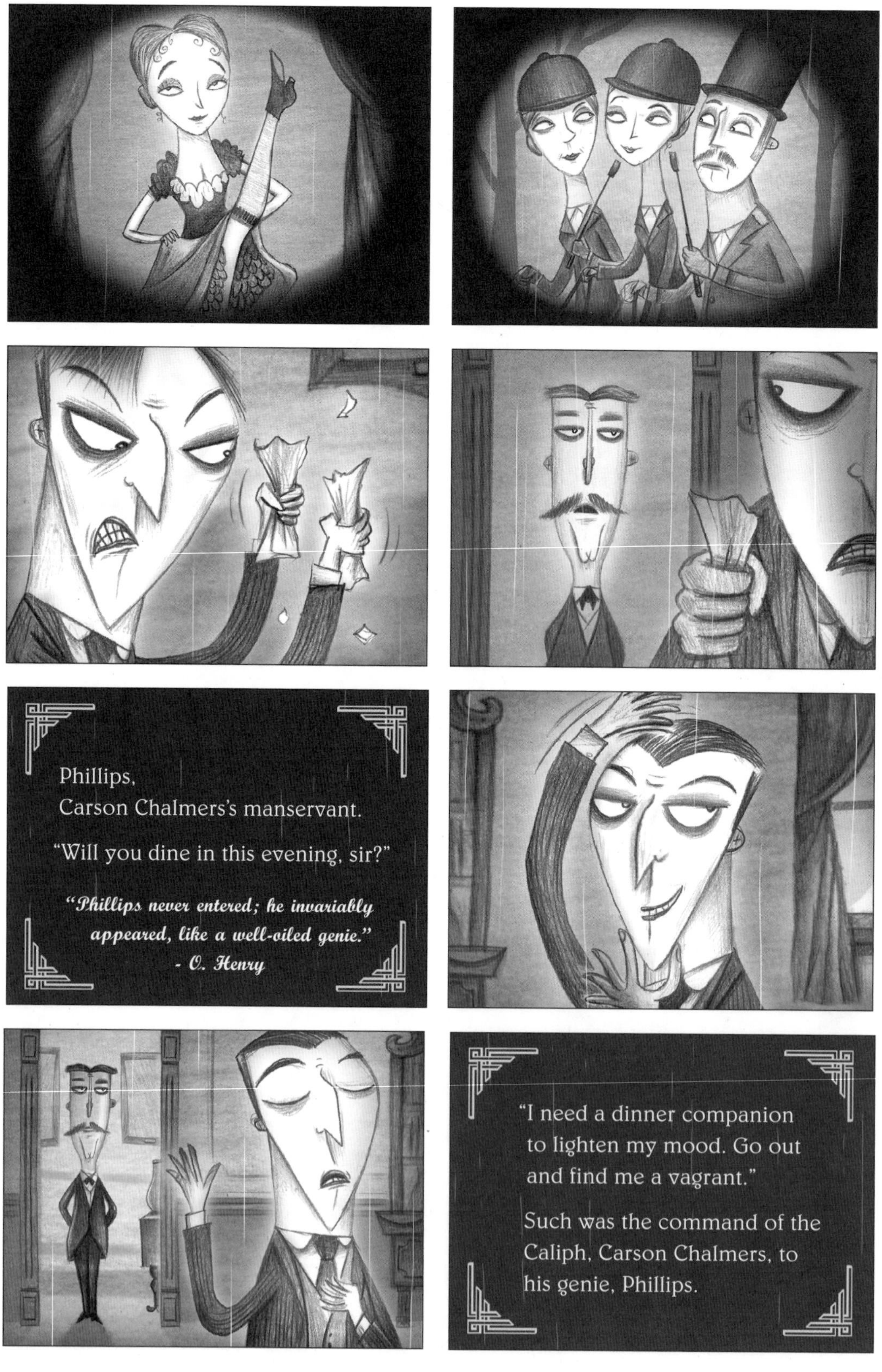
Phillips,
Carson Chalmers's manservant.
"Will you dine in this evening, sir?"
"Phillips never entered; he invariably appeared, like a well-oiled genie."
- O. Henry
"I need a dinner companion to lighten my mood. Go out and find me a vagrant."
Such was the command of the Caliph, Carson Chalmers, to his genie, Phillips.

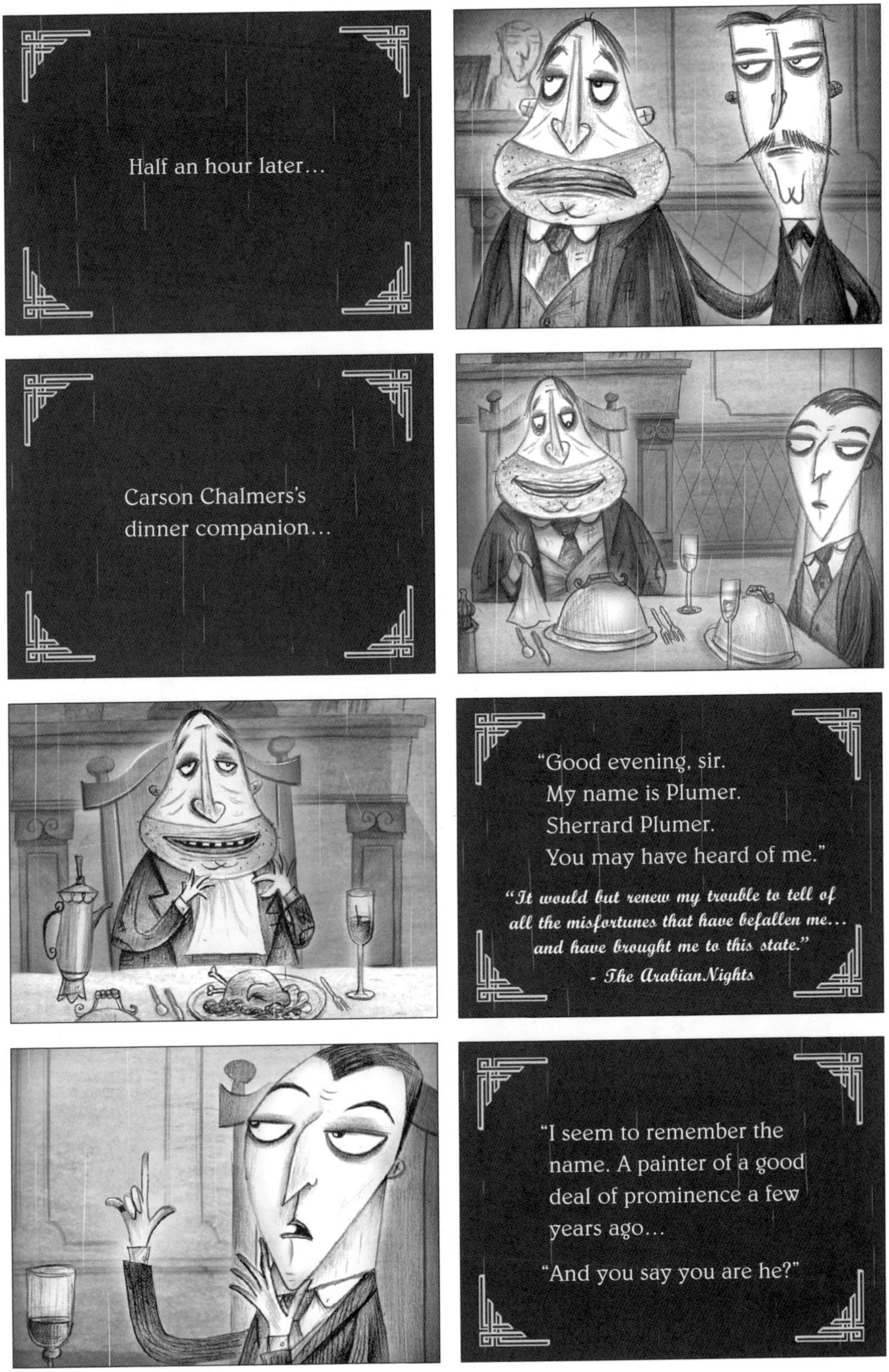
Half an hour later...
Carson Chalmers's dinner companion...
"Good evening, sir. My name is Plumer. Sherrard Plumer. You may have heard of me."
"It would but renew my trouble to tell of all the misfortunes that have befallen me... and have brought me to this state." - The ArabianNights
"I seem to remember the name. A painter of a good deal of prominence a few years ago...
"And you say you are he?"

"That's better! Now, my jovial ruler of Baghdad, I'm your tale-telling Scheherazade all the way to the toothpicks."

"This situation does not seem a novel one to you, Mr. Plumer."

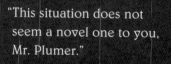

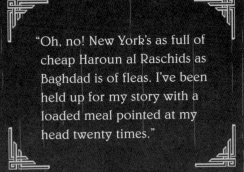

"Oh, no! New York's as full of cheap Haroun al Raschids as Baghdad is of fleas. I've been held up for my story with a loaded meal pointed at my head twenty times."

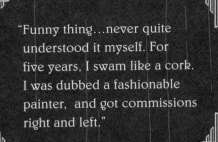

"Funny thing…never quite understood it myself. For five years, I swam like a cork. I was dubbed a fashionable painter, and got commissions right and left."

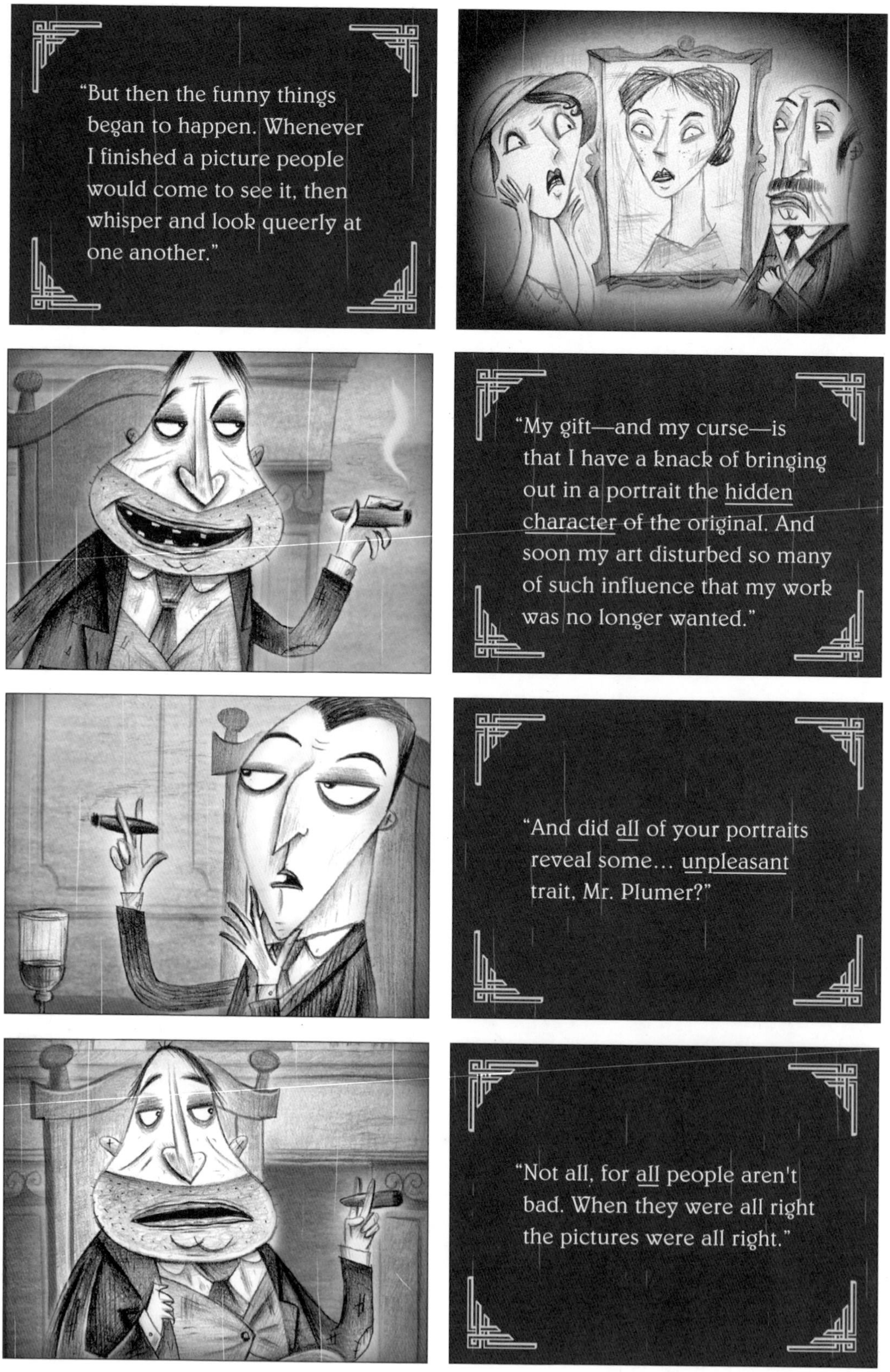
"But then the funny things began to happen. Whenever I finished a picture people would come to see it, then whisper and look queerly at one another."
"My gift—and my curse—is that I have a knack of bringing out in a portrait the hidden character of the original. And soon my art disturbed so many of such influence that my work was no longer wanted."
"And did all of your portraits reveal some… unpleasant trait, Mr. Plumer?"
"Not all, for all people aren't bad. When they were all right the pictures were all right."

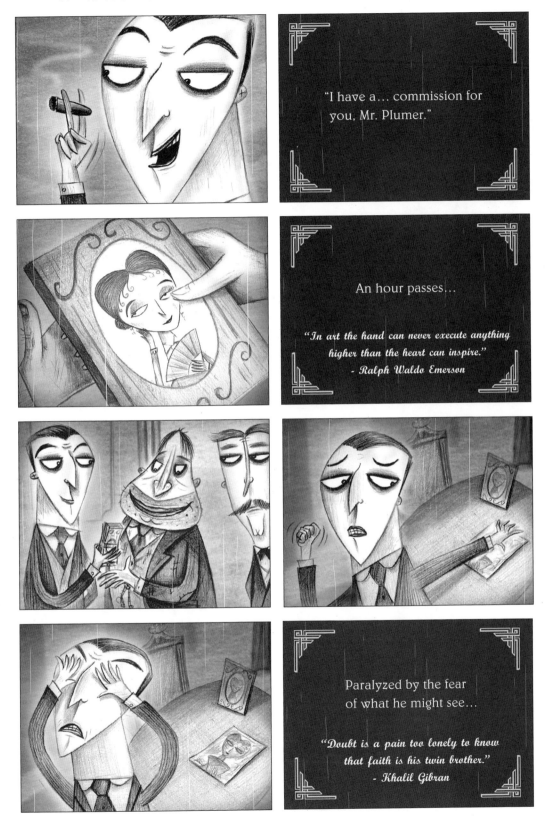

"I have a... commission for you, Mr. Plumer."

An hour passes...

"In art the hand can never execute anything higher than the heart can inspire."
- Ralph Waldo Emerson

Paralyzed by the fear of what he might see...

"Doubt is a pain too lonely to know that faith is his twin brother."
- Khalil Gibran

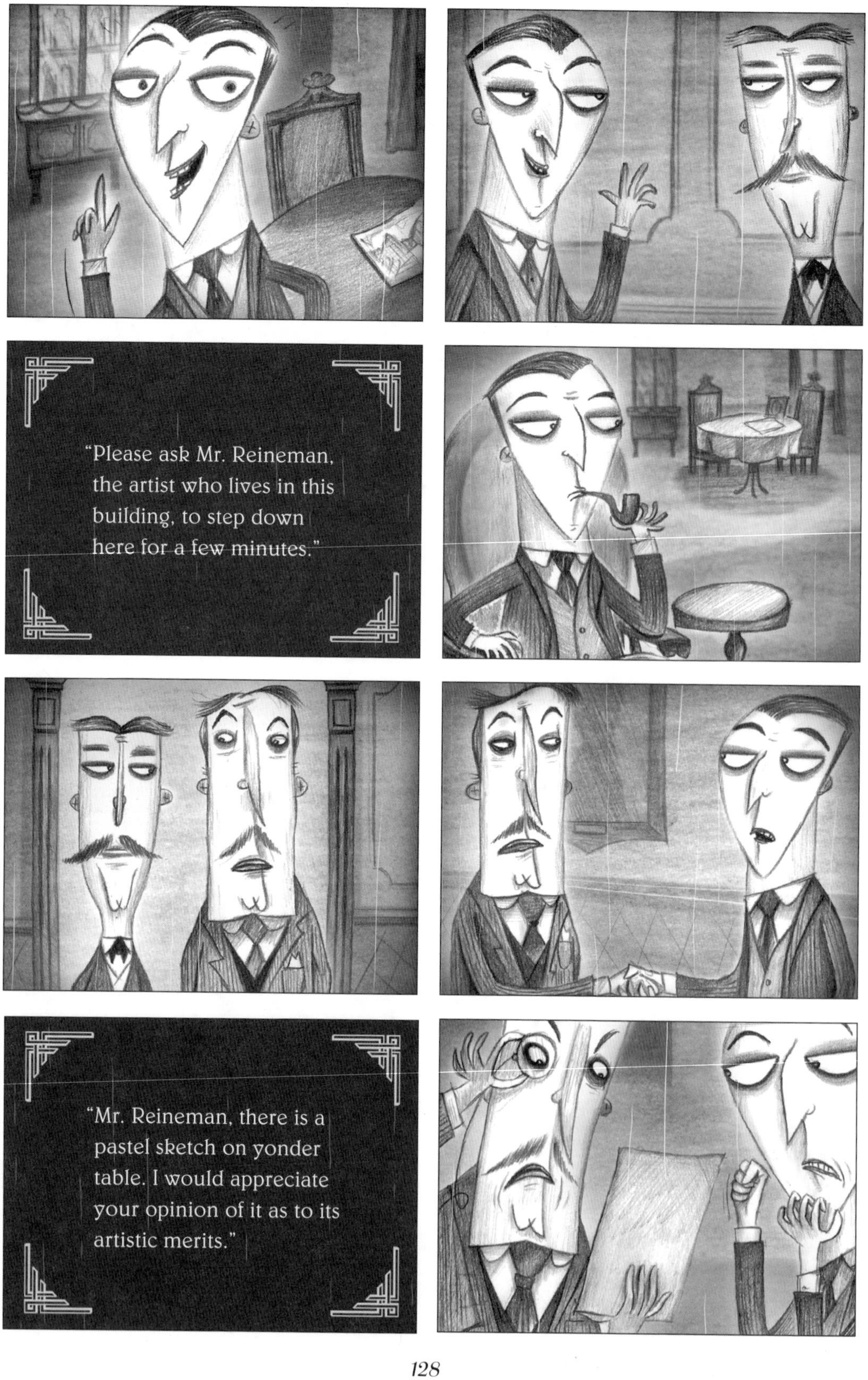
"Please ask Mr. Reineman, the artist who lives in this building, to step down here for a few minutes."
"Mr. Reineman, there is a pastel sketch on yonder table. I would appreciate your opinion of it as to its artistic merits."

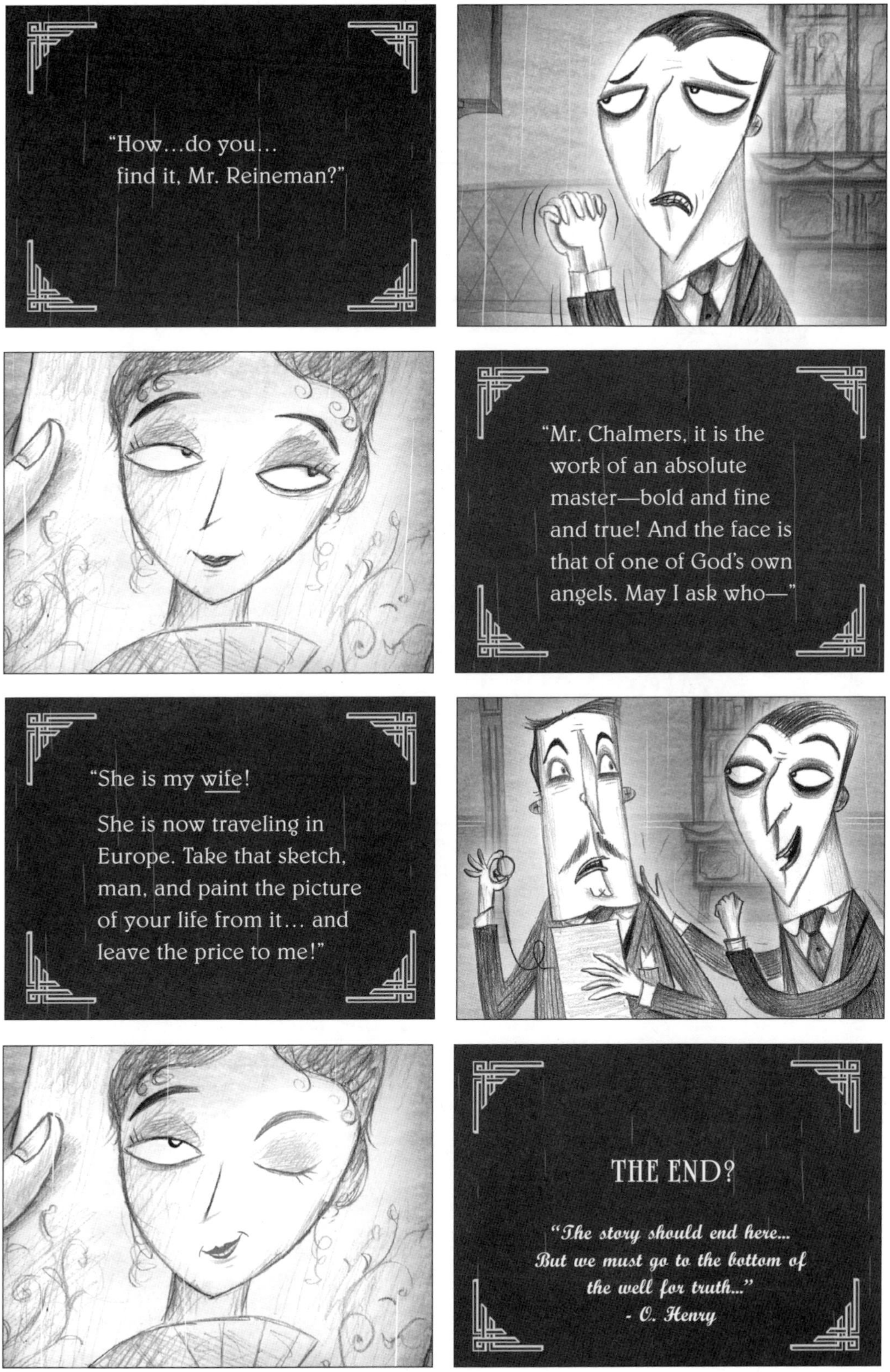
"How...do you...
find it, Mr. Reineman?"
"Mr. Chalmers, it is the work of an absolute master—bold and fine and true! And the face is that of one of God's own angels. May I ask who—"
"She is my wife!
She is now traveling in Europe. Take that sketch, man, and paint the picture of your life from it... and leave the price to me!"
THE END?
"The story should end here... But we must go to the bottom of the well for truth..."
- O. Henry

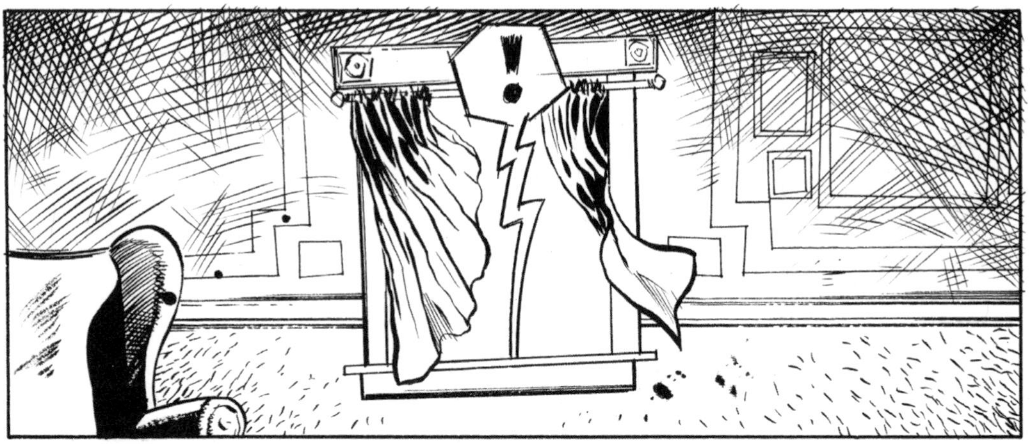

AN HOMAGE to O. HENRY

The Eye of the Beholder

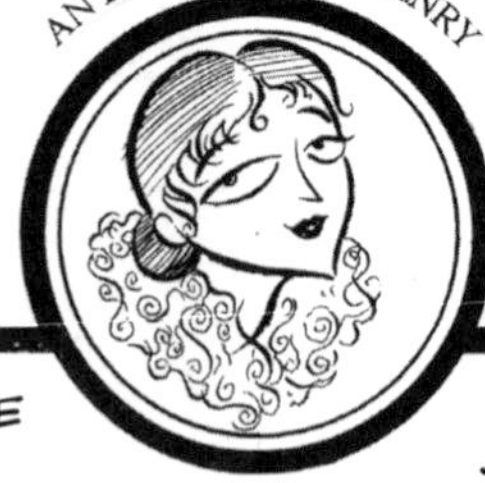

STORY BY MORT CASTLE
& TOM POMPLUN

DRAWN BY S. SHAW,
JOURNEYMAN CARTOONIST

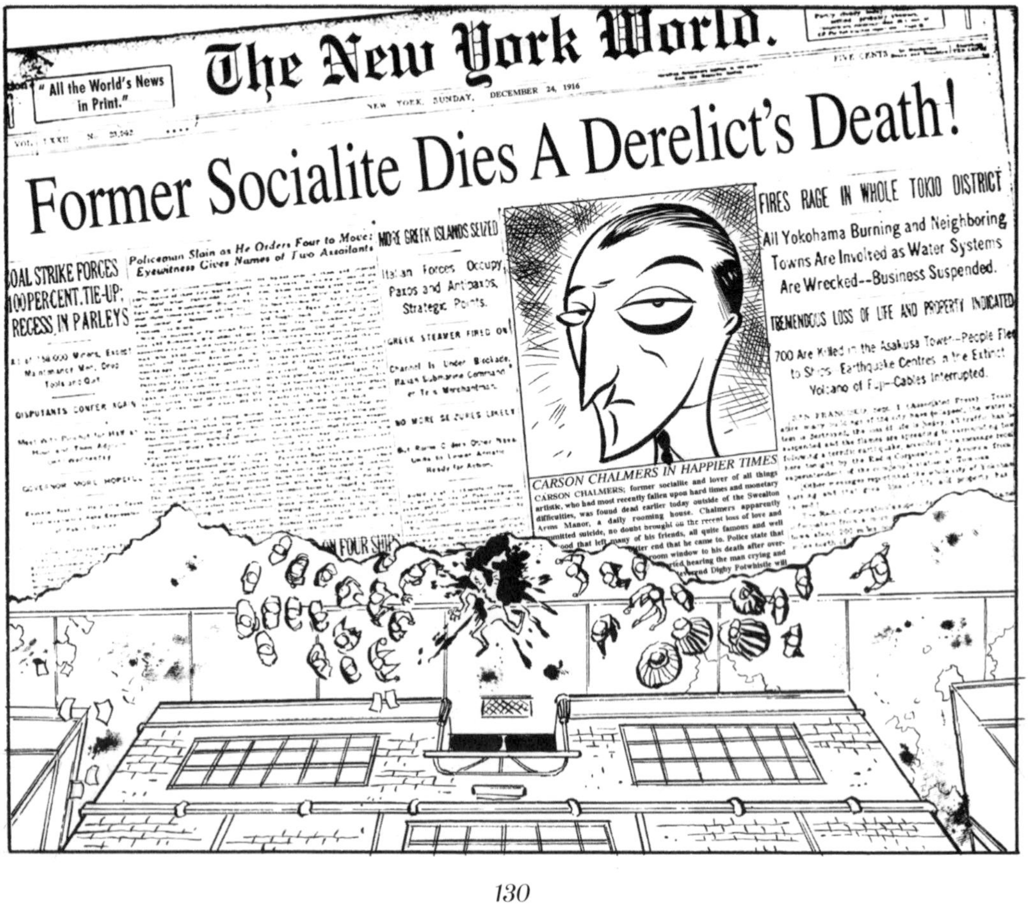
The New York World.
"All the World's News in Print."
NEW YORK, SUNDAY, DECEMBER 24, 1916
Former Socialite Dies A Derelict's Death!
COAL STRIKE FORCES 100PERCENT. TIE-UP; RECESS IN PARLEYS
Policeman Slain as He Orders Four to Move; Eyewitness Gives Names of Two Assailants
MORE GREEK ISLANDS SEIZED
Italian Forces Occupy Paxos and Antipaxos, Strategic Points.
GREEK STEAMER FIRED ON
NO MORE SEIZURES LIKELY
FIRES RAGE IN WHOLE TOKIO DISTRICT
All Yokohama Burning and Neighboring Towns Are Involved as Water Systems Are Wrecked--Business Suspended.
TREMENDOUS LOSS OF LIFE AND PROPERTY INDICATED
700 Are Killed in the Asakusa Tower--People Flee to Ships. Earthquake Centres in the Extinct Volcano of Fuji--Cables Interrupted.
CARSON CHALMERS IN HAPPIER TIMES
CARSON CHALMERS; former socialite and lover of all things
artistic, who had most recently fallen upon hard times and monetary
difficulties, was found dead earlier today outside of the Swealton
Arms Manor, a daily rooming house. Chalmers apparently
mitted suicide, no doubt brought on the recent loss of love and
ood that left many of his friends, all quite famous and well
tter end that he came to. Police state that
room window to his death after over-
rted hearing the man crying and
everend Digby Potwhistle will

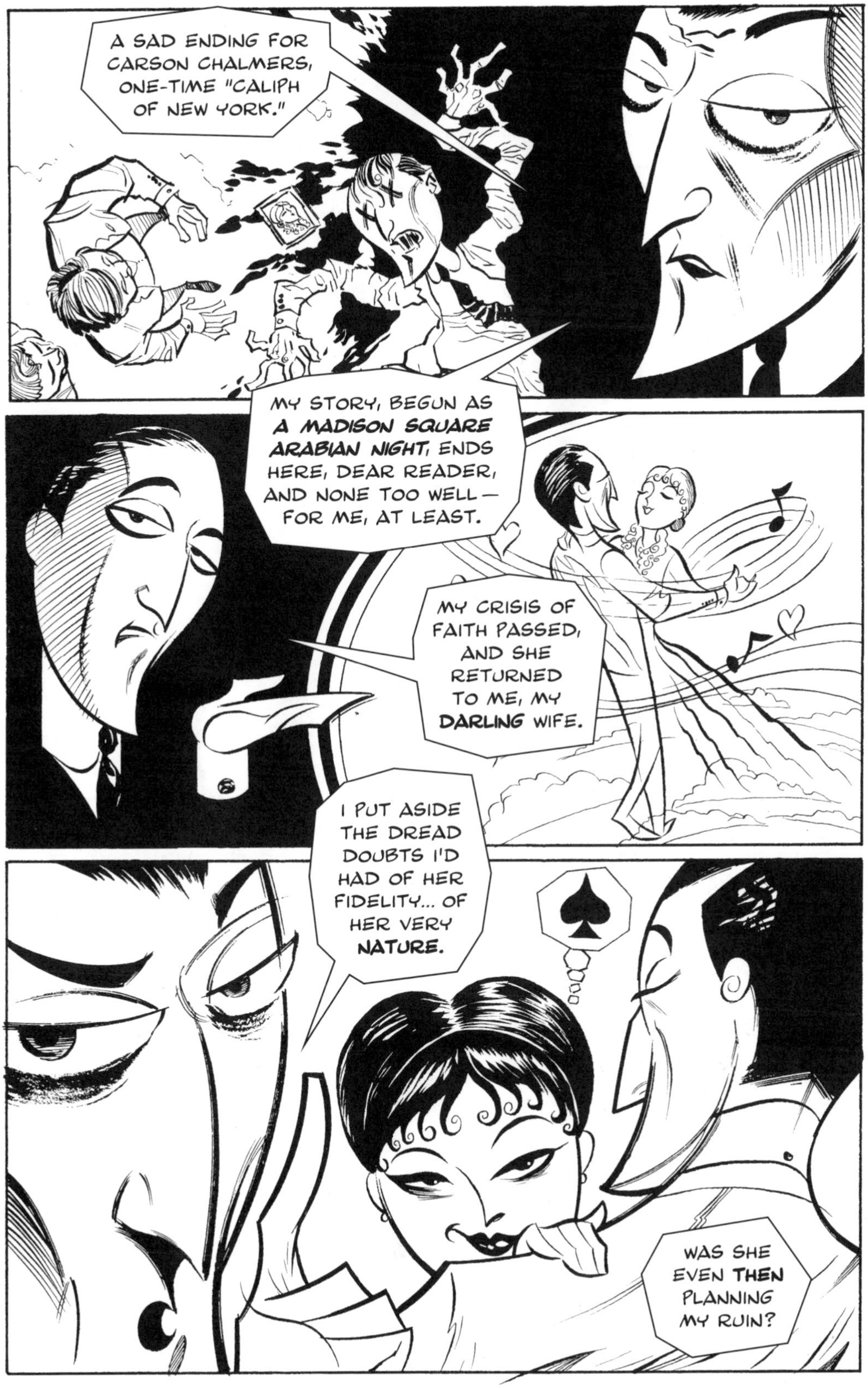
A SAD ENDING FOR CARSON CHALMERS, ONE-TIME "CALIPH OF NEW YORK."
MY STORY, BEGUN AS **A MADISON SQUARE ARABIAN NIGHT**, ENDS HERE, DEAR READER, AND NONE TOO WELL— FOR ME, AT LEAST.
MY CRISIS OF FAITH PASSED, AND SHE RETURNED TO ME, MY **DARLING** WIFE.
I PUT ASIDE THE DREAD DOUBTS I'D HAD OF HER FIDELITY... OF HER VERY **NATURE.**
WAS SHE EVEN **THEN** PLANNING MY RUIN?

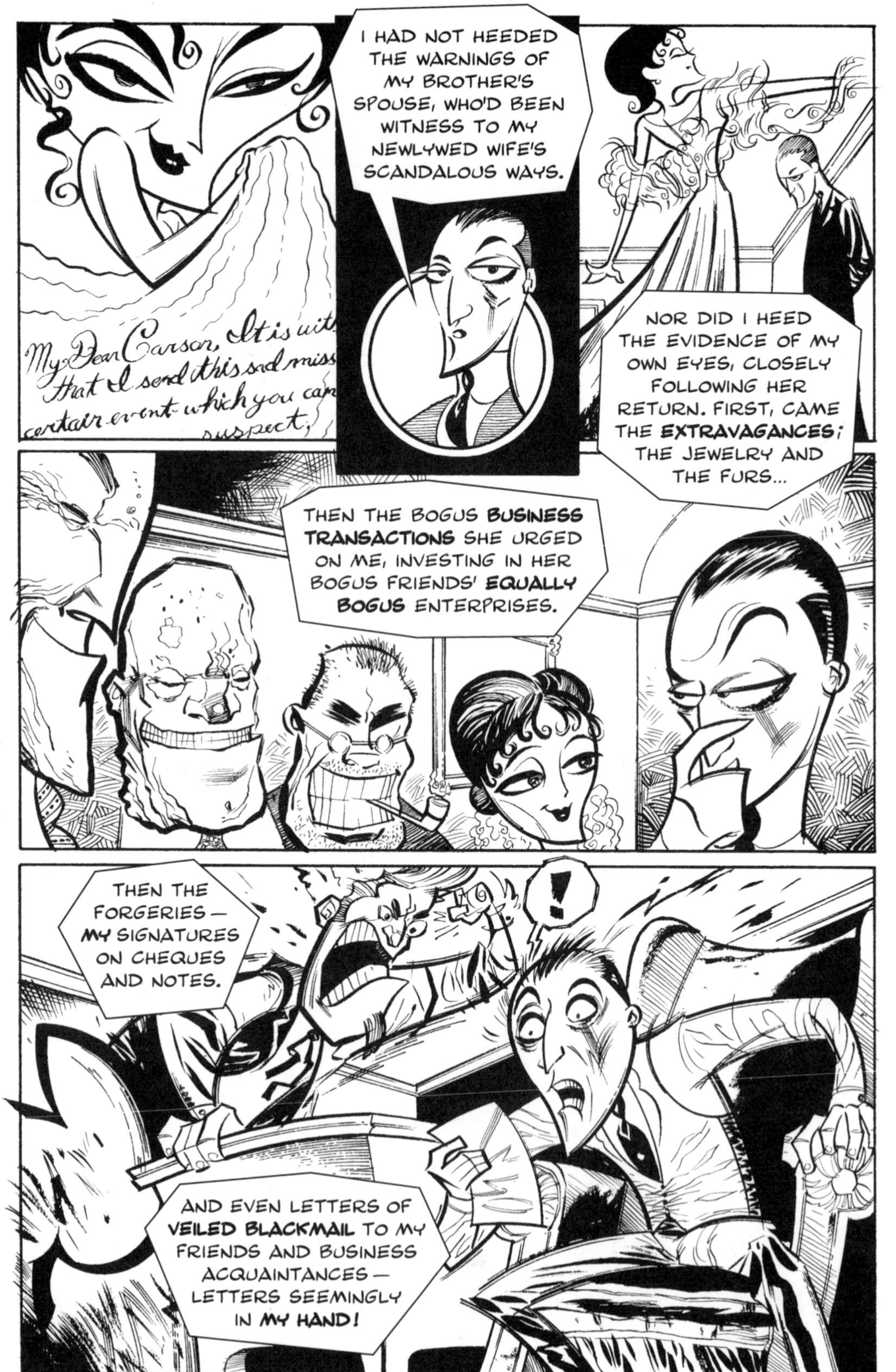
My Dear Carson, It is wit
that I send this sad miss
certain event which you can
suspect,
I HAD NOT HEEDED THE WARNINGS OF MY BROTHER'S SPOUSE, WHO'D BEEN WITNESS TO MY NEWLYWED WIFE'S SCANDALOUS WAYS.
NOR DID I HEED THE EVIDENCE OF MY OWN EYES, CLOSELY FOLLOWING HER RETURN. FIRST, CAME THE **EXTRAVAGANCES**; THE JEWELRY AND THE FURS...
THEN THE BOGUS **BUSINESS TRANSACTIONS** SHE URGED ON ME, INVESTING IN HER BOGUS FRIENDS' **EQUALLY BOGUS** ENTERPRISES.
THEN THE FORGERIES — **MY** SIGNATURES ON CHEQUES AND NOTES.
!
AND EVEN LETTERS OF **VEILED BLACKMAIL** TO MY FRIENDS AND BUSINESS ACQUAINTANCES — LETTERS SEEMINGLY IN **MY HAND**!

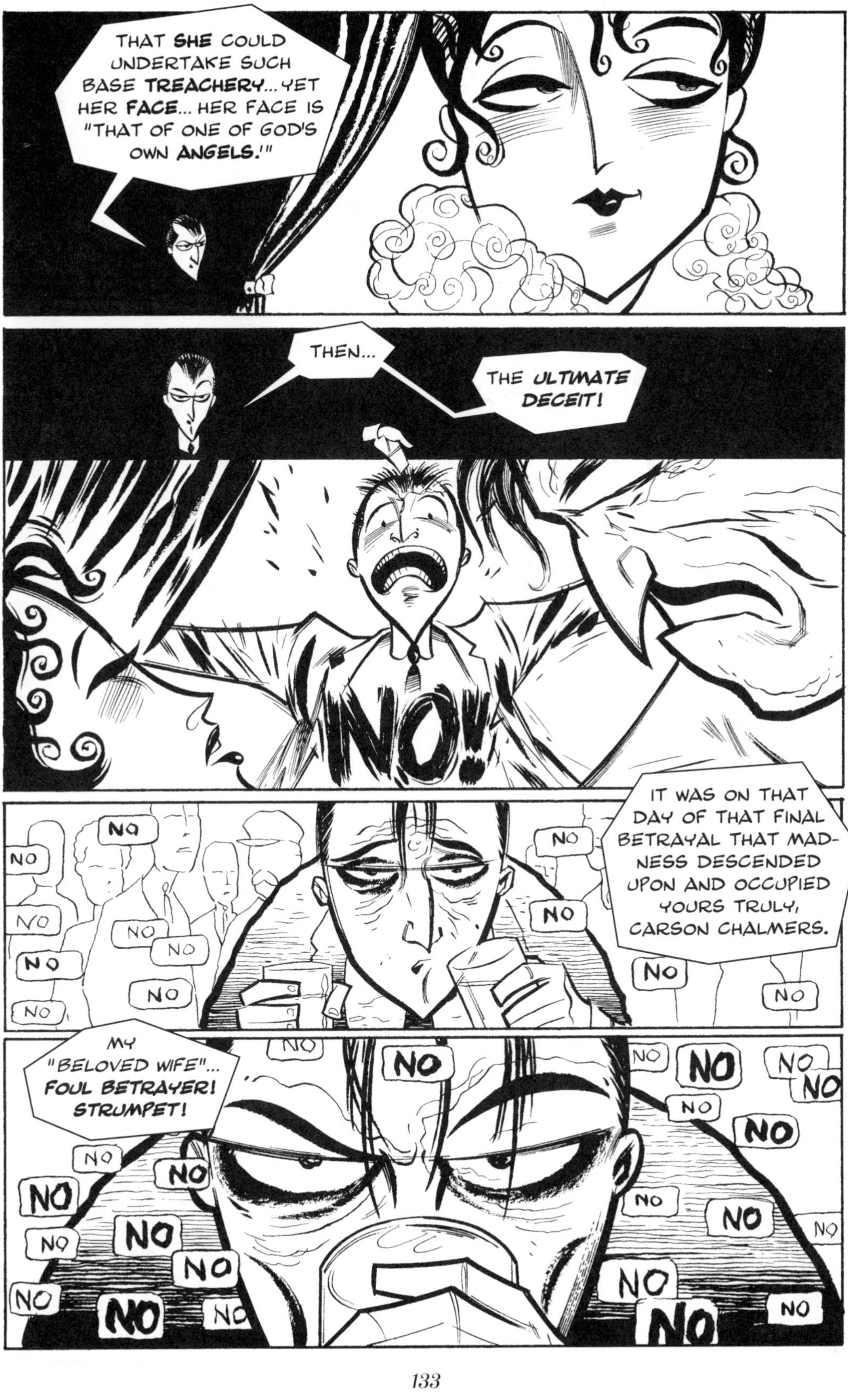
THAT SHE COULD UNDERTAKE SUCH BASE TREACHERY... YET HER FACE... HER FACE IS "THAT OF ONE OF GOD'S OWN ANGELS."
THEN...
THE ULTIMATE DECEIT!
NO!!
IT WAS ON THAT DAY OF THAT FINAL BETRAYAL THAT MADNESS DESCENDED UPON AND OCCUPIED YOURS TRULY, CARSON CHALMERS.
MY "BELOVED WIFE"... FOUL BETRAYER! STRUMPET!
NO

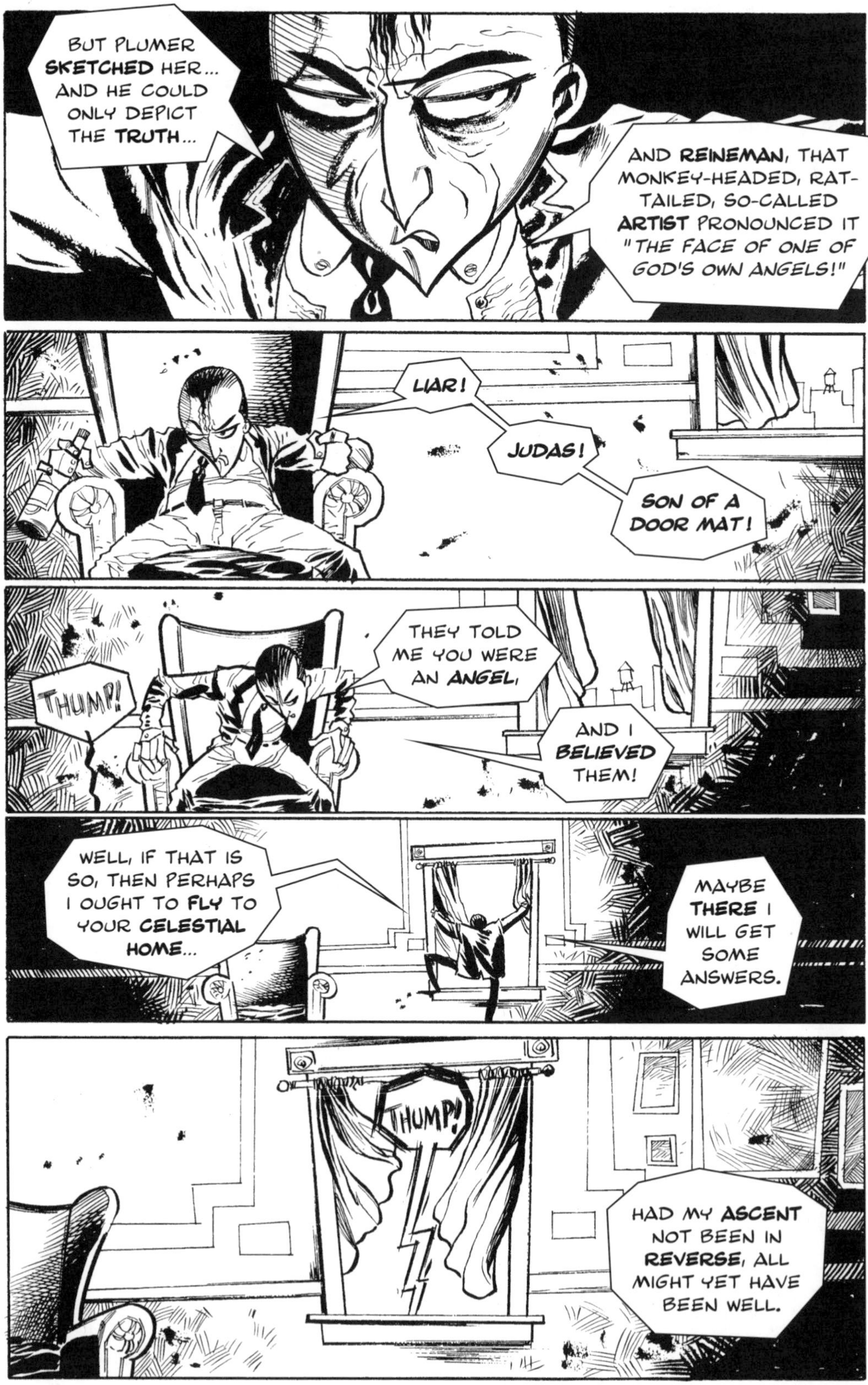
BUT PLUMER SKETCHED HER... AND HE COULD ONLY DEPICT THE TRUTH...
AND REINEMAN, THAT MONKEY-HEADED, RAT-TAILED, SO-CALLED ARTIST PRONOUNCED IT "THE FACE OF ONE OF GOD'S OWN ANGELS!"
LIAR!
JUDAS!
SON OF A DOOR MAT!
THUMP!
THEY TOLD ME YOU WERE AN ANGEL,
AND I BELIEVED THEM!
WELL, IF THAT IS SO, THEN PERHAPS I OUGHT TO FLY TO YOUR CELESTIAL HOME...
MAYBE THERE I WILL GET SOME ANSWERS.
THUMP!
HAD MY ASCENT NOT BEEN IN REVERSE, ALL MIGHT YET HAVE BEEN WELL.

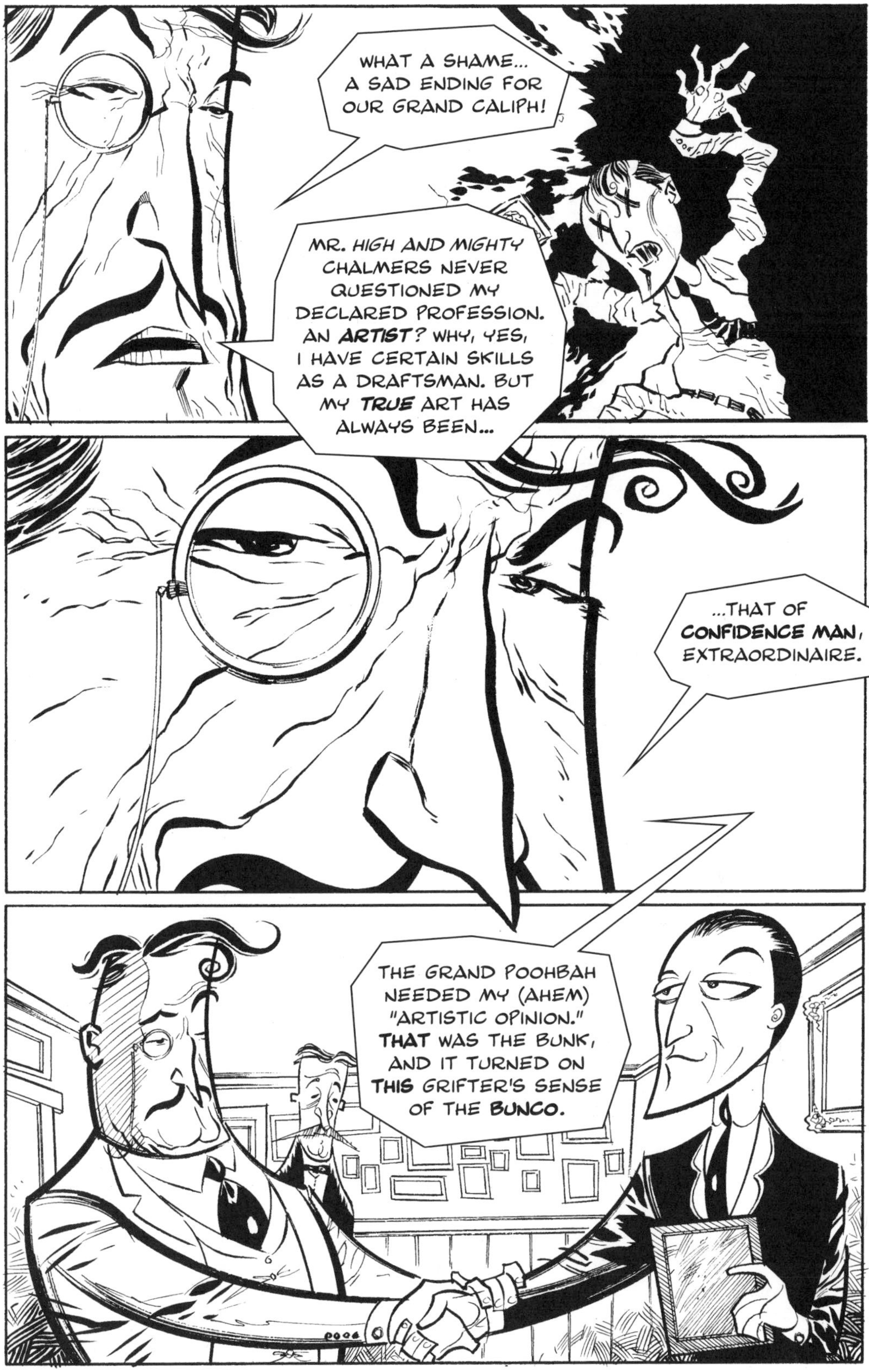
WHAT A SHAME... A SAD ENDING FOR OUR GRAND CALIPH!
MR. HIGH AND MIGHTY CHALMERS NEVER QUESTIONED MY DECLARED PROFESSION. AN ARTIST? WHY, YES, I HAVE CERTAIN SKILLS AS A DRAFTSMAN. BUT MY TRUE ART HAS ALWAYS BEEN...
...THAT OF CONFIDENCE MAN, EXTRAORDINAIRE.
THE GRAND POOHBAH NEEDED MY (AHEM) "ARTISTIC OPINION." THAT WAS THE BUNK, AND IT TURNED ON THIS GRIFTER'S SENSE OF THE BUNCO.

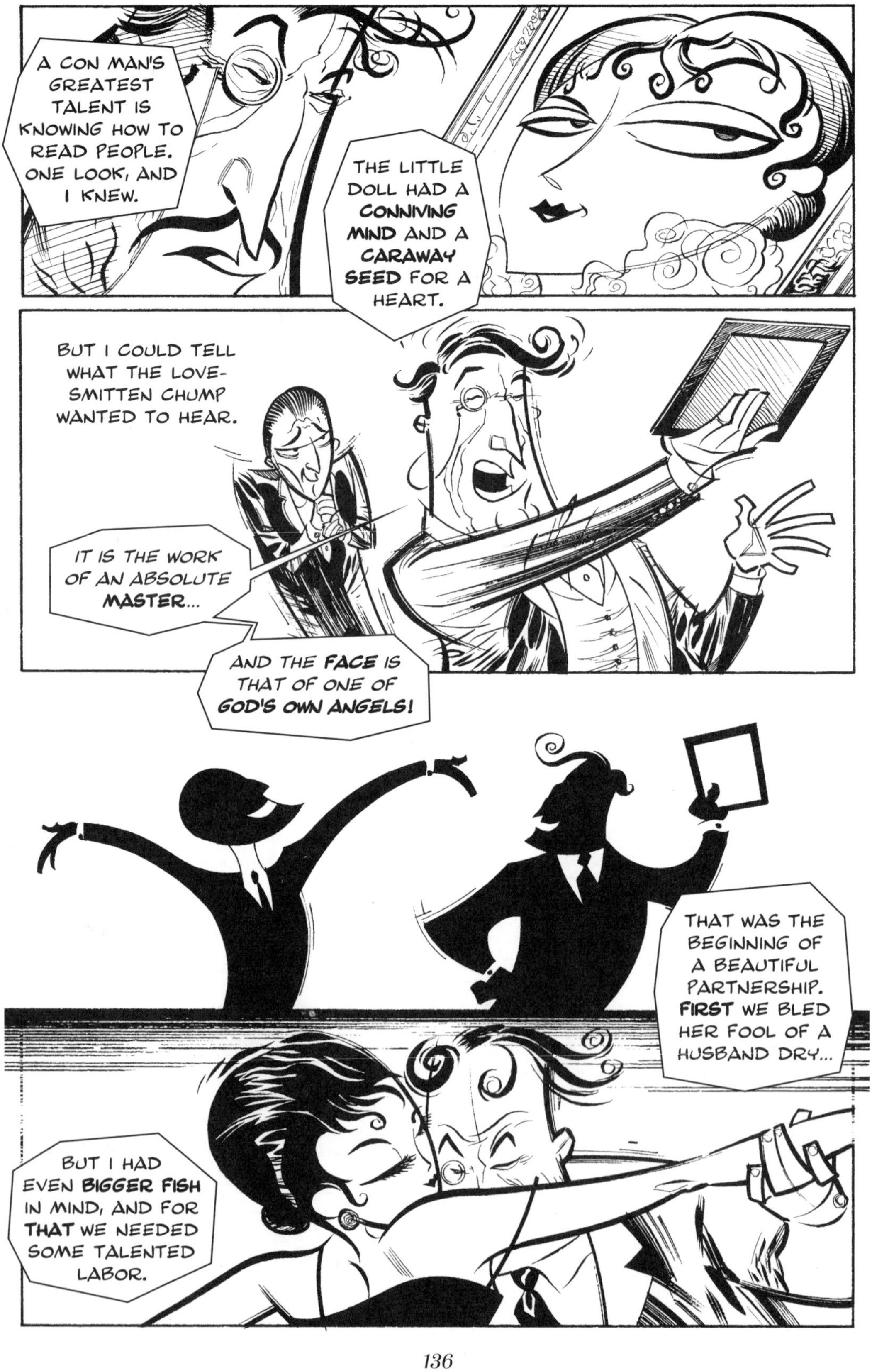
A CON MAN'S GREATEST TALENT IS KNOWING HOW TO READ PEOPLE. ONE LOOK, AND I KNEW.
THE LITTLE DOLL HAD A CONNIVING MIND AND A CARAWAY SEED FOR A HEART.
BUT I COULD TELL WHAT THE LOVE-SMITTEN CHUMP WANTED TO HEAR.
IT IS THE WORK OF AN ABSOLUTE MASTER...
AND THE FACE IS THAT OF ONE OF GOD'S OWN ANGELS!
THAT WAS THE BEGINNING OF A BEAUTIFUL PARTNERSHIP. FIRST WE BLED HER FOOL OF A HUSBAND DRY...
BUT I HAD EVEN BIGGER FISH IN MIND, AND FOR THAT WE NEEDED SOME TALENTED LABOR.

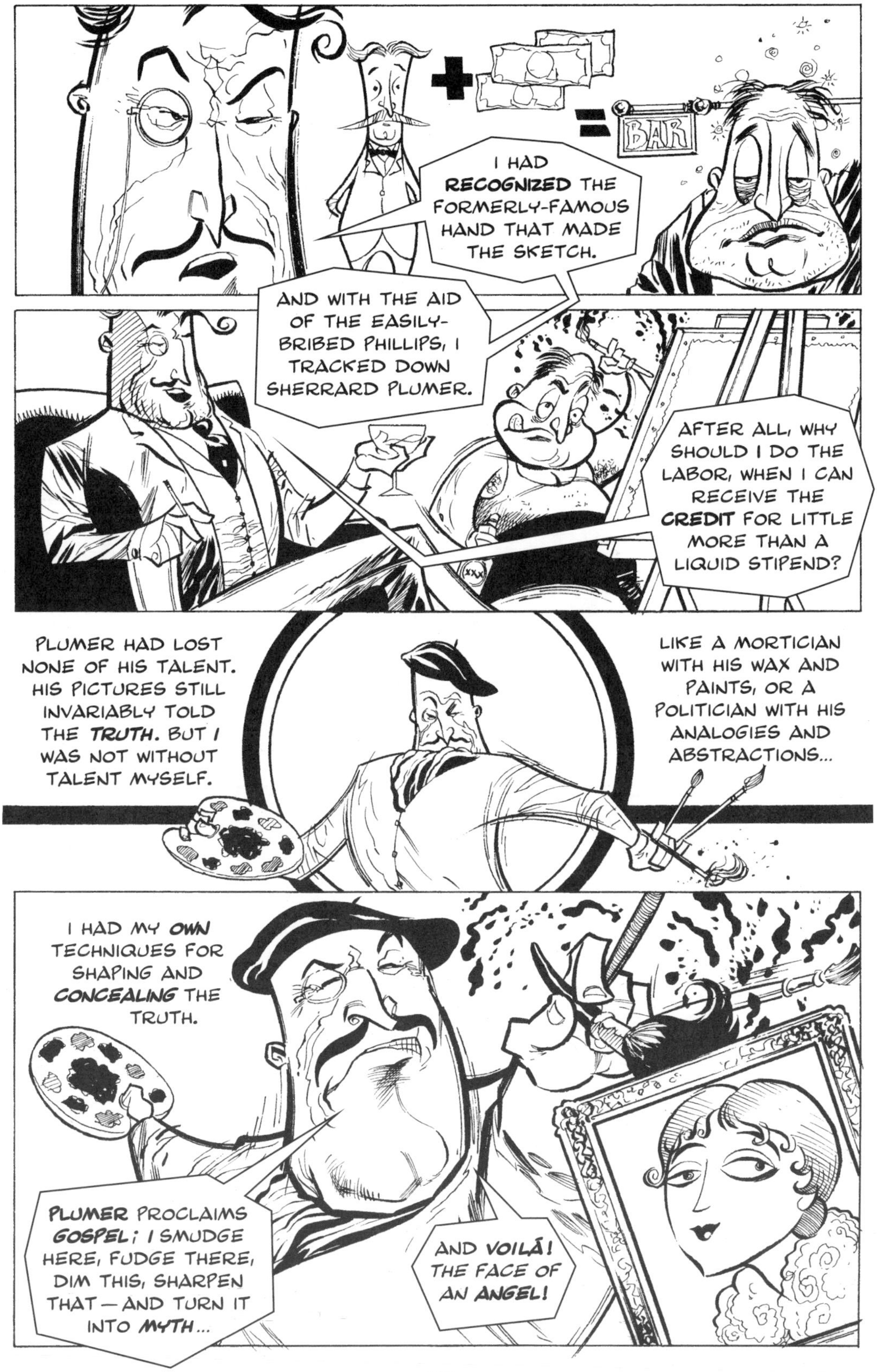
BAR
I HAD **RECOGNIZED** THE FORMERLY-FAMOUS HAND THAT MADE THE SKETCH.
AND WITH THE AID OF THE EASILY-BRIBED PHILLIPS, I TRACKED DOWN SHERRARD PLUMER.
AFTER ALL, WHY SHOULD I DO THE LABOR, WHEN I CAN RECEIVE THE **CREDIT** FOR LITTLE MORE THAN A LIQUID STIPEND?
XXX
PLUMER HAD LOST NONE OF HIS TALENT. HIS PICTURES STILL INVARIABLY TOLD THE ***TRUTH***. BUT ***I*** WAS NOT WITHOUT TALENT MYSELF.
LIKE A MORTICIAN WITH HIS WAX AND PAINTS, OR A POLITICIAN WITH HIS ANALOGIES AND ABSTRACTIONS...
I HAD MY ***OWN*** TECHNIQUES FOR SHAPING AND ***CONCEALING*** THE TRUTH.
PLUMER PROCLAIMS ***GOSPEL***; ***I*** SMUDGE HERE, FUDGE THERE, DIM THIS, SHARPEN THAT — AND TURN IT INTO ***MYTH***...
*AND **VOILÀ**! THE FACE OF AN **ANGEL**!*

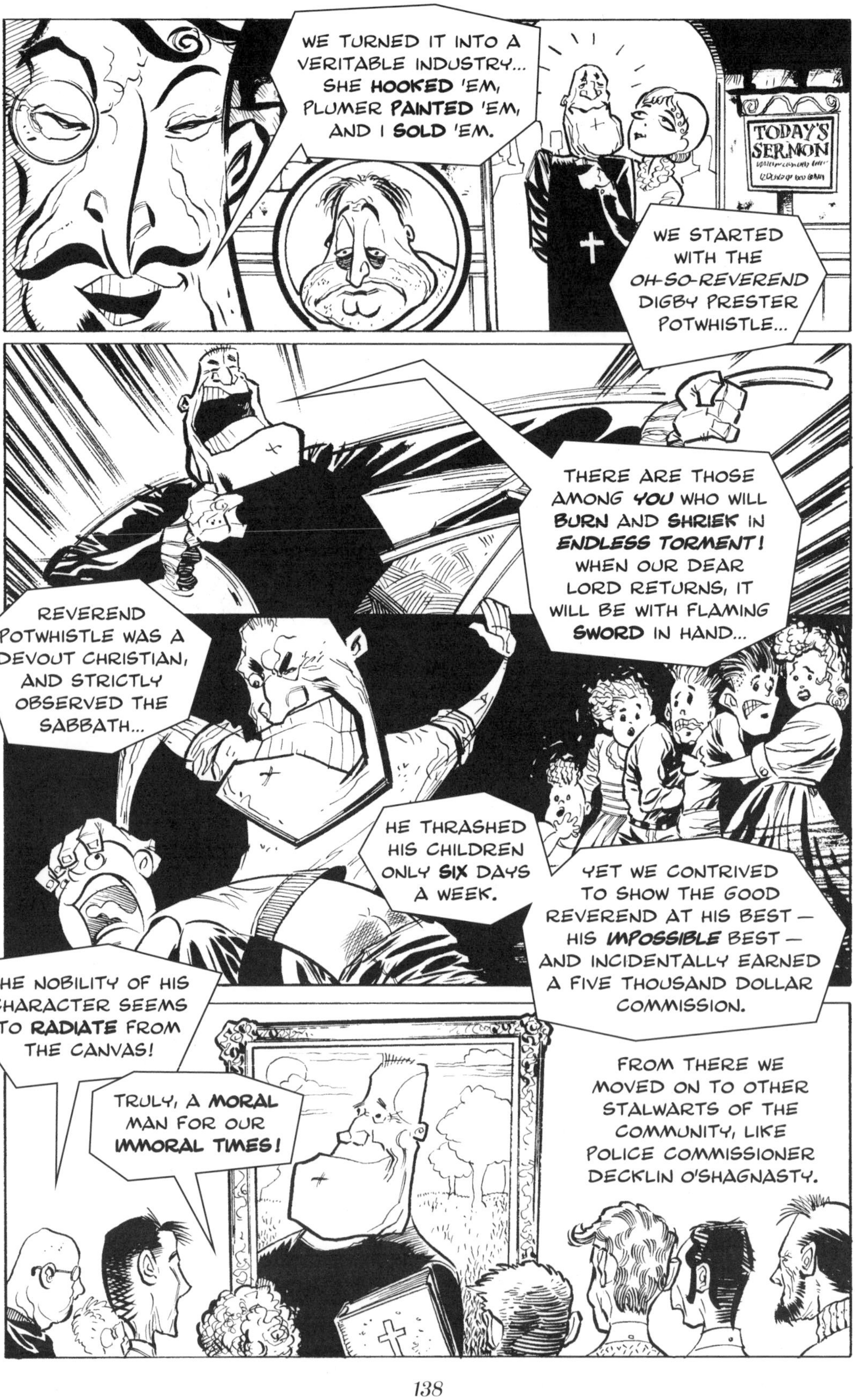
WE TURNED IT INTO A VERITABLE INDUSTRY... SHE **HOOKED** 'EM, PLUMER **PAINTED** 'EM, AND I **SOLD** 'EM.
TODAY'S SERMON
WE STARTED WITH THE *OH-SO-REVEREND* DIGBY PRESTER POTWHISTLE...
THERE ARE THOSE AMONG ***YOU*** WHO WILL **BURN** AND **SHRIEK** IN ***ENDLESS TORMENT!*** WHEN OUR DEAR LORD RETURNS, IT WILL BE WITH FLAMING **SWORD** IN HAND...
REVEREND POTWHISTLE WAS A DEVOUT CHRISTIAN, AND STRICTLY OBSERVED THE SABBATH...
HE THRASHED HIS CHILDREN ONLY **SIX** DAYS A WEEK.
YET WE CONTRIVED TO SHOW THE GOOD REVEREND AT HIS BEST — HIS ***IMPOSSIBLE*** BEST — AND INCIDENTALLY EARNED A FIVE THOUSAND DOLLAR COMMISSION.
THE NOBILITY OF HIS CHARACTER SEEMS TO **RADIATE** FROM THE CANVAS!
TRULY, A **MORAL** MAN FOR OUR **IMMORAL TIMES!**
FROM THERE WE MOVED ON TO OTHER STALWARTS OF THE COMMUNITY, LIKE POLICE COMMISSIONER DECKLIN O'SHAGNASTY.

THIS STALWART PROTECTOR AND DEFENDER OF THE FOUR MILLION HAD RISEN THROUGH THE RANKS DUE TO HIS BRAVERY AND POWERS OF DEDUCTION —

NOTWITHSTANDING A FEW WELL-PLACED BRIBES.

THERE IS AN **ART** TO THE EXTRACTING OF A CONFESSION!

OR MAYOR WINSTON C. WIDEBOTTOM; AN UPSTANDING CIVIL SERVANT WHO RADIATED INTELLIGENCE...

AND OWED HIS POSITION *NOT AT ALL* TO HIS ASSOCIATIONS WITH THE CITY'S CRIMELORDS.

IT'S **SPLENDID**! WHO'D HAVE THOUGHT YOU COULD CAPTURE MY CHARACTER SO **PERFECTLY**!

HIC

THE POSSIBILITIES WERE **ENDLESS.** AS THAT CURRENTLY-POPULAR AUTHOR **O. HENRY** HAS WRITTEN, "IT WAS BEAUTIFUL AND SIMPLE, AS ALL TRULY GREAT SWINDLES ARE."

BUT PLUMER'S **FINEST** WORK WAS A CANVAS WHICH I LEFT **UNTOUCHED**; THE WEDDING PORTRAIT OF MYSELF AND THE FORMER MRS. CHALMERS.

THE PICTURE WAS **PERFECT** AS HE PAINTED IT, AND **CERTAINLY** NEEDED NO RETOUCHING BY **ME**!

JACK LONDON AND O. HENRY

by ***Carl Sandburg***
illustrated by ***Milton Knight***

Both were jailbirds; no speechmakers at all;
speaking best with one foot on a brass rail;
a beer glass in the left hand and the right
hand employed for gestures.

And both were lights snuffed out... no warning
...no lingering:

Who knew the hearts of these boozefighters?

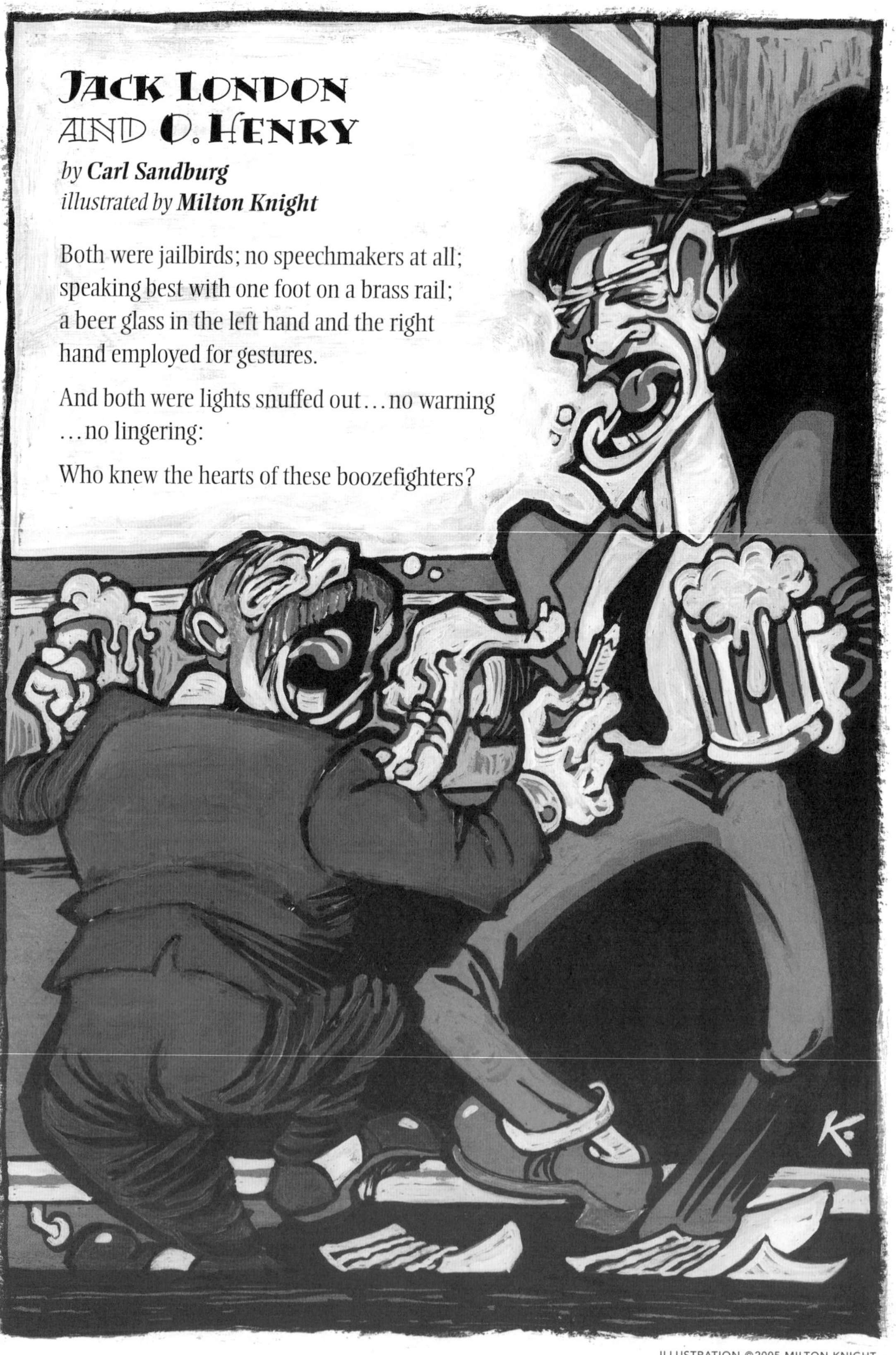

O. HENRY

O. Henry is the pen name of William Sydney Porter. The master of the surprise ending was born in 1862 in Greensboro, North Carolina. Porter left school at age fifteen, worked a number of jobs, then moved to Texas in 1882 where he became a ranch hand, then a pharmacist, and a bookkeeper. He married in 1887, and briefly published a humorous weekly, *The Rolling Stone*. When that paper failed, he joined *The Houston Post* as a reporter and columnist. He also worked as, most unfortunately, a bank clerk. He was accused of embezzlement, and fled, first to New Orleans, and then to Honduras to escape trial. While in Honduras he received word that his wife was terminally ill. He returned to Austin, and shortly after her death in 1897 he was convicted and sentenced to five years in a federal penitentiary in Ohio. It was while in prison that he adopted the pen name O. Henry (taken from the name of one of his guards) and began to write fiction. He was released from prison after three years and moved to New York City, where he wrote for *The New York World* and other publications. O. Henry was a prolific and extremely popular writer, and before his death in 1910 published over 600 short stories.

ESAO ANDREWS *(front cover)*

Painter, illustrator, skateboard designer and occasional comics artist Esao Andrews grew up in Mesa, Arizona and currently resides in Brooklyn, New York in what he claims is "a drunken splendor" with his dog Soybean. A frequent contributor to the *Meathaus* comics anthology, Esao is now concentrating on paintings for several future gallery shows. His haunting painting of *The Bottle Imp* appears on the back cover of *Graphic Classics: Robert Louis Stevenson*. Esao's very entertaining website can be visited at www.esao.net.

SHARY FLENNIKEN *(page 2)*

Shary Flenniken is a cartoonist, editor, author and screenwriter. She is best known for her irreverent comic strip *Trots & Bonnie*, about precocious preteens, which appeared in various underground comics and *National Lampoon*. Shary's graphic stories and comic strips have appeared in *Details*, *Premiere*, *Harvey*, and *Mad* magazines, as well as in *Graphic Classics: H.G. Wells*, *Graphic Classics: Ambrose Bierce*, *Graphic Classics: Mark Twain* and *Graphic Classics: Robert Louis Stevenson*. Her artwork can also be seen in *When a Man Loves A Walnut*, *More Misheard Lyrics* by the "very cool" Gavin Edwards, *Nice Guys Sleep Alone* by "big-time loser" Bruce Feirstein, and *Seattle Laughs*, a "truly wonderful" book edited by

Shary. She is currently teaching comedy writing and cartooning while working on a book of fairy tales and a series of novels that she claims are "not even remotely autobiographical." You can contact Shary and find out how to purchase original artwork at www.sharyflenniken.com.

JOHNNY RYAN *(page 4)*

Johnny Ryan was born in Boston in 1970. As a boy, he says, "First I wanted to be a cartoonist, then I wanted to be a physicist, then I wanted to be gay, and then a cartoonist again." He now lives in Los Angeles and is the creator of the award-winning *Angry Youth Comix*. His work has also been published in *Nickelodeon Magazine*, *Goody Good Comics*, *Measles* and *LCD*. "Comics used to be fun and crazy and weird and gross," says Johnny. "Now, they're a serious art form... it's as if everyone was having a big crazy orgy and then your grandparents walked in. They really sucked the life out of the party." Johnny's conversion of Bierce's *A Dog's Bequest* to an affectionate *Peanuts* parody appeared in *Graphic Classics: Ambrose Bierce*. And he transformed *The Whole Duty of Children* into a *Dennis the Menace* pastiche in *Graphic Classics: Robert Louis Stevenson*. When editor Tom Pomplun was selecting an artist for *The Ransom of Red Chief*, his first thought was Johnny, who seems born for the role.

MARK A. NELSON *(page 16)*

Mark Nelson was a professor of art at Northern Illinois University for twenty years. From 1998 to 2004 he was a senior artist at Raven Software, doing conceptual work, painting digital skins and creating textures for computer games. Mark is now the lead instructor of the Animation Department of Madison Area Technical College in Madison, Wisconsin. His comics credits include *Blood and Shadows* for DC, *Aliens* for Dark Horse Comics, and *Feud* for Marvel. He has worked for numerous publishers, and his art is represented in *Spectrum #4, 5, 6, 8, 10* and *From Pencils to Inks: The Art of Mark A. Nelson* (2004 Baron Publishing). Mark's comics and illustrations have appeared in *Graphic Classics: Edgar Allan Poe*, *Graphic Classics: Arthur Conan Doyle*, *Graphic Classics: H.P. Lovecraft*, *Graphic Classics: Jack London*, *Graphic Classics: Ambrose Bierce*, *Horror Classics*, *Rosebud 18* and *The Best of Rosebud*, all from Eureka Productions.

LISA K. WEBER *(page 32, back cover)*

Lisa is a graduate of Parsons School of Design in New York City, where she is currently employed in the fashion industry, designing prints and characters for teenage girls' jammies, while freelancing work on children's books and character design for animation. Other projects include her "creaturized" opera posters and playing cards. Lisa has provided illustrations for *Graphic Classics: Edgar Allan Poe, Graphic Classics: H.P. Lovecraft, Graphic Classics: Ambrose Bierce, Graphic Classics: Bram Stoker, Graphic Classics: Mark Twain* and *Graphic Classics: Robert Louis Stevenson.* Illustrations from her in-progress book *The Shakespearean ABCs* were printed in *Rosebud 25.* More of Lisa's art can be seen online at www.creatureco.com.

RACHEL MASILAMANI (page 40)
Rachel Masilamani lives and works in Las Cruces, New Mexico. Her stories have appeared in a number of comics anthologies, and in her self-published series, *RPM Comics.* The first issue of *RPM Comics* in 2000 received a grant award from the Xeric Foundation, a nonprofit corporation founded by *Teenage Mutant Turtles* creator Peter Laird. The Foundation offers financial assistance to self-publishing comics creators. You can contact Rachel at rpm77@lycos.com.

TOM NEELY (page 46)
Tom Neely is a painter, cartoonist, and animator living in Los Angeles. His work has been featured in galleries in San Francisco and Los Angeles, in magazines, literary journals and comics, and in *Graphic Classics: Robert Louis Stevenson.* He was the curator of *Mini*Mart,* a successful show of emerging alternative cartoonists, at the Harmony Gallery in 2003. He recently completed *Brother, Can You Spare a Job?* is a seven-minute animated political cartoon, currently being screened online (www.brothercanyouspareajob.com) and at film festivals around the world. He is currently working on paintings for an upcoming solo show, his first graphic novel and an animated music video for The Muffs. Tom says he likes playing his banjo, watching cartoons, and rollerskating—but not all at the same time. Visit his website at www.iwilldestroyyou.com.

ANTONELLA CAPUTO (page 48)
Antonella Caputo was born and educated in Rome, Italy, and is now living in England. She has been an architect, archaeologist, art restorer, photographer, calligrapher, interior designer, theater designer, actress and theater director. Antonella's first published work was *Casa Montesi,* a weekly comic strip that appeared in *Il Journalino.* She has since written comedies for children and scripts for comics in Europe and the U.S., before joining Nick Miller as a partner in Sputnik Studios. Her collaborations with Nick ~ve appeared in *Graphic Classics: H.G. Wells,*

Graphic Classics: Jack London, Graphic Classics: Ambrose Bierce, Graphic Classics: Mark Twain and *Graphic Classics: Robert Louis Stevenson.* She is now working on *The Time Machine* with artist Seth Frail for the second edition of *Graphic Classics: H.G. Wells* and on an adaptation of one of Arthur Conan Doyle's Brigadier Gerard stories for *Adventure Classics: Graphic Classics Volume 12.*

RICK GEARY (page 48)
Rick is best known for his thirteen years as a contributor to *The National Lampoon.* His work has also appeared in Marvel, DC, and Dark Horse comics, *Rolling Stone, Mad, Heavy Metal, Disney Adventures, The Los Angeles Times,* and *The New York Times Book Review.* He is a regular cartoonist in *Rosebud.* Rick has written and illustrated five children's books and published a collection of his comics, *Housebound with Rick Geary.* The fifth volume in his continuing book series *A Treasury of Victorian Murder* is *The Beast of Chicago* (NBM Publishing, 2003). More of Rick's work has appeared in the *Graphic Classics* anthologies *Edgar Allan Poe, Arthur Conan Doyle, H.G. Wells, H.P. Lovecraft, Jack London, Ambrose Bierce* and *Mark Twain.* You can also view his art at www.rickgeary.com.

GERRY ALANGUILAN (page 66)
Gerry Alanguilan is a licensed architect who chooses to write and draw comic books. In his native Philippines he has created comics including *Timawa, Crest Hut Butt Shop, Dead Heart* and *Wasted. Wasted* has received acclaim abroad from writers like Warren Ellis and Steven Grant, and has been filmed in the Philippines. In America, he has contributed inks on such titles as *X-Men, Fantastic Four, Wolverine, X-Force, Darkness, Stone* and *High Roads,* working with pencillers Leinil Francis Yu and Whilce Portacio. He is currently inking *Superman: Birthright* for DC Comics and is putting together *Komikero,* a portfolio of his sketches, illustrations and comics. Gerry's comics and illustrations also appear in *Graphic Classics: H.P. Lovecraft, Graphic Classics: Jack London* and *Graphic Classics: Bram Stoker.*

ROD LOTT (page 76)
Based in Oklahoma City, Rod Lott is a freelance writer and graphic designer in the worlds of journalism, advertising and beyond. For the past ten years, he has served as editor and publisher of the more-or-less quarterly magazine *Hitch: The Journal of Pop Culture Absurdity.* Rod's humorous essays have been published in anthologies including *More Mirth of a Nation, 101 Damnations* and *May Contain Nuts.* Rod